Inspired by turn-of-the-century American apothecaries, farmhouse living of the northern East Coast, and intimate British tea rooms, Kitten and the Bear is beloved for its cozy feeling of nostalgia, blue-ribbon collection of signature scones, and hand-crafted, small-batch fruit preserves made using time-honoured cooking methods.

Sophie and Bobby, artisanal jam makers and co-founders of Kitten and the Bear, share a heart-warming collection of over 90 recipes to create your own sweet world of glistening jars of jams, jellies, and marmalades, and homespun delights from flaky buttermilk scones and traditional spreads to savoury treats and hand-crafted drinks. Full of magical flavours and the comfort of home, the recipes range from Strawberry, Raspberry, and Cream Jam; Sunshine Peach Jam; Pink Apple and Lilac Jelly; Lemon Cream Marmalade; Morning Glory Scones; Blueberry Crumble Scones; and Orange Blossom Angel Food Cake with Fresh Peaches; to Savoury Cheese Sables with Cranberries and Walnuts; Clotted Cream and Potato Quiche; Lavender London Cream; and Baked Apple Toddy. Refined yet understated, the recipes in the *Kitten and the Bear Cookbook* were written to create homemade delights using easily accessible ingredients and equipment you already have in your pantry, while offering a thorough lesson in jam making theory and the art of preserving.

Embracing the fairy-tale spirit, tradition, and sweet world of Kitten and the Bear, the recipes deliver delicious preserves and baked goods to share and enjoy everyday moments with family and friends.

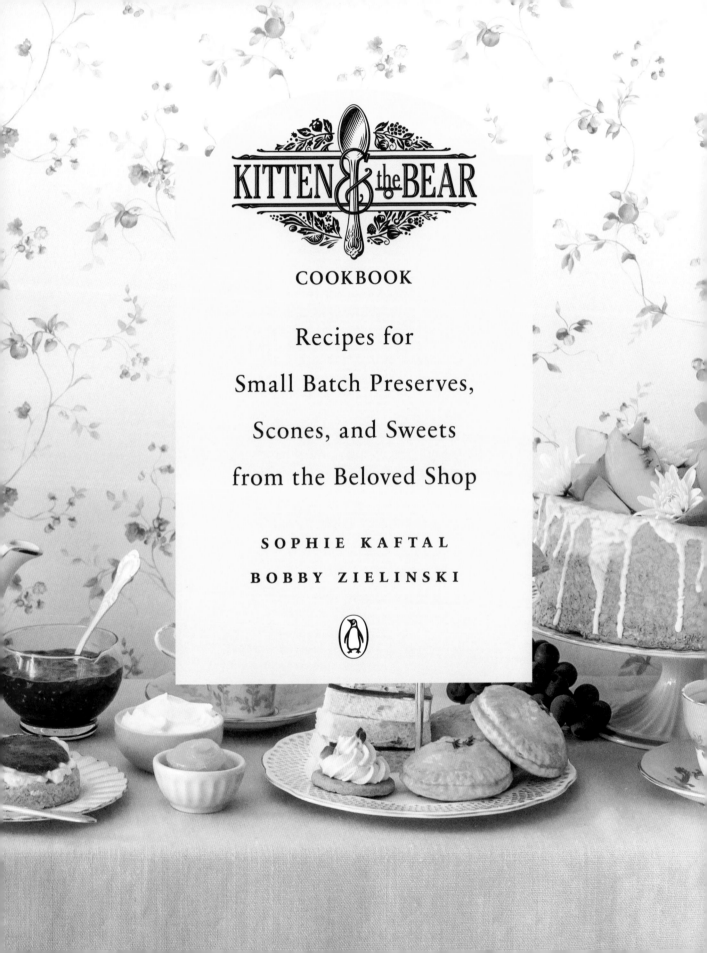

KITTEN & the BEAR

COOKBOOK

Recipes for
Small Batch Preserves,
Scones, and Sweets
from the Beloved Shop

SOPHIE KAFTAL
BOBBY ZIELINSKI

PENGUIN
an imprint of Penguin Canada, a division
of Penguin Random House Canada Limited

Canada • USA • UK • Ireland • Australia • New Zealand
• India • South Africa • China

First published 2024

www.penguinrandomhouse.ca

LIBRARY AND ARCHIVES CANADA CATALOGUING IN PUBLICATION
Title: Kitten and the Bear cookbook : recipes for small batch preserves, scones,
and sweets from the beloved shop / Sophie Kaftal and Bobby Zielinski.
Names: Kaftal, Sophie, author. | Zielinski, Bobby, author.
Description: Includes index.
Identifiers: Canadiana (print) 20230199984 | Canadiana (ebook) 20230200001 |
ISBN 9780735239593 (hardcover) | ISBN 9780735239609 (EPUB)
Subjects: LCSH: Cooking (Jam) | LCSH: Jam. | LCSH: Baked products. |
LCSH: Canning and preserving. | LCGFT: Cookbooks.
Classification: LCC TX612.J3 K34 2024 | DDC 641.85/2—dc23

Cover and interior design by Lisa Jager
Cover and food photography by Johanna Martin
Food and prop styling by Sophie Kaftal and Johanna Martin
Lifestyle photography by Andrea Charbonneau
Illustrations by Melody Tam

Printed in China

10 9 8 7 6 5 4 3 2 1

Penguin
Random House
PENGUIN CANADA

To our children, there is nothing sweeter than you.

CONTENTS

Kitten and the Bear:
Our Story

At Kitten and the Bear, we handcraft traditional fruit preserves and buttermilk scones using time-honoured methods. Our years spent learning the art of preserving has given us a great appreciation for tradition, heritage, and the power of the human touch. With this book, we strive to pass on an experience that is genuine and true to the timeless practice of jam making while putting our own contemporary spin on this artisanal inheritance.

Refined yet understated, the recipes in this book were written to create beautiful, homespun delights using easily accessible ingredients and equipment you already have in your pantry, while offering a thorough lesson in jam making theory and the art of preserving.

Kitten and the Bear is us—partners in every way, a husband-and-wife team. When we met, we were working long hours in separate industries. Like two ships passing in the night, we barely saw each other. We shared one day a week, eating, creating, and imagining a world that brought us closer together.

We started Kitten and the Bear in 2012 with a handful of jars of jam sold at farmers' markets and through a home-made website, renting space at a co-op kitchen. Over time, ten jars became twenty, and twenty jars became forty.

Since then, we have been on a journey that has been as personal as it has been professional, an adventure full of "pinch me" moments. Kitten and the Bear started as the little jam company that could, and has followed a winding path from that simple website, to a tiny storefront in Toronto's West End, to a secret-garden-style tearoom,

a pandemic-era take-out window, to finally arrive at what it is today: a bustling production kitchen brimming with glistening jars of jam and racks of freshly baked scones. A journey that began as a dream, our story is of a lifestyle reimagined—spending our days together, creating, our children running around our legs, stirring pots of bubbling jam, and the culmination of the last ten years: writing this book.

Kitten and the Bear was born as a way for us to create a new story for ourselves—a fairy tale life full of beauty, tradition, and the art of daily ritual. There is no greater joy than welcoming you into our sweet little world and sharing a moment where the smell of butter and strawberries almost feels like magic. Join us in savouring the simple things in life. As they say, the moments in between the moments are always the sweetest!

With love and gratitude,
Sophie and Bobby

About Our Book

The joy of preserving comes from starting with something raw and creating something that feels like a prize. Of course, it is a bonus to be able to open a jar of sunshine in the middle of winter, but the greatest joy comes with the experience of making something out of what feels like nothing and the ability and freedom to make an heirloom recipe all your own.

With this book, we hope to offer inspiration and knowledge to embolden you to throw some fruit and sugar in a pan—add lavender or bourbon if desired—and be rewarded with a creation of your own. Making homemade preserves for yourself and sharing them with loved ones is as gratifying as cooking a homemade meal. It may not be perfect the first few times, but that does not make the beauty of a day in the kitchen and joy of sharing your result any less special. As with everything in life, it will get better over time. Whether or not you use the best-quality ingredients or the most expensive equipment, the overall gratification from the process will be the same.

Historically, the rhythm of preserving came from the flow of the seasons and availability of fruit. Now, with our modern access to produce year-round, this rhythm has transformed into the creation of edible poetry that speaks to each season in its own way. If Christmas means orange zest and winter spices, or summer means juicy stone fruit and fresh florals, let's create a preserve that speaks to that sensory memory! The beauty of jam is in its encapsulating quality—its ability to hold the ambiance of a season within its glistening glass walls.

Therefore, the jam recipes in this book are organized for ease of use by category of fruit—berries; stone fruit; tree fruit; citrus; and tropical, vine, and other. Then, within each section, you will find the flow of recipes by seasonal ambiance, starting with warm weather jams and ending with wintery and holiday recipes. Finally, you will find sections for our favourite teatime accoutrements, including scones and traditional spreads, sweet and savoury delights, and hand-crafted drinks.

All About Preserving

Types of Preserves

Jam

A fruit spread of fruit pulp or pieces cooked with sugar and lemon juice. Jam can be made from many different fruits and have many different textures, from soft and saucy to firmly set and cuttable. As we do not use any added pectin or stabilizers, our preserves vary in texture based on the quantity of natural pectin in the fruit, the methodology, and the proportion of sugar and lemon juice used.

Jelly

A clear, firmly set spread with no fruit pieces whatsoever. Jellies are made by boiling fruit in water to extract the pectin and flavour, and then straining out the fruit pulp through muslin or a fine-mesh sieve to produce a flavourful stock. This stock is then mixed with sugar and lemon juice in the proper proportion, and cooked to a lovely, clear consistency.

Marmalade

Typically made with the whole citrus fruit, including thinly sliced zest and pith. The most traditional marmalade is made with bitter Seville oranges, but it can be made with virtually any citrus fruit, including lemons, clementines, kumquats, Buddha's hand, citrons, limes, and many other types of oranges. Our marmalade is rustic, made with hand-cut citrus sliced crosswise to include the whole fruit, which is then boiled in water and softened until it is the perfect texture. It is then mixed with reduced citrus stock to give the final product a bit of space between the slices, ensuring a lovely, firm set and spreadable consistency, with pieces of zest that you can bite through without pulling the whole strip off your toast.

Jamalade

Made with a base of fleshy fruit, such as stone fruit, berries, or tropical varieties, and blended with slices of citrus zest and flesh. For jamalades, we typically start with jam as a canvas and add blanched marmalade cuts that candy while they cook within the jam. The addition of citrus adds complexity and a unique texture, and it is a fun and stress-free way to work with citrus, allowing you to focus on the palate of flavours rather than a perfect set.

Jam Making Theory

The Pectin:Sugar: Acid Ratio

When making traditional fruit preserves of any type, there are three main ingredients: fruit, sugar, and lemon juice. The proportion and balance of these elements will dictate the cooking process, as well as the final texture and flavour of your preserve. Let's look at each in turn to understand how they work in harmony.

Pectin: Pectin is a naturally occurring molecule that holds the cells of plant matter together. Fruits vary in the amount of natural pectin in their cells, with firm, seedy fruit such as apples, quince, citrus, and seedy berries (like raspberries and blackberries) containing the most pectin, and soft fruits such as blueberries, strawberries, rhubarb, and stone fruit containing the least pectin. Boiling jam with sugar and lemon juice causes fruit to break down, releasing the pectin in their cells and forming a molecular gel network that gives jam its characteristic texture after cooling.

Sugar: Sugar's role in jam making is three-fold: adding sweetness, helping to activate the pectin reaction, and ensuring safe preservation. To be suitably preserved, all jam must fall within 55 to 70 Brix, which is a direct measure of sugar concentration. You may have heard the rule that jam sets at 220°F (105°C); however, this is a commonly misunderstood metric. Although heat is, of course, necessary, it is not temperature that directly triggers the pectin reaction. Since molten sugar reaches higher temperatures than water, the 220°F (105°C) baseline is simply a result of sugar concentration and how much evaporation you have achieved. (See Temperature, page 13.) Therefore, preserves with lower starting sugar ratios typically need to be cooked longer to achieve the proper final sugar concentration, and jams with higher starting sugar ratios may be cooked for less time to achieve the same ending sugar concentration. Of course, these contrasting preparations will yield two vastly different preserves in terms of texture, freshness of flavour, and brightness of colour. (See Sugar Concentration, page 10.)

Acid: Lemon juice (or, chemically speaking, citric acid) is the most common acid used in traditional fruit preservation as it lends a lovely brightness that marries extremely well with fruity flavours. Acid is also particularly important in jam making because in high concentrations and combined with sugar, it allows the natural pectin to form its gel network. Though fruit does contain natural levels of acidity, additional acid is almost always necessary to allow jam to set.

Sugar Concentration

We have learned that it is the balance of fruit (pectin), sugar, and acid (lemon juice) that ultimately dictates the style, nuance, and success of a recipe. As you will see throughout this book, we push and pull the sugar and lemon juice proportions depending on the base fruit and desired results. Are we looking to make a velvety compote-like jam, or do we want pieces of fruit floating in our jam? Do we want something cuttable and firm or saucy and soft? To make these creative choices, we consider the fruit we are working with and then edit the starting sugar ratio.

It is tempting to reduce the amount of sugar in jam recipes, as its volume can be quite jarring; however, the starting sugar ratio of a recipe does not equate to the perceived sweetness or resulting sugar content of the final product. Sugar is hygroscopic, meaning that it attracts and bonds with water (see Maceration, page 12). Low-sugar recipes need to be cooked longer to evaporate their water content and achieve a jammy texture. They can therefore end up tasting sweeter—or even having a higher final sugar concentration—than high-sugar-ratio recipes (for example, fruit butters).

Perceived sweetness can usually be correlated to an improper balance of acidity, rather than purely to sugar concentration. Tart versus sweet jams have little to do with the starting sugar concentration in the recipe; the perceived flavour balance can instead be due to a

plethora of variables, including the raw flavour of the fruit used (for example, sour cherries versus sweet cherries), length of cooking time, amount of reduction, and amount of lemon juice.

At Kitten and the Bear, our recipes tend to fall within the three basic tiers of starting sugar ratio outlined below.

Low Sugar: These jams start at a 45 to 55 percent sugar to fruit ratio (for example, 450 g/2¼ cups of sugar to 1 kg of fruit). This proportion is best suited to fleshy, pulpy fruits with high water content, such as plums, pears, tomatoes, and sweet cherries. As low-sugar jams are cooked for a longer time (on average, 35 to 40 minutes of boiling), this proportion gives the fruit time to break down and fall apart, resulting in a homogenous, soft-set, velvety texture that is more compote-like. These recipes will require more stirring to prevent the high proportion of fruit content from sticking to the bottom of the pan, with the goal being to achieve the most evaporation of water content (rather than triggering the pectin reaction). Therefore, the texture in the pot won't change very much as the jam cools.

Mid-Sugar: These jams start at a 55 to 65 percent sugar to fruit ratio (for example, 550 g/2¾ cups of sugar to 1 kg of fruit). This proportion is best suited to fruits that have average, middle-of-the-road pectin levels, such as apricots, peaches, sour cherries, and wild blueberries. Jams with mid-sugar levels will have a glistening texture, with chunks of fruit floating in their own jammy ocean. The cooking time of these recipes will be closer to 15 to 20 minutes, thus fruit will be breaking down, but the texture will not be fully homogeneous. Adding sugar creates space between the pieces of fruit, thus requiring less stirring than their low-sugar cousins. Finally, these recipes rely on both evaporation/reduction and the pectin reaction to set. They will set up a bit more so as they cool.

High Sugar: These jams start at a 65 to 80 percent sugar to fruit ratio (for example, 650 g/3¼ cups of sugar to 1 kg of fruit). This proportion is best suited to fruits with very high natural pectin content, such as apples, currants, raspberries, blackberries, and citrus fruits. Recipes that use a high proportion of sugar will cook very quickly, between 10 and 20 minutes of boiling time, and rely almost exclusively on the pectin reaction to set. Therefore, they require the least amount of stirring and will look practically liquid when entering the jar. After 12 to 48 hours, they will set into a lovely jelly-like texture with pieces of fruit suspended within. For marmalade and seedy berries, a high-sugar ratio is necessary, as the sugar gives the fruit room to breathe.

Additional Methods to Control the Outcome

Maceration: For the vast majority of jam recipes in this book, we use maceration as an important tool to achieve flavourful, beautifully textured preserves. In jam making, maceration is the process of soaking fruit in sugar and lemon juice before cooking. Maceration's purpose is manyfold: First, it softens the fruit and begins the process of breaking down the cell walls to release the flavour and aroma of the fruit into the jam liquid. During this process, sugar also enters the fruit structure through osmosis, resulting in a candying effect, higher concentration of flavours, and better structure and preservation of the fruit pieces within your jam.

Second, and most important, sugar is hygroscopic, meaning that it attracts and bonds with water molecules, creating a syrupy texture (as opposed to oils, which are hydrophobic and repel water). Because of this characteristic, allowing fresh fruit to soak in sugar will draw the water content out of the fruit, dissolving the sugar crystals gradually and allowing for greater and faster evaporation during the cooking process. A shorter cooking time and greater evaporation, coupled with the candying effect of the sugar soak, mean the fruit pieces have

a better chance of maintaining their shape (especially in high-sugar-ratio recipes).

Throughout this book, you will notice that the average maceration time for most fruits is 12 to 24 hours (overnight) in your fridge. However, we do occasionally skip maceration for tender, thin-skinned fruit such as raspberries and blueberries. At the other end of the spectrum, we may extend maceration time for very tough, fibrous produce such as rhubarb that needs lots of time to soften or in recipes in which we want the resulting jam to consist of whole candied pieces of fruit.

Reduction: Reduction is an important factor in jam making. All jams, regardless of sugar ratio, require some degree of moisture evaporation. As mentioned earlier (see Sugar Concentration, page 10), low-sugar jams that depend less on the pectin reaction require more evaporation to thicken, and high-sugar jams that rely on the pectin reaction to set rely less on evaporation. It is the play between sugar concentration (aka, reduction) and pectin that will ultimately dictate the texture and richness of your jams.

Temperature: Sugar reacts very differently at specific temperature stages; thus, it is an important factor in all candy work and will determine whether your sugar will flow, sheet, snap, or crack. When working with non-fruit sugar syrups (for example, sugar in water), temperature is directly correlated with sugar concentration, and the results of sugar cooking are fully predictable. However, the metric of temperature is complicated when fruit pulp and pectin are introduced, and as we have discussed previously (see The Pectin:Sugar:Acid Ratio, page 9), temperature does not directly trigger a pectin reaction. In practice, you may use 220°F (105°C) as the average temperature at which jam sets; however, know that not all jams will reach 220°F (105°C), especially particularly low-sugar jams, or if you prefer your jam saucier in texture or fresher in flavour.

The Three Main Ingredients

Sugar

We have spoken in the previous sections about why sugar is an important ingredient in jam making; however, there are many different types of sugars out there, as well as alternative sweeteners that may be used in place of sugar. The sugar that we always prefer, and the most popular for jam making, is classic white granulated table sugar. Granulated sugar is usually made with either refined sugar cane or sugar beets, depending on the refinery, but both yield the white table sugar we all know and love. This sugar has uniform and perfectly sized crystals that dissolve slowly and evenly, and, as the refining process strips the sugar of molasses, it dissolves clear and will not muddy the colour or flavour of your jams.

Speaking of molasses, brown and raw sugar may also be used for jam making. Brown sugar is refined sugar that has had the molasses added back in during its processing, and it is also slightly more acidic. Therefore, expect a darker colour and a more caramelized, rich flavour in your jams, as well as a denser texture. Raw sugar

is similar to brown sugar in that it contains molasses; however, in this case the molasses has never been removed, as it is still in its raw, unrefined state. Regardless of its processing, you can still expect a browner colour and an earthy, molasses taste in your jams. If you prefer to use brown or raw sugar in your preserves, we recommend substituting only a portion of the white sugar, 1:1 (for example, in our Baked Apple and Brown Sugar Jam, page 115).

Of all the sugar substitutes available, the only one that we recommend for jam making is liquid honey. This is a great alternative for those who prefer low-refined-sugar diets or for children over the age of twelve months. Honey has a lovely, floral sweetness and will impart its delicate flavour to your preserve. We like to use liquid wildflower honey, which is light in colour and thus will still allow the bright colours of your fruit to shine. As honey will not activate a pectin reaction in the same way that sugar does, we must thicken these jams with a combination of pectin-rich fruits and evaporation. A great example of this is in our Children's Strawberry and Honey Jam (page 49), which uses cranberries to increase the natural pectin levels and add much needed body to this otherwise saucy jam.

Fruit

There is much romance to the art of jam making, conjuring images of linen-lined baskets overflowing with still-warm-from-the-sun fruit. Although in-season, sun-ripened fruit is a gorgeous start to a jam making journey, it is absolutely not necessary to make lovely and tasty preserves. Farm-fresh, conventional, grocery store, bruised, or frozen fruit are absolutely suitable for jam making (if not preferred in some cases!) and can all be substituted for each other, 1:1. Regardless of fruit quality, your homemade jam will still be vastly superior to commercial varieties.

Acid

Lemon juice is the most common acid in jam making, and though it is best to use freshly squeezed, you may use bottled or frozen unsweetened lemon juice in a 1:1 substitution. If you are using concentrated lemon juice, be sure to check the packaging for the dilution ratio to make it equivalent to freshly squeezed.

How to Add Flavourings

A plethora of flavours can be used in preserve making to create something all your own. Knowing when to add these ingredients is important to make sure their flavours come through as intended.

Fresh Herbs

Add fresh herbs to your jam at the very end of the cooking process, when your jam is fully cooked and off the heat. Submerge full sprigs of your herbs within the jam and allow them to infuse for about 5 minutes. Then, remove the sprigs with heatproof tongs and place the sprigs on a heatproof plate. Use your spatula to press on the leaves and scrape away as much jam as possible back into the pot for every drop of flavour.

Dried Herbs and Ground Spices

Add dried herbs and ground spices into your jam at the very beginning of the cooking process to give the dehydrated bits as much time as possible to absorb liquid, rehydrate, and become tender. If added at the end of cooking or when most of the water has already been boiled off, they will float on top of the jam and add a gritty, textured mouth-feel to your preserve.

Whole Spices

Add whole spices into your jam at the very beginning of the jam-making process. You may even add whole spices into the maceration to give them the longest time to infuse. Depending on the size of the spice pod and how much you would like to add to the jam, you may either use a large tea infuser/spice ball or allow them to float freely. Remove them at the very end of the cooking process, or simply leave them in each jar as decoration!

Fresh Florals

Fresh florals are perhaps the most delicate infusion because of the fragile nature of fresh blossoms. The goal is to keep your florals whole and as fresh as possible, as withering will dramatically change their flavour. Therefore, it is best to add your fresh florals at the very end of the cooking process, off the heat. Pluck your blossoms off their stems directly into the pot to catch all of their fragrant pollen. Stir gently to distribute, and jar immediately. The exception to this rule is when making floral jellies using a tea-like infusion (such as Pink Apple and Lilac Blossom Jelly, page 101). In this method, strain your fruit stock directly over top of the florals and steep before adding the sugar and lemon.

Spirits and Essences

Any alcohol-based flavourings, including spirits, extracts, and liqueurs, should be added after the initial boil, when the foam on your jam has subsided and has been skimmed off (if necessary) and there are still at least 5 to 10 minutes of cooking time left so that you boil off any residual alcohol content. If you are working with a gas stove, be sure to turn off the flame when adding spirits for safety's sake, and then turn the flame back on to continue cooking your preserve.

Wine and Port

To truly impart wine flavours into a preserve, quite a bit of volume is necessary, which means that this additional water content will need to be boiled off for the jam to set. Therefore, we recommend adding the wine or port into the maceration liquid to start the infusion as early as possible and allow the fruit to soak up those rich wine flavours during the sugar's osmosis. Expect wine-infused jams to boil for longer than usual to achieve the necessary reduction.

Sourcing and Preparing Your Fruit

A Note on Measuring Fruit

For the recipes in this book, all the measurements given for fruit should be the weight of the fully prepared fruit. For example, "1.5 kg of peaches" means 1.5 kg of diced peaches with the peels and stones already removed. Therefore, be sure to buy extra when purchasing your fruit to account for any waste.

For berries, purchase only 25 to 50 g extra per kilogram for the nominal weight of the greens of strawberries or a few soft blueberries. For stone fruit jams in which the stone is removed and skin is included (plums, nectarines), purchase 100 to 200 g per kilogram extra. For stone and tree fruit jams where the skin and stones/cores are removed, account for a bit more weight in waste—300 to 500 g per kilogram—using your best judgment.

For a more practical method, when you are at the grocery store, use the produce scale to weigh the amount of fruit the recipe calls for, and then add one to two pieces of fruit or one clamshell for low-waste fruits such as citrus and berries. For high-waste fruits, for example, peaches, apples, or bananas, add two to three additional pieces of fruit.

Unique Fruit Preparation

Type of Fruit	Preparation
Berries	1. Wash berries well. Sort through and discard any mushy or mouldy ones. 2. For strawberries, remove the greens by inserting a small paring knife into the top of the berry and spin to twist the knife around the stem end.
Stone Fruit— Peaches (skins removed)	1. Fill a large bowl with ice water. Bring a large, wide rondo or stock pot of water to a boil over high heat. Working in batches, about three peaches at a time, submerge the peaches in the boiling water and blanch for 1 minute or until you notice the skin beginning to crack and peel. Using a slotted spoon, remove the blanched peaches from the boiling water and plunge them into the ice water until cool enough to handle, 1 to 2 minutes. 2. Once you have blanched all the peaches, peel the skins off the fruit and discard. Cut each peach in half, and remove and discard the stone. Dice each half into ½-inch cubes. Weigh the prepared peaches to the specifications in the recipe.
Citrus— Marmalade Cuts (zest included)	1. Wash the fruit well, scrubbing each fruit with mild soap and hot water to remove any wax. 2. Cut each fruit lengthwise into 1-inch-thick wedges. Then, cut each wedge crosswise in delicate triangle shaped slices no more than ⅛ inch thick. (These will be the strips of zest in your finished marmalade.) 3. Weigh the prepared slices to the specifications of the recipe. 4. If your recipe includes citrus stock, you may add any seeds, pith, or scraps you have collected while cutting the slices to the stock mixture for an extra hit of pectin.

The Five Stages of Cooking

1. Bring the jam to a boil on high heat, about 5 minutes.

2. Most jams will start to foam. Lower the heat to keep it as hot as possible without the mixture overflowing or sputtering. Do not skim; the foam will collapse on its own once the sugar has reached a high enough concentration.

3. Once the foam subsides, you will be able to turn the heat back up. Manage the heat to keep the jam as hot as possible without sputtering.

4. After about 10 to 20 minutes (for most recipes), the jam will start to thicken. The fruit will be broken down, and the bubbles will become smaller and evenly distributed across the surface of the jam. Remove from the heat and skim any foam from the surface, as needed.

5. Test for doneness using the wrinkle test and sheet test (page 21). If necessary, bring back to a boil for 3 to 5 minutes or until the jam is done. Jar and process.

Canning Step-by-Step

Testing for Doneness

After you have collected your fruit, chosen your recipe, infused your flavours, and cooked your jam to the perfect consistency, the final step is the canning process. Though this tends to be the source of intimidation for many home cooks, following a simple set of instructions will ensure your jam is perfectly preserved and ready to be stashed away in the pantry.

There are a number of metrics that you may use to ensure your preserve is set. However, please remember that for the traditional jam recipes in this book (for example, recipes with no additional packaged pectin added), there is no wrong outcome! It should be an enjoyable process, so try not to get too hung up on achieving a perfect set. If your jam comes out too saucy or too thick, there are plenty of uses for over- or under-set jam to ensure no effort goes to waste. However, the following are the best ways to test jam for doneness.

Temperature: We have spoken at length about the importance of temperature in jam making, and although temperature is not a 100 percent guaranteed metric, it does give you a good sense of sugar concentration and therefore how close your jam is to being done. Aim for approximately 220°F (105°C); however, do not be alarmed if your jam never reaches, or goes slightly above, this temperature. As long as you have reached at least 200°F (100°C), your jam is safe for canning. Regardless, we always recommend using a secondary test for doneness (or your intuition) to confirm how close your jam is to being done.

Wrinkle Test: Since set is a result of both temperature and reduction (lack of water), our go-to way to test for doneness is the wrinkle test. When you sense that your jam is getting close to being done with the cooking process, remove it from the heat and scoop a small amount of jam onto a spoon or ceramic plate that has been kept in the freezer. This will cool the jam down quickly and will give a good estimate of how the preserve will set up once it is jarred and sitting in your fridge. Allow the jam to cool for 3 to 5 minutes, and then slightly push the jam with the tip of your finger. A jam that is set will have formed a skin and will wrinkle when nudged. During this 5-minute wait, we also recommend not touching the pot of jam at all—after you test your jam on the spoon, you can also give the pot of jam a push with the tip of your spatula. If done, the pot of jam will also have formed a skin and will wrinkle when moved.

Sheet Test: Sheeting may take a bit of practice to be able to identify; however, it is a very quick and useful tool to check for doneness throughout the cooking process without having to remove your jam from the heat. Jam can be considered set when sheets, or wide planes of jam, fall from the spatula, rather than drips or ribbon-like liquid or syrup. To test for sheeting, dip your spatula completely in the pot of jam, and then raise it above the pot, rotating it gently to allow the jam to cool slightly while keeping the spatula horizontal. Continue to rotate for a minute or so away from the steam coming from the pot, and then gently rotate so that you are looking at the wide, flat side of your spatula, allowing the jam to run down the flat side and back into the pot. If the jam drips in drops, the jam is not adequately thickened and will need to continue to boil. If the jam runs in a sheet, or large sections that are ½ to 1 inch thick, your preserve is likely set! Proceed with the wrinkle test if you are still unsure or continue to the canning process.

Processing

Processing your finished jars of jam to be stashed away in the pantry tends to be the part of preserve making that gives the most anxiety. However, though it is an important part of the process, it does not have to be scary! Following a few simple steps makes for easy and, most importantly, safe results.

Step 1: Sterilize Your Jars

The most important factor in successful canning is cleanliness. Be sure to start with a perfectly clean and sanitary workspace, including tabletops and any tools you will be using during the canning process. Some of your tools may have plastic or rubber parts that cannot be heat-sanitized. A good wash in hot water and dish soap is sufficient.

Water Bath Sterilizing: To sanitize the jars, lids, and rings, begin by bringing a large, wide pot of water to a boil. The water level will rise significantly once the jars are submerged, so make sure the pot has high enough walls to accommodate the size of jar you are using. If you have hard or mineralized water where you live (for example, you find a white powdery film in your tea kettle), we recommend using bottles of distilled water to keep your jars crystal clear.

Once the water is at a rolling boil, submerge your jars using canning tongs, allowing water to fill each jar as you place it. Then, add the lids and rings. Boil for 10 minutes (adjusting for altitude).

Remove the jars, lids, and rings from the boiling water using canning tongs. Be careful when you lift the jars, as they will be filled with boiling water—pour this water back out into the pot. Place all of your materials upright on a clean kitchen towel and allow any residual water to evaporate.

Oven Sterilizing: As an alternative to water bath canning, you may also sterilize your jars in the oven. This is our preferred method, as removing the boiled empty jars from the water bath can be cumbersome and dangerous.

To oven sterilize, simply preheat your oven to 250°F (120°C). Arrange your jars, lids, and rings on a clean baking sheet, and place in the oven for a minimum of 30 minutes, or until your jam is ready to can.

Once your jam is finished cooking, remove the tray from the oven and allow the jars to rest and cool for a minute or two. Then, proceed with filling the warm jars with jam.

Step 2: Fill Your Jars

Using two heatproof plastic pitchers (or one large silicone ladle and one pitcher), scoop a portion of jam out of the pot, and pour it into the second clean pitcher. Whichever tool you use for scooping jam (either pitcher or ladle) should stay in the pot to keep your workspace clean.

This method allows you to move across your countertop without dripping jam as you go.

Place a canning funnel (optional) in the top of your first jar and pour the jam into the jar. Work slowly, as it is easier to top up an underfilled jar than clean up an overflowed jar. Continue until you have canned all of your jam. Then, go back and check the fill line of each jar, topping up if necessary—you should leave ¼ inch empty at the top of the jar (called the headspace).

Step 3: Cap Your Jars

To ensure a good seal, the rims of the jars must be perfectly clean and free of any jam or stickiness. Dampen a new piece of paper towel with warm water and run a clean finger around each jar rim. If you encounter any jam, wipe it away with the paper towel. Give it a minute or two to dry before capping—it will evaporate quickly since the jar will be warm.

To cap a mason jar, place the flat cap on the top of the jar. Then, screw the ring on top until finger tight. There is no need to use an undue amount of strength, as mason jars are specially designed for this purpose. Simply tighten as you would any condiment jar during ordinary use.

Step 4: Process Your Jars

For this step, a water bath is necessary. However, it is safer and much less cumbersome once the jars are full of preserves. Simply bring a large pot (as described on the previous page) to a boil, and submerge your full jars of jam using canning tongs. Boil at a simmer for 10 minutes (adjusting for altitude), ensuring the water is not sputtering or making your jars bounce around the bottom uncontrollably. Remove the jars from the water carefully, again using tongs, and place on a clean kitchen towel.

Step 5: Cool Your Jars and Store

Arrange your hot jars about 1 inch apart in a cool place where they will be able to rest undisturbed for a minimum of 12 hours. During this time, resist the urge to move or tip your jars at all, as the pectin is in the process of activating and setting your jam.

Once your jam is completely cool, is it safely preserved, and the jars are ready to store in a cool, dry, and (most importantly) dark place. Your preserves will last up to 1 year for red and purple jams, and up to 9 months for yellow jams (such as peach, apricot, and banana).

Tools and Equipment

Cooking Vessel

In this book, our goal is to make jam making easy and accessible using tools and ingredients from your own kitchen. The vessel in which you make your jam is no exception. The choices range from very fancy to the simplest of saucepans, but your jam will be equally delicious no matter what your jam has been boiled in. In this section, we have detailed our favourite jam-making vessels: the copper preserving pan, the stainless steel maslin, and the Dutch oven.

Copper Preserving Pan: Starting with the grandest, the copper preserving pan is deeply rooted in history and tradition, sometimes even being passed down through generations of jam makers. Historically, pure copper pans were prized for jam making as it was thought to lend a shiny, glistening look to the preserve through its metallic properties. We now know that the conductive properties of copper ensure a high cooking temperature and unrivalled uniformity in heat distribution (of superior importance in all confectionery work), while the quintessential wide shape of the pan is engineered to allow for the quickest evaporation of moisture. These come in three or four standard sizes, our recommendation being the smallest size (10.5 L/11 quarts) for home use.

As these pans are made of uncoated copper inside and out, they can only be used for sugar work, as the sugar prevents the copper from leaching into the contents. Therefore, this pan may be used exclusively for jam, caramel, and other high-sugar recipes. It cannot be used for any savoury or acidic applications such as stews, soups, chutneys, or pickling brines.

Stainless Steel Maslin Pan: A maslin, though also a traditional pan for jam making, is made of stainless steel and can thus be used for any recipe regardless of composition. Maslins are also easily accessible and tend to be on the less pricey end of the spectrum, depending on manufacturer and quality. These pans typically include a number of fun features to aid in your jam making, such as graded measurement markings on the interior, a spout for pouring, and a hinged handle, and some even come with a glass lid (which is excellent for jelly and marmalade making). When purchasing a maslin, look particularly for an encapsulated bottom or double-bottomed variety to ensure even heat distribution. These pans may also be used on any stove top,

including induction! In terms of size, these are relatively standard at an 8.5 L (9-quart) capacity.

Dutch Oven: Finally, Dutch ovens are one of our favourite vessels for home jam making, as they are iconic and versatile. A staple in any household, they are useful in a wide variety of applications, including preserving, making savoury stews, sauces, and soups, and even bread baking! Made of thick, enamelled cast iron, these heavy-duty pots are superb conductors of heat—similar to a copper preserving pan—and ensure extremely even heat distribution. All the recipes in this book have been tested in Dutch ovens, and our recommendation is the most classic and flexible 7 L (7.5-quart) size or larger.

Note: Copper preserving pans and maslin pans are shaped specifically for jam making and thus have slightly larger capacity and tall, sloped sides to give lots of room for the jam to foam and bubble. Dutch ovens are slightly shallower; therefore (especially if you are using a 6 or 7 L/6.5- to 7.5-quart pot), expect to be more diligent about heat and foam management as your jams are bubbling away.

Non-Reactive Containers with Lids (plastic or glass)

For mixing and macerating ingredients, any large glass, ceramic, or food-grade plastic will work just fine! The bigger the better, as it is always easier to mix chunky ingredients with lots of room. A tight-fitting lid is ideal, but a layer of plastic wrap works equally well.

Try to stay away from disposable plastics, such as reused takeaway food containers, as these plastics are not a good choice to hold high-acid foods for elongated periods of time.

Heatproof Plastic Measuring Pitchers

When filling your jars (see Canning Step-by-Step, Step 2: Fill Your Jars, page 21), a heat-resistant plastic liquid measuring pitcher is the best choice. Though glass pitchers are lovely for measuring ingredients, using plastic for canning negates any risk of glass chipping inside your jam. Depending on the size of your pot, you may also use a second pitcher—one pitcher to sink into the pot for scooping jam and a second clean pitcher to transfer your jam into its jars.

Heatproof Silicone Ladle

When scooping your jam out of the pot, a large ladle is a great tool to safely and cleanly transfer your preserve from the pot to a clean pitcher, which will then be used to pour the jam into the jars. Our preference is a silicone ladle, as anything metal can scratch or damage the inside of your Dutch oven or copper pan.

Heatproof Rubber Spatula

Flexible, soft silicone or rubber spatulas are perfect for transferring your maceration mixture, as well as for stirring and scraping all of that hard work out of the pan. The longer the handle, the better to avoid splatter burns—we particularly like 16.5-inch spatulas, which have a handle about 12 inches in length.

Candy Thermometer

A digital high-temperature thermometer is a great tool for monitoring the doneness of your jam, but it is not essential. There are many options, including traditional candy thermometers and digital thermometers at all price points; however, if you are interested in a splurge, the digital varieties with a long, tethered probe are particularly luxurious for jam making. Dip the probe into your preserve, have a digital read in seconds, and watch the temperature slowly climb as the jam boils.

Canning Funnel

Though not necessary if you have a steady hand, a wide-mouth funnel will help keep your jars tidy and their rims clean during the canning process. Canning funnels usually feature an enlarged opening that will sit perfectly within the jar, keeping your hands free for scooping and pouring your jam. It is easy to overfill when using a funnel, so move slowly at the beginning to get a good sense of what a full jar looks like inside the mouth of the funnel.

Canning Tongs

If you are processing your jars in the water bath canning method, canning tongs are necessary. These are tongs that have a wide, rounded, rubberized grip that fits perfectly around standard jam jars to enable you to lift them in and out of their hot water bath safely. Before you use them the first time, be sure to practise by lifting a full jar of jam an inch or two over a padded surface, such as a folded kitchen towel. Jam-filled jars can be surprisingly heavy, and you may have to squeeze tighter than you might expect.

Glass Jars with Lug or Mason Caps

Jam jars come in a number of varieties, including mason style, lug cap, threaded cap, or Weck. For home canning, mason jars are our best recommendation, as they are easy to use, are relatively foolproof, and can be found widely in supermarkets and hardware stores, especially during the harvest seasons. Mason jars are made up of three parts—a tempered glass jar, a threaded metal ring, and a self-sealing lid. They come in many styles, including various mouth openings and volume capacities from 125 mL (4 ounces/½ cup) to 2 L (½ gallon/8 cups). The threaded rings and glass jars may be reused indefinitely with a simple sanitizing as long as no chips or cracks are present; however, the lids are one-time use and must be replaced with a new lid every time the jar is used. The lids have a sealing compound around their outer rim called plastisol. When you tighten the threaded ring, it presses the compound into the warm rim of the jar, which softens it and forms a gasket.

You will also notice that each lid has a convex pop top, which makes it easy to see (and hear!) that your jars have sealed properly.

As they cool, a vacuum is created inside the jar and the lid will be sucked downward. A quick press on each jar will reassure you that each jar is properly sealed. The rings should then be removed and used for the next batch! These may be used indefinitely as long as they are rust-free and free of any dents. And yes—you read that correctly! This means that your jars should be stored cap only, without the ring, as a fail-safe for identifying unsealed jars.

If you get your new and used lids mixed up, you can always tell whether a lid has been used by looking at the soft red or white material on its underside. If it is used, you will notice a full indent in the material where it has previously been sealed to a jar. If it is new, it will be plump and pristine.

PART ONE

Preserves

Berries

Strawberry, Raspberry, and Cream Jam

YIELD six 250 mL (8-ounce) jars

This elegant, dessert-like preserve is full of red berry sweetness and decadent creaminess. Whole, plump strawberries and a sprinkle of raspberries are blended with balanced notes of vanilla for a transparent, creamy linger. For our most beloved flavour, the trick is using flavourful, fresh berries and choosing a sweetly scented vanilla that appeals to your personal palate.

From whole Madagascar bean to high-quality flavouring, there are many types of vanilla to choose from, and each has its own unique profile. Though it may seem like culinary sacrilege, we opt for a naturally derived vanilla flavouring in our kitchen for this recipe to achieve that rich, vanilla-cake-like nuance. Vanilla, birthday cake, and whipped cream flavoured vodkas also make great choices and are readily accessible.

1.25 kg hulled strawberries
250 g raspberries
1 kg (5 cups) granulated sugar
125 mL (½ cup) lemon juice
1 tablespoon natural vanilla flavouring

1. **Macerate the fruit:** Combine the strawberries, raspberries, sugar, and lemon juice in a large non-reactive container, and toss gently to evenly coat. Cover with a lid and macerate in the fridge overnight for at least 12 hours but no more than 24.

2. **The next day, make the jam:** Sterilize your jars and lids by following the instructions on page 23.

3. Remove the macerated fruit from the fridge. Scrape the fruit mixture and all the juices into your preserving pan. Bring to a boil over high heat, stirring constantly, until the juices run from the berries and the sugar is dissolved. Once it boils, the mixture will begin to foam. Adjust the heat as needed to keep it as hot as possible without allowing the mixture to overflow or sputter. Continue to cook, stirring constantly and scraping the bottom of the pan to distribute the heat evenly and melt the foam back down into the mixture, about 5 minutes.

4. Once the foam subsides, boil over high heat (adjust the heat if the jam sputters) for another 10 to 15 minutes, stirring frequently. As the jam cooks, gradually reduce the heat to medium-low if needed to prevent scorching, and stir constantly until it becomes thicker, slightly syrupy, and the bubbles are smaller and evenly distributed across the surface. Remove from the heat and skim any foam from the surface.

5. Gently stir to evenly distribute the fruit within the syrup, and then test for doneness. The jam should pass the wrinkle test or sheet test and reach at least 200°F (100°C) on a candy thermometer (see page 21). If the jam still seems too loose, boil for another 3 to 5 minutes and check

recipe continues

the set again. Once set, remove from the heat. Immediately add the vanilla and stir vigorously to incorporate.

6. Pour the jam into the sterilized jars, leaving ¼ inch of headspace, and process by following the instructions on page 23. Arrange the hot jars about 1 inch apart in a cool place, and let sit undisturbed for at least 12 hours.

VARIATION: You can substitute the vanilla flavouring with 60 mL (¼ cup) of vanilla, birthday cake, or whipped cream flavoured vodka. Add the vodka toward the end of cooking when the jam is 3 to 5 minutes from being set. Stir vigorously to allow any alcohol to burn off. (Make sure your head is not over the pot, as the alcohol vapour has a very strong smell.)

NOTES

Strawberry, Gooseberry, and Elderflower Jam

YIELD six 250 mL (8-ounce) jars

A classic seasonal pairing, elderflowers, springtime strawberries, and gooseberries all appear at the market around late June to early July. The tartness and high natural pectin content of green gooseberries elevates and brightens this strawberry preserve in flavour and colour by ensuring a quick cooking time. Fresh elderflowers are a lovely addition, as they decorate every spoonful and impart their delicate perfume.

Fresh elderflower blossoms are not readily available on a commercial scale, but they grow abundantly in both white and pink varieties in our northern climate. Ensure your elderflowers are picked on a warm, dry day and use them as soon as you get into the kitchen. When they are freshly picked, the blooms will be bright, firm, and easily removed from their stems. While your jam is cooking, pluck the blossoms over a bowl or piece of parchment paper to catch all their fragrant pollen, ensuring no portion of the stem makes its way into the jam, as the stems are not edible. Toss the blossoms into the jam at the very end of the cooking process, off the heat—the best strategy with any fresh floral or herb for a delicate infusion and to avoid wilting.

750 g hulled strawberries
750 g topped and tailed green gooseberries, divided
    (375 g left whole; 375 g cut in half)
1 kg (5 cups) granulated sugar
125 mL (½ cup) lemon juice
5 g (⅓ cup) fresh elderflower blossoms

1. Macerate the fruit: Combine the strawberries, whole and halved gooseberries, sugar, and lemon juice in a large non-reactive container, and toss gently to evenly coat. Cover with a lid and macerate in the fridge overnight for at least 12 hours but no more than 24.

2. The next day, make the jam: Sterilize your jars and lids by following the instructions on page 23.

3. Remove the macerated fruit from the fridge. Scrape the fruit mixture and all the juices into your preserving pan. Bring to a boil over high heat, stirring constantly, until the juices run from the berries and all the sugar is dissolved. Once it boils, the mixture will begin to foam. Adjust the heat as needed to keep it as hot as possible without allowing the mixture to overflow or sputter. Continue to cook, stirring constantly and scraping the bottom of the pan to distribute the heat evenly and melt the foam back down into the mixture, about 5 minutes.

4. Once the foam subsides, boil over high heat (adjust the heat if the jam sputters) for another 10 to 15 minutes, stirring frequently. As the jam cooks, gradually reduce the heat to medium-low if needed to prevent scorching, and stir constantly until it becomes

recipe continues

thicker, slightly syrupy, and the bubbles are smaller and evenly distributed across the surface. Remove from the heat and skim any foam from the surface.

5. Gently stir to evenly distribute the fruit within the syrup, and then test for doneness. The jam should pass the wrinkle test or sheet test and reach at least 200°F (100°C) on a candy thermometer (see page 21). If the jam still seems too loose, boil for another 3 to 5 minutes and check the set again. Once set, remove from the heat. Immediately add the elderflower blossoms and stir to evenly distribute them within the jam. Let sit for 1 to 2 minutes. Stir again to re-incorporate any blossoms that floated to the top.

6. Pour the jam into the sterilized jars, leaving ¼ inch of headspace, and process by following the instructions on page 23. Arrange the hot jars about 1 inch apart in a cool place, and let sit undisturbed for at least 12 hours.

VARIATION: You can substitute the fresh elderflower blossoms for 2 to 3 tablespoons of elderflower syrup, cordial, or liqueur. Add toward the end of cooking, when the jam is 3 to 5 minutes from being set. You may need to add 3 to 5 minutes onto the total cooking time to account for additional evaporation.

NOTES

Strawberry and Rhubarb Pie Jam

YIELD six 250 mL (8-ounce) jars

Nostalgic as a warm summer's day, strawberry and rhubarb is such a historic pairing that it is practically a flavour unto itself. The addition of warming pie spices and vanilla evokes images of red-and-white checkered picnic blankets, sundresses, and wicker baskets.

Easy as pie, the trick to a successful pectin-free strawberry and rhubarb preserve is to choose the reddest rhubarb you can find. Often these varieties will be less fibrous and yield a brighter colour and superior texture than their green, stalky counterparts. Additionally, macerate the rhubarb for an extra day, and then cook the jam until it is practically as thick as you will want the end product to be. A high-water content and low natural pectin in both fruits can yield a soupy, compote-like preserve, so cook diligently and stir often until it is thick enough that you get a clean gap on the bottom of the pan for a moment when you scrape with your spatula.

750 g topped and tailed rhubarb
1 kg (5 cups) granulated sugar
750 g hulled strawberries
125 mL (½ cup) lemon juice
1 teaspoon ground cinnamon
1 teaspoon ground cardamom
1 teaspoon pure vanilla extract

1. **Prepare the rhubarb and macerate the fruit:** Slice the rhubarb stalks crosswise into ½-inch chunks. Individual rhubarb fibres may not break down during cooking, so the length of each piece of fruit should not exceed the length of the bowl of a teaspoon to avoid an overly stringy preserve.

2. Combine the rhubarb and sugar in a large non-reactive container, and toss gently to evenly coat. Cover with a lid and macerate at room temperature for at least 12 hours but no more than 24.

3. After the first maceration period, add the strawberries and lemon juice to the fruit mixture and stir to combine. Re-cover and macerate in the fridge overnight for at least another 12 hours but no more than 24 (24 to 48 hours total maceration).

4. **The next day, make the jam:** Sterilize your jars and lids by following the instructions on page 23.

5. Remove the macerated fruit from the fridge. Scrape the fruit mixture and all the juices into your preserving pan. Add the cinnamon, cardamom, and vanilla and stir gently to combine. Bring to a boil over high heat, stirring constantly, until the juices run from the berries and the sugar is dissolved. The rhubarb will look dense and stalky, but it will break down during the cooking process. Once it boils, the mixture will begin to foam. Adjust the heat as needed to keep it as hot as possible without allowing the mixture to overflow or sputter.

recipe continues

Continue to cook, stirring constantly and scraping the bottom of the pan to distribute the heat evenly and melt the foam back down into the mixture, about 5 minutes.

6. Once the foam subsides, boil over high heat (adjust the heat if the jam sputters) for another 10 to 15 minutes, stirring frequently. As the jam cooks, gradually reduce the heat to medium-low if needed to prevent scorching, and stir constantly until it becomes thicker and slightly syrupy and the bubbles are smaller and evenly distributed across the surface. Remove from the heat and skim any foam from the surface.

7. Gently stir to evenly distribute the fruit within the syrup, and then test for doneness. The jam should pass the wrinkle test or sheet test and reach at least 200°F (100°C) on a candy thermometer (see page 21). If the jam still seems too loose, boil for another 3 to 5 minutes and check the set again. Once set, remove from the heat.

8. Pour the jam into the sterilized jars, leaving ¼ inch of headspace, and process by following the instructions on page 23. Arrange the hot jars about 1 inch apart in a cool place, and let sit undisturbed for at least 12 hours.

Golden Raspberry and Golden Plum Jam

YIELD six 250 mL (8-ounce) jars

This golden preserve is so lovely, it shimmers both in flavour and in colour. Early Golden plums are the gems of our Niagara growing region, brightening the palate of farmers' markets and local groceries in early summer. Puckeringly tart, they are the best fruit to blend into your homemade preserves if you prefer sour jams and spreads. Pair with any berry—strawberries, raspberries, and sour cherries are some of our favourites—to cut through the richness and add a bit of body to a pure berry preserve.

For this recipe, we chose golden raspberries for a stunning gold-on-gold result. One of our rarest berries here in Ontario, golden raspberries bloom in two seasons—early July and late August. As opposed to their rich, red cousins, golden raspberries boast a mild raspberry flavour with a hint of lemon candy.

1.25 kg pitted and halved Early Golden plums*
1 kg (5 cups) granulated sugar
60 mL (¼ cup) lemon juice
250 g golden raspberries
1 lemon

1. **Macerate the fruit:** Combine the plums, sugar, and lemon juice in a large non-reactive container, and toss gently to evenly coat. Cover with a lid and macerate in the fridge overnight for at least 12 hours but no more than 24.

2. **The next day, make the jam:** Sterilize your jars and lids by following the instructions on page 23.

3. Remove the macerated fruit from the fridge. Scrape the fruit mixture and all the juices into your preserving pan. Bring to a boil over high heat, stirring constantly, until the juices run from the fruit and the sugar is dissolved. Once it boils, the mixture will begin to foam. Adjust the heat as needed to keep it as hot as possible without allowing the mixture to overflow or sputter. Continue to cook, stirring constantly and scraping the bottom of the pan as needed to distribute the heat evenly and melt the foam back down into the mixture, about 5 minutes.

4. Once the foam subsides, boil over high heat (adjust the heat if the jam sputters) for another 5 to 8 minutes, stirring frequently, until the plums are broken down and the jam appears homogeneous with no pockets of liquid between pieces of fruit. If necessary, mash the plums with a potato masher to encourage the fruit to break down.

5. Add the raspberries and stir to combine. Continue to boil for another 5 minutes. As the jam cooks, gradually reduce the heat to medium-low if needed to prevent scorching, and stir constantly. Golden plums have melting flesh and high acidity,

recipe continues

so when combined with the high natural pectin content in the raspberries, the jam may appear liquidy while hot, but it will set when it cools. Remove from the heat and skim any foam from the surface.

6. Gently stir to evenly distribute the fruit within the syrup, and then test for doneness. The jam should pass the wrinkle test or sheet test and reach at least 200°F (100°C) on a candy thermometer (see page 21). You will notice that once the jam is off the heat, a matte skin will quickly form on the surface. If the jam still seems too loose, boil for another 3 to 5 minutes and check the set again. Once set, remove from the heat.

7. Zest the lemon over the pan. Stir thoroughly to evenly distribute the flavour.

8. Pour the jam into the sterilized jars, leaving ¼ inch of headspace, and process by following the instructions on page 23. Arrange the hot jars about 1 inch apart in a cool place, and let sit undisturbed for at least 12 hours.

VARIATION: If Early Golden plums are not available, substitute 1:1 for Shiro plums, Mirabelle plums, or apricots. Red raspberries can easily substitute for golden, also at a 1:1 proportion. The resulting jam will be slightly richer and berry-forward.

*You will need about 1.5 kg of whole plums. See **A NOTE ON MEASURING FRUIT** (page 19).

NOTES

Farmers' Market Jam

YIELD six 250 mL (8-ounce) jars

A trip to the farmers' market is the perfect start to a full jam-making experience! In our market blend preserve, we chose a combination of strawberries, raspberries, blackberries, and blueberries, but feel free to substitute any berries you gather. Full fruit and rustic, it's the best of summer preserved in a jar.

An homage to the roots of jam making, this recipe lets you flex your creative muscles. Experiment with different combinations of as many varieties of berries as you can find. Just be sure to keep the total weight of all fruit constant (1.5 kg total). Do not feel shy about adding a little bit of flair either—a sprinkle of lavender, a splash of gin, or leaves from a couple of sprigs of fresh mint—this jam is sure to be a delicious, custom creation that is all your own!

750 g hulled strawberries
250 g raspberries
250 g blackberries
250 g blueberries
1 kg (5 cups) granulated sugar
125 mL (½ cup) lemon juice

1. **Macerate the fruit:** Combine the strawberries, raspberries, blackberries, blueberries, sugar, and lemon juice in a large non-reactive container, and toss gently to evenly coat. Cover with a lid and macerate in the fridge overnight for at least 12 hours but no more than 24.

2. **The next day, make the jam:** Sterilize your jars and lids by following the instructions on page 23.

3. Remove the macerated fruit from the fridge. Scrape the fruit mixture and all the juices into your preserving pan. Bring to a boil over high heat, stirring constantly, until the juices run from the berries and the sugar is dissolved. Once it boils, the mixture will begin to foam. Adjust the heat as needed to keep it as hot as possible without allowing the mixture to overflow or sputter. Continue to cook, stirring constantly and scraping the bottom of the pan as needed to distribute the heat evenly and melt the foam back down into the mixture, about 5 minutes.

4. Once the foam subsides, boil over high heat (adjust the heat if the jam sputters) for another 10 to 15 minutes, stirring frequently. As the jam cooks, gradually reduce the heat to medium-low if needed to prevent scorching, and stir constantly until it becomes thicker, slightly syrupy, and the bubbles are smaller and evenly distributed across the surface. Remove from the heat and skim any foam from the surface.

5. Gently stir to evenly distribute the fruit within the syrup, and then test for doneness. The jam should pass the wrinkle test

recipe continues

or sheet test and reach at least 200°F (100°C) on a candy thermometer (see page 21). If the jam still seems too loose, boil for another 3 to 5 minutes and check the set again. Once set, remove from the heat.

6. Pour the jam into the sterilized jars, leaving ¼ inch of headspace, and process by following the instructions on page 23. Arrange the hot jars about 1 inch apart in a cool place, and let sit undisturbed for at least 12 hours.

Children's Strawberry and Honey Jam

YIELD six 250 mL (8-ounce) jars

We are not shy with our sugar; however, sometimes it is best to start the little ones off slow! For this jam with no added sugar, we use a touch of honey for its sweetness and natural anti-microbial properties, as well as a handful of fresh cranberries whose extremely high natural pectin content helps to add stability, thickness, and a little tang. Perfect for guilt-free lunchtime PB&Js or slathered between layers of vanilla cake for a special birthday treat. (Please note, this recipe is not suitable for babies under one year old, as it is not recommended that children under this age consume honey.)

350 g fresh cranberries
250 mL (1 cup) water
1.15 kg hulled strawberries
750 mL (3 cups) liquid honey
2 tablespoons lemon juice

1. Sterilize your jars and lids by following the instructions on page 23.

2. Place the cranberries in a stainless steel maslin pan or Dutch oven (see Note) and cover with the water. Simmer over low heat for 2 to 3 minutes, until the cranberries puff up and burst and fall apart when stirred. Pass the cranberry sauce through a food mill into a medium bowl. (Alternatively, you can mash the cranberries thoroughly with a potato masher in the pot to completely break them down, and then push the purée through a strainer into a medium bowl to remove the skins.) You should have about 350 g of purée.

3. Combine the strawberries, warm cranberry purée, honey, and lemon juice in the same pot over low heat, stirring and scraping the bottom of the pan constantly, until the juices run from the berries. Gradually increase the heat as the fruit starts to float in the syrup until the mixture is simmering over medium heat. The mixture will begin to foam. Continue to simmer, stirring constantly to distribute the heat evenly and melt the foam back down into the mixture, about 5 minutes.

4. Once the foam subsides, simmer for 50 to 60 minutes, stirring frequently. As the jam cooks, gradually reduce the heat to low if needed to prevent scorching, and stir constantly until the jam is almost as thick as desired. Remove from the heat and skim any foam from the surface.

5. Gently stir to evenly distribute the fruit within the syrup, and then test for doneness. The jam should pass the wrinkle test or sheet test and reach at least 200°F (100°C) on a candy thermometer (see page 21). If the jam still seems too loose, boil for another 3 to 5 minutes and check the set again. Once set, remove from the heat.

recipe continues

6. Pour the jam into the sterilized jars, leaving ¼ inch of headspace, and process by following the instructions on page 23. Arrange the hot jars about 1 inch apart in a cool place, and let sit undistributed for at least 12 hours.

NOTE: Because of the sugar-free nature of this jam, we do not recommend using a copper preserving pan for this recipe. Use a double-bottomed stainless steel pot, maslin pan, or Dutch oven.

Blackberry, Plum, and Violet Jam

YIELD six 250 mL (8-ounce) jars

Inspired by vintage violet candies, this floral preserve is our quintessential teatime companion. Blackberries and flavourful, blue-skinned plums are subtly blended with violet for a traditional, fruit-forward preserve. There is something eternally whimsical and feminine about violets, which is perhaps why they are frequently seen delicately sugared atop dainty petit fours and painted on vintage teacups.

750 g pitted and diced black plums*
750 g blackberries
1 kg (5 cups) granulated sugar
125 mL (½ cup) lemon juice
60 mL (¼ cup) crème de violette (violet liqueur), or to taste

1. **Macerate the fruit:** Combine the plums, blackberries, sugar, and lemon juice in a large non-reactive container, and toss gently to evenly coat. Cover with a lid and macerate in the fridge overnight for at least 12 hours but no more than 24.

2. **The next day, make the jam:** Sterilize your jars and lids by following the instructions on page 23.

3. Remove the macerated fruit from the fridge. Scrape the fruit mixture and all the juices into your preserving pan. Bring to a boil over high heat, stirring constantly, until the juices run from the berries and the sugar is dissolved. Once it boils, the mixture will begin to foam. Adjust the heat as needed to keep it as hot as possible without allowing the mixture to overflow or sputter. Continue to cook, stirring constantly and scraping the bottom of the pan as needed to distribute the heat evenly and melt the foam back down into the mixture, about 5 minutes.

4. Once the foam subsides, boil over high heat (adjust the heat if the jam sputters) for another 10 to 15 minutes, stirring frequently. As the jam cooks, gradually reduce the heat to medium-low if needed to prevent scorching, and stir constantly until it becomes thicker and slightly syrupy and the bubbles are smaller and evenly distributed across the surface. Remove from the heat and skim any foam from the surface.

5. Gently stir to evenly distribute the fruit within the syrup, and then test for doneness. The jam should pass the wrinkle test or sheet test and reach at least 200°F (100°C) on a candy thermometer (see page 21). If the jam still seems too loose, boil for another 3 to 5 minutes and check the set again. Once set, remove from the heat. Immediately pour in the crème de violette. Stir vigorously to incorporate the flavour and allow any alcohol to burn off. (Make sure your head is not over the pot, as the alcohol vapour has a very strong smell.)

recipe continues

6. Pour the jam into the sterilized jars, leaving ¼ inch of headspace, and process by following the instructions on page 23. Arrange the hot jars about 1 inch apart in a cool place, and let sit undisturbed for at least 12 hours.

VARIATION: If you are lucky enough to source fresh culinary-grade violet blossoms or have a crop in your garden, let the jam cool for about 5 minutes off the heat before adding 250 mL (1 cup) of fluffy blossoms to get the most out of their delicate perfume. Include the whole flower, not just the petals, as much of their essence is held in the pollen.

*You will need about 900 g of whole plums. See **A NOTE ON MEASURING FRUIT** (page 19).

Raspberry and Black Currant Jam

YIELD six 250 mL (8-ounce) jars

With the perfect balance of earthy and sweet, this lovely preserve is a nod to days of old. Black currant jam is particularly coveted by traditionalists, making this blend extra special. Fresh black currants come into season mid- to late summer in Ontario and are some of our most prized crops. Musky and ever-so-slightly savoury, currants add a delicate earthiness that makes this preserve a perfect pairing for cheese scones or a brie en croûte.

Raspberries and black currants are both seedy fruits, so for this recipe we remove a portion of the seeds using a simple metal strainer during the cooking process. This will yield a more palatable, less crunchy jam. However, if you prefer heavily textured jams or do not have a heatproof strainer on hand, feel free to leave the seeds as nature intended. Your jam will be delightful regardless.

1.25 kg raspberries
250 g black currants
1.2 kg (6 cups) granulated sugar
90 mL (6 tablespoons) lemon juice

1. Sterilize your jars and lids by following the instructions on page 23.

2. Combine the raspberries, black currants, sugar, and lemon juice in your preserving pan over low heat, stirring and scraping the bottom of the pan constantly, until the juices run from the berries and the sugar is dissolved. Gradually increase the heat as the fruit starts to float in the syrup until the mixture is boiling over high heat. The mixture will foam minimally. Adjust the heat as needed to keep it as hot as possible without allowing the mixture to overflow or sputter. Continue to cook, stirring constantly and scraping the bottom of the pan to distribute the heat evenly and melt the foam back down into the mixture, about 5 minutes.

3. Once the jam reaches a boil, reduce the heat to low and quickly scoop out about a quarter of the mixture using a plastic heatproof measuring pitcher. Holding a metal strainer over the pot, pour the scooped mixture into the strainer so it runs back into the pot. Using the back of a ladle or large spoon, push the fruit pulp through the strainer and back into the pot to separate the seeds. Fruit pulp tends to cling to the bottom of the strainer, so be sure to scrape the bottom over the pot. Discard the seeds.

4. Continue to boil the mixture over high heat for 5 to 7 minutes, stirring frequently. As this is a high-sugar-ratio recipe (see Sugar Concentration, page 10), we are relying on the pectin reaction, rather than reduction, to set the jam. The mixture will look liquidy while hot, but will set when it cools. Remove from the heat and skim any foam from the surface.

recipe continues

5. Gently stir to evenly distribute the fruit within the syrup, and then test for doneness. The jam should pass the wrinkle test or sheet test and reach at least 200°F (100°C) on a candy thermometer (see page 21). If the jam still seems too loose, boil for another 3 to 5 minutes and check the set again. Once set, remove from the heat.

6. Pour the jam into the sterilized jars, leaving ¼ inch of headspace, and process by following the instructions on page 23. Arrange the hot jars about 1 inch apart in a cool place, and let sit undisturbed for at least 12 hours.

VARIATIONS: If you cannot find fresh black currants at your local farmers' market, substitute with frozen black currant purée or good-quality preserved black currants in juice or syrup, available at most European grocers or specialty food stores. Substitute jarred black currants, strained from their liquid, in a 1:1 ratio, or 250 mL (1 cup) of frozen black currant purée. Add the fruit to the raspberries at the beginning of the recipe and continue as written.

You can make a classic raspberry jam by substituting the 250 g black currants with an equal amount of raspberries (1.5 kg total fruit for the recipe).

Saskatoon Berry, Apple, and Thyme Jam

YIELD six 250 mL (8-ounce) jars

Despite the name, the Saskatoon berry, also called the Service berry, can be found growing from the north/central United States all the way up to Alaska. These small, dark reddish-purple berries have a fruity, woodsy-like flavour with large crunchy seeds in the middle. Though a traditional food source in Indigenous cultures, these lovely and productive trees have become more popular as ornamental brush than for their fruit-bearing capabilities. With a close eye you may spot many Saskatoon berry trees dotting parks, lawns, and gardens right in your neighbourhood! Urban foraging is always a satisfying adventure, though be sure to give your fruit a good scrub with a mild dish soap and a thorough rinse before consuming.

   Paired with cubes of apple and a hint of thyme, this savoury preserve is full fruit and rustic. It pairs equally well with a hefty slice of crunchy toasted sourdough and butter or spooned over warm brie.

1 kg peeled and cored green apples,* divided (500 g cut into 8 wedges; 500 g diced into ¼-inch cubes)
250 mL (1 cup) water

500 g Saskatoon berries
1 kg (5 cups) granulated sugar
125 mL (½ cup) lemon juice
Leaves from 6 sprigs fresh thyme

1. Sterilize your jars and lids by following the instructions on page 23.

2. Combine the 500 g apple wedges and water in a small saucepan. Cover with the lid slightly ajar and simmer over low heat for about 15 minutes, or until the apples have softened and can be easily mashed. Pass the apples and their cooking liquid through a food mill directly into your preserving pan. (Alternatively, you can use an immersion blender or potato masher in the pan to completely break down the apples, and then push the purée through a strainer into a medium bowl.)

3. Combine the Saskatoon berries, 500 g apple cubes, sugar, and lemon juice in your preserving pan with the apple purée over low heat, stirring and scraping the bottom of the pan until the juices run from the berries and the sugar is dissolved. Gradually increase the heat as the fruit starts to float in the syrup until the mixture is boiling over high heat. The mixture may foam minimally. Adjust the heat as needed to keep it as hot as possible without allowing the mixture to overflow or sputter. Continue to boil over high heat (adjust the heat if the jam sputters) for 15 to 20 minutes, stirring frequently. As the jam cooks, gradually reduce the heat to medium-low to prevent scorching, and stir constantly. The apple pieces will begin to turn translucent and purple from the surrounding syrup. Once the apples are no longer opaque, your jam should be close to set and the fruit will suspend in the preserve. The jam will become thicker, slightly syrupy, and the bubbles will be smaller

recipe continues

and evenly distributed across the surface. For this recipe, this is a very good sign that your jam is reduced to the proper consistency. Remove from the heat and skim any foam from the surface.

4. Gently stir to evenly distribute the fruit within the syrup, and then test for doneness. The jam should pass the wrinkle test or sheet test and reach at least 200°F (100°C) on a candy thermometer (see page 21). If the jam still seems too loose, boil for another 3 to 5 minutes and check the set again. Once set, remove from the heat. Sprinkle the thyme leaves into the pan and stir to combine evenly.

5. Pour the jam into the sterilized jars, leaving ¼ inch of headspace, and process by following the instructions on page 23. Arrange the hot jars about 1 inch apart in a cool place and let sit undisturbed for at least 12 hours.

*You will need about 1.5 kg of whole apples. See **A NOTE ON MEASURING FRUIT** (page 19).

Strawberries and Chocolate Jam

YIELD six 250 mL (8-ounce) jars

Inspired by chocolate-dipped strawberries, this classic strawberry jam is kissed with a splash of chocolate liqueur for an elegant, romantic preserve. Adding chocolate directly to jams, as in our Dark Cherry, Plum, and Cocoa Jam (page 95), gives a jam-meets-chocolate-spread texture—brown, gooey, and rich. We opted for transparent chocolate liqueur (crème de cacao) in this recipe to maintain a vibrant red strawberry colour, glossy texture, and light, fruity flavour with a delicate cocoa nuance. Adding a second day of maceration allows the strawberries extra time to soak up the sugar and to candy, encouraging them to hold their shape during the cooking process and making it taste like you are pulling chocolate-covered strawberries out of the jar.

1.5 kg hulled strawberries
1 kg (5 cups) granulated sugar
125 mL (½ cup) lemon juice
60 mL (¼ cup) crème de cacao white liqueur

1. **Macerate the fruit:** Combine the strawberries, sugar, and lemon juice in a large non-reactive container, and toss gently to evenly coat. Cover with a lid and macerate in the fridge overnight for at least 12 hours but no more than 24.

2. After the first maceration period, transfer the fruit mixture and all the juices into your preserving pan. Heat gently over medium-low heat just until the mixture reaches a slow simmer, about 5 minutes. Remove from the heat. Transfer the mixture back into the non-reactive container and let cool at room temperature. Cover with a lid, return to the fridge, and macerate overnight for at least 12 hours but no more than 24.

3. **The next day, make the jam:** Sterilize your jars and lids by following the instructions on page 23.

4. Remove the macerated fruit from the fridge. Scrape the fruit mixture and all the juices into your preserving pan. Bring to a boil over high heat, stirring constantly, until the juices run from the berries and the sugar is dissolved. Once it boils, the mixture will begin to foam. Adjust the heat as needed to keep it as hot as possible without allowing the mixture to overflow or sputter. Continue to cook, stirring constantly and scraping the bottom of the pan to distribute the heat evenly and melt the foam back down into the mixture, about 5 minutes.

5. Once the foam subsides, boil over high heat (adjust the heat if the jam sputters) for another 10 to 15 minutes, stirring frequently. As the jam cooks, gradually reduce the heat to medium-low if needed to prevent scorching, and stir constantly until it becomes thicker and slightly syrupy and the bubbles are smaller and evenly distributed across the surface.

6. Remove from the heat. Immediately pour in the chocolate liqueur and stir

recipe continues

vigorously to incorporate the flavour and allow any alcohol to burn off. (Make sure your head is not over the pot, as the alcohol vapour has a very strong smell.)

7. Return to the heat and bring back to a boil for another 5 minutes to evaporate the chocolate liqueur. Remove from the heat and skim any foam from the surface.

8. Gently stir to evenly distribute the fruit within the syrup, and then test for doneness. The jam should pass the wrinkle test or sheet test and reach at least 200°F (100°C) on a candy thermometer (see page 21). If the jam still seems too loose, boil for another 3 to 5 minutes and check the set again. Once set, remove from the heat.

9. Pour the jam into the sterilized jars, leaving ¼ inch of headspace, and process by following the instructions on page 23. Arrange the hot jars about 1 inch apart in a cool place, and let sit undisturbed for at least 12 hours.

NOTES

Wild Blueberry and Chai Jam

YIELD six 250 mL (8-ounce) jars

The richness of wild blueberries meets the warmth of chai spices and black tea in this bold, flavourful preserve. As wild blueberries lack the fleshiness of their cultivated counterparts, wild blueberry jam is notoriously deep, dark, and sweet. We choose to embrace the innate syrupy set of this special preserve and cook this jam hot and fast for the freshest taste possible and to keep the berries whole and plump. It is perfect spooned over pancakes or waffles, drizzled over ricotta toast, or swirled into yogurt.

2 tablespoons loose-leaf chai tea leaves
125 mL (½ cup) boiling water
1.5 kg wild blueberries

1 kg (5 cups) granulated sugar
175 mL (¾ cup) lemon juice

1. **Make the chai concentrate:** Steep the tea in the boiling water, covered, for 8 to 10 minutes. You will notice that there is quite a bit of tea for a small amount of water. This is to increase the strength of the concentrate without making it taste overly extracted and bitter. Strain the tea through a fine-mesh strainer into a small bowl, pushing firmly on the leaves to squeeze out every drop of concentrate.

2. **Make the jam:** Sterilize your jars and lids by following the instructions on page 23.

3. Combine the blueberries, sugar, tea concentrate, and lemon juice in your preserving pan over very low heat, stirring and scraping the bottom of the pan constantly, until the juices run from the berries and the sugar is dissolved. Gradually increase the heat as the fruit starts to float in the syrup until the mixture is boiling over high heat. The mixture may foam minimally. Adjust the heat as needed to keep it as hot as possible without allowing the mixture to overflow or sputter.

4. Continue to boil over high heat (adjust the heat if the jam sputters) for 12 to 15 minutes, stirring frequently. As the jam cooks, gradually reduce the heat to medium-low if needed to prevent scorching, and stir constantly until it becomes thicker and slightly syrupy and the bubbles are smaller and evenly distributed across the surface. For this recipe, this is a very good sign that your jam is reduced to the proper consistency. Remove from the heat and skim any foam from the surface.

5. Gently stir to evenly distribute the fruit within the syrup, and then test for doneness. The jam should pass the wrinkle test or sheet test and reach at least 200°F (100°C) on a candy thermometer (see page 21). If the jam still seems too loose, boil for another 3 to 5 minutes and check the set again. Once set, remove from the heat.

6. Pour the jam into the sterilized jars, leaving ¼ inch of headspace, and process by following the instructions on page 23. Arrange the hot jars about 1 inch apart in a cool place, and let sit undisturbed for at least 12 hours.

Stone Fruit

Sour Cherry and Rhubarb Jam

YIELD six 250 mL (8-ounce) jars

Sour cherries are such a delicate and oh-so-lovely fruit. We eagerly await their arrival at the market every summer. They come into season in late July, just as rhubarb is bidding its farewell, which makes this jam a special and fleeting midsummer treat. A tart and rustic cousin of the forever-classic strawberry and rhubarb, sour cherries and rhubarb are a truly lovely pair. Their sweet-and-sour flavour palate is elegant enough for scones and jam, and down to earth enough for sourdough heels torn off the loaf.

This preserve is full fruit and rustic, filled with an abundance of texture from the cherries (kept whole) and quintessentially stringy rhubarb, and therefore benefits heavily from a two-day maceration. Late-crop rhubarb tends to be tougher and greener than early season harvests, so choose the pinkest and thinnest rhubarb you can find for a superior texture and brightest possible colour.

A little tip—a cherry pitter may be too rough for these delicate fruits, so use a firm drinking straw to remove the stones. Pluck off the stem and push the straw straight through. The stone will pop right out of the bottom.

750 g topped and tailed rhubarb
750 g stemmed and pitted sour cherries*
900 g (4½ cups) granulated sugar
125 mL (½ cup) lemon juice

1. **Prepare the rhubarb:** Slice each stalk crosswise into ½-inch chunks. Individual rhubarb fibres may not break down during cooking, so the length of each piece of fruit should not exceed the length of the bowl of a teaspoon to avoid an overly stringy preserve.

2. **Macerate the fruit:** Combine the rhubarb, sour cherries, sugar, and lemon juice in a large non-reactive container, and toss gently to evenly coat. Cover with a lid and macerate in the fridge for at least 48 hours (2 overnights).

3. **Two days later, make the jam:** Sterilize your jars and lids by following the instructions on page 23.

4. Remove the macerated fruit from the fridge. Scrape the fruit mixture and all the juices into your preserving pan. Bring to a boil over high heat, stirring constantly, until the juices run from the fruit and the sugar is dissolved. Once it boils, the mixture will begin to foam. Adjust the heat as needed to keep it as hot as possible without allowing the mixture to overflow or sputter. Continue to cook, stirring constantly and scraping the bottom of the pan to distribute the heat evenly and melt the foam back down into the mixture, about 5 minutes.

5. Once the foam subsides, boil over high heat (adjust the heat if the jam sputters) for another 10 minutes, stirring frequently.

recipe continues

As the jam cooks, gradually reduce the heat to medium-low if needed to prevent scorching, and stir constantly until it becomes thicker and slightly syrupy and the bubbles are smaller and evenly distributed across the surface. Remove from the heat and skim any foam from the surface.

6. Gently stir to evenly distribute the fruit within the syrup, and then test for doneness. The jam should pass the wrinkle test or sheet test and reach at least 200°F (100°C) on a candy thermometer (see page 21). If the jam still seems too loose, boil for another 3 to 5 minutes and check the set again. Once set, remove from the heat.

7. Pour the jam into the sterilized jars, leaving ¼ inch of headspace, and process by following the instructions on page 23. Arrange the hot jars about 1 inch apart in a cool place, and let sit undisturbed for at least 12 hours.

*You will need about 975 g of whole cherries. See **A NOTE ON MEASURING FRUIT** (page 19).

Golden Plum and Lavender Jam

YIELD six 250 mL (8-ounce) jars

Inspired by lemon lavender shortbread, this tart and floral preserve is puckeringly sour and ever-so-slightly floral from the addition of dried lavender blossoms. It is equally refreshing in summer as it is a welcome hit of sunshine in the depths of winter. We like to make this bright and happy preserve during Early Golden plum season in the Niagara region of Ontario (around mid-July) and tuck it away to enjoy year-round.

There are a handful of varieties of yellow plums that appear at the market throughout July, and each results in a slightly different preserve. When choosing your plums, try to find the Early Golden variety with a slightly blushed skin—these are guaranteed to have a free stone (no struggling to cut the fruit away from the pit), have lovely melting flesh, and yield a warm, golden-coloured preserve.

1.5 kg pitted and halved Early Golden plums*
1 kg (5 cups) granulated sugar
125 mL (½ cup) lemon juice
1 heaping tablespoon dried culinary lavender blossoms, or to taste

1. **Macerate the fruit:** Combine the plums, sugar, and lemon juice in a large non-reactive container, and toss gently to evenly coat. Cover with a lid and macerate in the fridge overnight for at least 12 hours but no more than 24.

2. **The next day, make the jam:** Sterilize your jars and lids by following the instructions on page 23.

3. Remove the macerated fruit from the fridge. Scrape the fruit mixture and all the juices into your preserving pan. Bring to a boil over high heat, stirring constantly, until the juices run from the fruit and the sugar is dissolved. Once it boils, the mixture will begin to foam. Adjust the heat as needed to keep it as hot as possible without allowing the mixture to overflow or sputter. Continue to cook, stirring constantly and scraping the bottom of the pan to distribute the heat evenly and melt the foam back down into the mixture, about 5 minutes.

4. Once the foam subsides, sprinkle in the lavender blossoms and stir to combine. Boil over high heat (adjust the heat if the jam sputters) for another 15 to 20 minutes, stirring frequently. The plums will soften and break down, and the jam will appear homogeneous with no pockets of liquid between pieces of fruit. As the jam cooks, gradually reduce the heat to medium-low if needed to prevent scorching, and stir constantly until it becomes thicker and slightly syrupy and the bubbles are smaller and evenly distributed across the surface. Remove from the heat and skim any foam from the surface.

5. Gently stir to evenly distribute the fruit within the syrup, and then test for doneness.

recipe continues

The jam should pass the wrinkle test or sheet test and reach at least 200°F (100°C) on a candy thermometer (see page 21). If the jam still seems too loose, boil for another 3 to 5 minutes and check the set again. Once set, remove from the heat.

6. Pour the jam into the sterilized jars, leaving ¼ inch of headspace, and process by following the instructions on page 23. Arrange the hot jars about 1 inch apart in a cool place, and let sit undisturbed for at least 12 hours.

*You will need about 1.8 kg of whole plums. See **A NOTE ON MEASURING FRUIT** (page 19).

Apricot, White Cherry, and Amaretto Jam

YIELD six 250 mL (8-ounce) jars

Apricots are one of our favourite fruits to work with, and we look forward to apricot season all year long. Fuzzy and adorable, these little golden orbs not only make stunning and relatively foolproof jam but are also a pleasure to work with and require very little prep work—simply wash and cut in half to remove the stone and you are done.

In this preserve, we chose to pair apricots with whole white cherries and a splash of amaretto. They are a natural marriage—the stone inside of an apricot contains a small kernel called the noyau. This kernel has a distinct almond flavour and is traditionally used to make amaretto. We've left the white cherries whole in this preserve, allowing them to float in a velvety, nutty apricot ocean. The addition of amaretto rounds out the profile, reminiscent of cherry almond cake and marzipan sweets.

750 g pitted and halved apricots*
750 g stemmed and pitted white cherries*
1 kg (5 cups) granulated sugar
125 mL (½ cup) lemon juice
60 mL (¼ cup) amaretto liqueur

1. **Macerate the fruit:** Combine the apricots, cherries, sugar, and lemon juice in a large non-reactive container, and toss gently to evenly coat. Cover with a lid and macerate in the fridge overnight for at least 12 hours but no more than 24.

2. **The next day, make the jam:** Sterilize your jars and lids by following the instructions on page 23.

3. Remove the macerated fruit from the fridge. Scrape the fruit mixture and all the juices into your preserving pan. Bring to a boil over high heat, stirring constantly, until the juices run from the fruit and the sugar is dissolved. Once it boils, the mixture will begin to foam. Adjust the heat as needed to keep it as hot as possible without allowing the mixture to overflow or sputter. Continue to cook, stirring constantly and scraping the bottom of the pan to distribute the heat evenly and melt the foam back down into the mixture, about 5 minutes.

4. Once the foam subsides, boil over high heat (adjust the heat if the jam sputters) for another 15 to 20 minutes, stirring frequently. The apricots will soften and break down, and the jam will appear homogeneous with no pockets of liquid between pieces of fruit. As the jam cooks, gradually reduce the heat to medium-low if needed to prevent scorching, and stir constantly until it becomes thicker and slightly syrupy and the bubbles are smaller and evenly distributed across the surface. Remove from the heat and skim any foam from the surface.

5. Gently stir to evenly distribute the fruit within the syrup, and then test for doneness.

recipe continues

The jam should pass the wrinkle test or sheet test or reach at least 200°F (100°C) on a candy thermometer (see page 21). If the jam still seems too loose, boil for another 3 to 5 minutes and check the set again. Once set, remove from the heat. Immediately pour in the amaretto and stir vigorously to incorporate the flavours and allow any alcohol to burn off. (Make sure your head is not over the pot, as the alcohol vapour has a very strong smell.)

6. Pour the jam into the sterilized jars, leaving ¼ inch of headspace, and process by following the instructions on page 23. Arrange the hot jars about 1 inch apart in a cool place, and let sit undisturbed for at least 12 hours.

*You will need about 900 g of whole apricots and 975 g of whole cherries. See **A NOTE ON MEASURING FRUIT** (page 19).

Sunshine Peach Jam

YIELD six 250 mL (8-ounce) jars

Golden peaches are blended with a hint of orange blossom water and a splash of yuzu juice for a preserve that is a bit floral and a tad citrusy—a bright and cheerful jam that brings to mind warm summer days and peach groves filled with sunshine!

All peaches fall into either the melting or the non-melting flesh category—melting flesh being ideal for jam making, and non-melting flesh being best suited for canned peaches. As the categories suggest, melting flesh cultivars will melt, or break down easily under heat, yielding a soft, full fruit, and velvety textured preserve. They are also freestone, meaning the flesh does not cling to the pit, which can be removed with a gentle twist. In contrast, non-melting flesh peaches will not break down under heat. Instead, the peaches will float in the syrup and may seem to turn even firmer when heated. These peaches are typically also clingstone, where the fruit clings to the pit and must be cut away. If you happen to find yourself surprised by non-melting flesh mid-batch, do not despair—toward the end of cooking, if your peaches still have not broken down, use an immersion blender or potato masher to break down the peaches manually. Your preserve will be equally peachy and delicious.

1.5 kg peeled, pitted, and ½-inch diced freestone peaches*
1 kg (5 cups) granulated sugar
150 mL (⅔ cup) lemon juice
20 mL (4 teaspoons) yuzu juice
27 mL (5½ teaspoons) orange blossom water

1. **Macerate the fruit:** Combine the peaches, sugar, and lemon juice in a large non-reactive container, and toss gently to evenly coat. Cover with a lid and macerate in the fridge overnight for at least 12 hours but no more than 24.

2. **The next day, make the jam:** Sterilize your jars and lids by following the instructions on page 23.

3. Remove the macerated fruit from the fridge. Scrape the fruit mixture and all the juices into your preserving pan. Bring to a boil over high heat, stirring constantly, until the juices run from the fruit and the sugar is dissolved. Once it boils, the mixture will begin to foam. Adjust the heat as needed to keep it as hot as possible without allowing the mixture to overflow or sputter. Continue to cook, stirring constantly and scraping the bottom of the pan to distribute the heat evenly and melt the foam back down into the mixture, about 5 minutes.

4. Once the foam subsides, boil over high heat (adjust the heat if the jam sputters) for another 10 minutes, stirring frequently. The peaches will begin to soften and become transparent. To encourage the fruit to break down, mash the peaches thoroughly with a potato masher. Boil for another 5 to 10 minutes until the jam appears homogeneous with no pockets of liquid between pieces

recipe continues

of fruit. As the jam cooks, gradually reduce the heat to medium-low if needed to prevent scorching, and stir constantly until it becomes thicker, slightly syrupy, and the bubbles are smaller and evenly distributed across the surface. Remove from the heat and skim any foam from the surface.

5. Gently stir to evenly distribute the fruit within the syrup, and then test for doneness. The jam should pass the wrinkle test or sheet test and reach at least 200°F (100°C) on a candy thermometer (see page 21). You'll be adding additional water content in the form of yuzu juice and orange blossom water, so you need to be sure that the jam has been sufficiently reduced. The jam must look thickened and no longer liquidy. If the jam still seems too loose, boil for another 3 to 5 minutes and check the set again. Once set, remove from the heat. Immediately pour in the yuzu juice and orange blossom water and stir vigorously to incorporate the flavour and encourage evaporation.

6. Pour the jam into the sterilized jars, leaving ¼ inch of headspace, and process by following the instructions on page 23. Arrange the hot jars about 1 inch apart in a cool place and let sit undisturbed for at least 12 hours.

*You will need about 2.25 kg of whole peaches. See A NOTE ON MEASURING FRUIT (page 19). For preparation instructions, see the chart UNIQUE FRUIT PREPARATION (page 19).

NOTES

Peach, Basil, and Lime Jam

YIELD six 250 mL (8-ounce) jars

This flavour pairing was one of the first peach preserves we ever made and continues to be a favourite! With a complex, cocktail-like flavour profile, this unassuming and adventurous jam is sure to be a crowd pleaser and conversation starter.

The trick to making this jam truly shine is achieving brightness of flavour and elegant texture—use perfectly ripe, melting flesh peaches, and the freshest basil you can find. Immerse the basil sprigs fully into the jam off the heat after the cooking process is complete. This allows them to infuse their green fragrance into the jam without leaving strands of herb behind. Squish the jam-soaked sprigs with your spatula to squeeze and scrape every infused drop of jam back into the pot. Once the basil is removed, grate lime zest directly over the pan to capture every spritz of citrus oil.

1.5 kg peeled, pitted, and ½-inch diced freestone peaches*
1 kg (5 cups) granulated sugar
60 mL (¼ cup) lemon juice
4 to 6 sprigs fresh basil
2 limes

1. **Macerate the fruit:** Combine the peaches, sugar, and lemon juice in a large non-reactive container, and gently toss to evenly coat. Cover with a lid and macerate in the fridge overnight for at least 12 hours but no more than 24.

2. **The next day, make the jam:** Sterilize your jars and lids by following the instructions on page 23.

3. Remove the macerated fruit from the fridge. Scrape the fruit mixture and all the juices into your preserving pan. Bring to a boil over high heat, stirring constantly, until the juices run from the fruit and the sugar is dissolved. Once it boils, the mixture will begin to foam. Adjust the heat as needed to keep it as hot as possible without allowing the mixture to overflow or sputter. Continue to cook, stirring constantly and scraping the bottom of the pan to distribute the heat evenly and melt the foam back down into the mixture, about 5 minutes.

4. Once the foam subsides, boil over high heat (adjust the heat if the jam sputters) for another 10 minutes, stirring frequently. The peaches will begin to soften and become transparent. To encourage the fruit to break down, mash the peaches thoroughly with a potato masher. Boil for another 5 to 10 minutes until the jam appears homogeneous with no pockets of liquid between pieces of fruit. As the jam cooks, gradually reduce the heat to medium-low if needed to prevent scorching, and stir constantly until it becomes thicker, slightly syrupy, and the bubbles are smaller and evenly distributed across the

recipe continues

surface. Remove from the heat and skim any foam from the surface.

5. Gently stir to evenly distribute the fruit within the syrup, and then test for doneness. The jam should pass the wrinkle test or sheet test and reach at least 200°F (100°C) on a candy thermometer (see page 21). If the jam still seems too loose, boil for another 3 to 5 minutes and check the set again. Once set, remove from the heat.

6. Using tongs, submerge the basil sprigs directly into the jam and let steep for 5 minutes. Remove the sprigs and transfer them to a heatproof plate. Use a spatula to press the basil leaves and scrape away as much jam as possible back into the pot. Zest the limes over the pan, and then cut each lime in half and squeeze the juice into the jam. Stir thoroughly to evenly distribute the flavour.

7. Pour the jam into the sterilized jars, leaving ¼ inch of headspace, and process by following the instructions on page 23. Arrange the hot jars about 1 inch apart in a cool place and let sit undisturbed for at least 12 hours.

*You will need about 2.25 kg of whole peaches. See **A NOTE ON MEASURING FRUIT** (page 19). For preparation instructions, see the chart **UNIQUE FRUIT PREPARATION** (page 19).

White Peach and Rose Petal Jam

YIELD six 250 mL (8-ounce) jars

Perhaps our most whimsical preserve, fresh rose petals impart their delicate perfume and decorate this velvety blush-pink spread. White peaches are at their most elegant adorned with wisps of pink petals, as their light colour and mild peach flavour blend perfectly with rose so that you are not quite sure where the peach ends and rose begins.

It is surprising to note that all rose petals are edible! However, please do not use roses from your local florist for culinary purposes, as these are not meant for consumption and are typically heavily sprayed with pesticides. Instead, opt for culinary, food-grade petals from your local farmers' market, or even better, pick from your own garden!

White peaches tend to oxidize and brown quickly, so it is best to dice them directly into the lemon juice to keep them bright in colour (see Step 1).

1.5 kg peeled, pitted, and ½-inch diced white peaches*
125 mL (½ cup) lemon juice
1 kg (5 cups) granulated sugar
25 g (1 cup) fresh culinary rose petals

1. **Prepare the peaches and macerate:** Place a large non-reactive container on a kitchen scale, pour in the lemon juice, and tare the scale to zero. As you are dicing the peaches, place them into the lemon juice and toss to completely coat. Scale out your prepared peaches to 1.5 kg.

2. Blanket the mixture with the sugar without stirring so that no air can reach the fruit. Cover with a lid and macerate in the fridge overnight for at least 12 hours but no more than 24.

3. **The next day (or same day) make the jam:** Sterilize your jars and lids by following the instructions on page 23.

4. Remove the macerated fruit from the fridge. Mix the fruit mixture thoroughly to saturate any dry sugar, and then pour the mixture and all the juices into your pre-serving pan. Bring to a boil over high heat, stirring constantly, until the juices run from the fruit and the sugar is dissolved. Once it boils, the mixture will begin to foam. Adjust the heat as needed to keep it as hot as possible without allowing the mixture to overflow or sputter. Continue to cook, stirring constantly and scraping the bottom of the pan to distribute the heat evenly and melt the foam back down into the mixture, about 5 minutes.

5. Once the foam subsides, boil over high heat (adjust the heat if the jam sputters) for another 10 minutes, stirring frequently. The peaches will begin to soften and become transparent. To encourage the fruit to break down, mash the peaches thoroughly with a potato masher. Boil for another 5 to 10 minutes until the jam appears homogeneous with no pockets of liquid between pieces

recipe continues

of fruit. As the jam cooks, gradually reduce the heat to medium-low if needed to prevent scorching, and stir constantly until it becomes thicker, slightly syrupy, and the bubbles are smaller and evenly distributed across the surface. Remove from the heat and skim any foam from the surface.

6. Gently stir to evenly distribute the fruit within the syrup, and then test for doneness. The jam should pass the wrinkle test or sheet test and reach at least 200°F (100°C) on a candy thermometer (see page 21). If the jam still seems too loose, boil for another 3 to 5 minutes and check the set again. Once set, remove from the heat. Sprinkle in the rose petals and stir. They will float at first, but simply continue to stir to encourage them to sink and disperse throughout the jam.

7. Pour the jam into the sterilized jars, leaving ¼ inch of headspace, and process by following the instructions on page 23. Arrange the hot jars about 1 inch apart in a cool place and let sit undisturbed for at least 12 hours.

VARIATION: If fresh rose petals are unavailable, feel free to use 8 g (⅓ cup) dried culinary rose petals (not buds) that can be found online or at local spice or tea shops. When your jam is heating on the stove, just before it starts to foam, scoop a small amount of warm syrup and place in a small bowl. Soak your dried petals in the warm syrup to saturate them with liquid during the cooking process. By the time you add them to the jam they will be rehydrated and heavy with syrup to allow them to sink and suspend within your jam, rather than float to the top. As with fresh blossoms and herbs, stir the syrup-laden petals into your pot at the very end of the cooking process off the heat for the best and freshest possible infusion.

*You will need about 2.25 kg of whole peaches. See **A NOTE ON MEASURING FRUIT** (page 19). For preparation instructions, see the chart **UNIQUE FRUIT PREPARATION** (page 19).

NOTES

Nectarine and Garam Masala Jam

YIELD six 250 mL (8-ounce) jars

In our opinion, nectarine jam is one of the most underrated preserves out there. It is elegant yet rustic, with natural notes of buckwheat honey, candied fruit, and cinnamon. Though at their peak at the height of summer (mid-August to early September), we love to stockpile our nectarine jam for autumn when that slight chill appears in the air. Be sure to allow your nectarines to ripen fully so that they are nice and soft to the touch for a velvety textured jam.

Garam masala, a traditional spice blend common in cuisines of the Indian subcontinent, is an unexpected yet lovely pairing for late summer red nectarines. Somewhat like a pie spice blend with a base of sweet spices such as cinnamon, nutmeg, cardamom, and clove, garam masala has the addition of savoury, warming notes—white and black peppercorn, cumin, fennel, mace, and coriander—though specific composition varies by region and the personal taste of the blender. None is considered more authentic than another, so either blend your own or find a spice house whose recipe you enjoy.

1.5 kg pitted and ½-inch diced red nectarines*
850 g (4¼ cups) granulated sugar
1 tablespoon garam masala
125 mL (½ cup) lemon juice

1. **Macerate the fruit:** Combine the nectarines, sugar, garam masala, and lemon juice in a large non-reactive container, and toss gently to evenly coat. Cover with a lid and macerate in the fridge overnight for at least 12 hours but no more than 24.

2. **The next day, make the jam:** Sterilize your jars and lids by following the instructions on page 23.

3. Remove the macerated fruit from the fridge. Scrape the fruit mixture and all the juices into your preserving pan. Bring to a boil over high heat, stirring constantly, until the juices run from the fruit and the sugar is dissolved. Once it boils, the mixture will begin to foam. Adjust the heat as needed to keep it as hot as possible without allowing the mixture to overflow or sputter.

Continue to cook, stirring constantly and scraping the bottom of the pan to distribute the heat evenly and melt the foam back down into the mixture, about 5 minutes.

4. Once the foam subsides, boil over high heat (adjust the heat if the jam sputters) for another 10 minutes, stirring frequently. The nectarines will begin to soften and become transparent. To encourage the fruit to break down, mash the nectarines thoroughly with a potato masher. Boil for another 5 to 10 minutes until the jam appears homogeneous with no pockets of liquid between pieces of fruit. As the jam cooks, gradually reduce the heat to medium-low if needed to prevent scorching, and stir constantly until it becomes thicker, slightly syrupy, and the

recipe continues

bubbles are smaller and evenly distributed across the surface. Remove from the heat and skim any foam from the surface.

5. Gently stir to evenly distribute the fruit within the syrup, and then test for doneness. The jam should pass the wrinkle test or sheet test and reach at least 200°F (100°C) on a candy thermometer (see page 21). If the jam still seems too loose, boil for another 3 to 5 minutes and check the set again. Once set, remove from the heat.

6. Pour the jam into the sterilized jars, leaving ¼ inch of headspace, and process by following the instructions on page 23. Arrange the hot jars about 1 inch apart in a cool place, and let sit undisturbed for at least 12 hours.

*You will need about 1.8 kg of whole nectarines. See **A NOTE ON MEASURING FRUIT** (page 19).

Damson Plum and Earl Grey Jam

YIELD six 250 mL (8-ounce) jars

Made with flavourful Damson plums, a coveted and traditional variety for jam making, this elegant preserve boasts a subtle citrusy note and black tea aromatics. Plums are a particularly perfect canvas for flavour additions, as they have a neutral, fruity flavour that allows even the most subtle ingredients to shine.

Earl Grey, the immensely popular black tea, has been considered a classic since the 1830s. Earl Grey is not a type of tea, rather, it is a blend—black tea scented with a robust portion of the aromatic oil of Italian bergamot, a prized citrus fruit. Add a little bit of teatime to your morning toast, yogurt parfait, or cheese board with this traditional jam, which uses both strongly brewed Earl Grey tea and a pure and organic culinary bergamot oil (which can be found easily online) to push the Earl Grey notes even further into the foreground.

1.5 kg pitted and ½-inch diced Damson plums*
1.2 kg (6 cups) granulated sugar
60 mL (¼ cup) lemon juice
2 tablespoons loose-leaf Earl Grey tea (or 3 tea bags)
125 mL (½ cup) boiling water
3 to 5 drops pure food-grade bergamot oil (optional)

1. Macerate the fruit: Combine the plums, sugar, and lemon juice in a large non-reactive container, and toss gently to evenly coat. Cover with a lid and macerate in the fridge overnight for at least 12 hours but no more than 24.

2. The next day, make the jam: Sterilize your jars and lids by following the instructions on page 23.

3. Prepare the Earl Grey tea concentrate: This jam tends to cook quickly, so it's best to make the tea concentrate before you start making the jam. In a glass carafe or measuring cup, steep the tea in the boiling water, covered, for 8 to 10 minutes. You will notice that there is quite a bit of tea for a small amount of water. This is to increase the strength of the concentrate without

making it taste overly extracted and bitter by extending the steep time. Strain the tea through a fine-mesh strainer into a clean measuring cup or small bowl, pushing firmly on the leaves to squeeze out every drop of concentrate. Set aside.

4. Remove the macerated fruit from the fridge. Scrape the fruit mixture and all the juices into your preserving pan. Bring to a boil over high heat, stirring constantly, until the juices run from the fruit and the sugar is dissolved. Once it boils, the mixture will begin to foam. Adjust the heat as needed to keep it as hot as possible without allowing the mixture to overflow or sputter. Continue to cook, stirring constantly and scraping the bottom of the pan to distribute

recipe continues

the heat evenly and melt the foam back down into the mixture, about 5 minutes.

5. Once the foam subsides, boil over high heat (adjust the heat if the jam sputters) for another 5 to 10 minutes, stirring constantly. (Damson plums make a thick preserve that sets quickly, so it is important to stir constantly and manage the heat carefully to prevent scorching. You may not be able to get the heat as high as with other jams, but that is fine.) The jam will very quickly appear homogeneous and jammy—very close to what the end, cooled result will be. Remove from the heat and skim any foam from the surface.

6. Gently stir to evenly distribute the fruit within the syrup, and then test for doneness. The jam should pass the wrinkle test or sheet test and reach at least 200°F (100°C) on a candy thermometer (see page 21). You'll be adding additional water content in the form of tea concentrate, so you need to be sure you have achieved enough reduction. If the jam still seems too loose, boil for another 3 to 5 minutes and check the set again. Once set, remove from the heat. You will also notice that once the jam is off the heat, a matte skin will quickly form on the surface.

7. Pour in the Earl Grey tea concentrate and bergamot oil, if using. Stir vigorously to incorporate the flavour and encourage evaporation.

8. Pour the jam into the sterilized jars, leaving ¼ inch of headspace, and process by following the instructions on page 23. Arrange the hot jars about 1 inch apart in a cool place, and let sit undisturbed for at least 12 hours.

*You will need about 1.8 kg of whole plums. See A NOTE ON MEASURING FRUIT (page 19).

NOTES

_____

_____

_____

_____

_____

_____

_____

_____

Greengage Plum and Wildflower Honey Jam

YIELD six 250 mL (8-ounce) jars

A holy grail fruit for jam making, the ancient Greengage (or Reine Claude) plum is a beauty, with a gorgeous sage green skin and dense golden flesh. Acclaimed for their unique honey-like flavour and bold look, they are traditionally used for preserving and prized in the French pastry arts for treats such as plum Tatins, crumbles, and galettes.

They are available more readily in Europe, particularly in southwest France, but interest in this historic plum has been rekindled in North America in recent years. They are not available on a commercial scale; however, if you happen upon Greengage plums at your local farmers' market or gourmet grocer (harvested from mid- to late September), be sure to pick up a handful—you won't be disappointed!

1.5 kg pitted and ½-inch diced Greengage plums*
450 g (2¼ cups) granulated sugar
325 mL (1⅓ cups) liquid honey
125 mL (½ cup) lemon juice

1. **Macerate the fruit:** Combine the plums, sugar, honey, and lemon juice in a large non-reactive container, and toss gently to evenly coat. Cover with a lid and macerate in the fridge overnight for at least 12 hours but no more than 24.

2. **The next day, make the jam:** Sterilize your jars and lids by following the instructions on page 23.

3. Remove the macerated fruit from the fridge. Scrape the fruit mixture and all the juices into your preserving pan. Bring to a boil over high heat, stirring constantly, until the juices run from the fruit and the sugar is dissolved. Once it boils, the mixture will begin to foam. Adjust the heat as needed to keep it as hot as possible without allowing the mixture to overflow or sputter. Continue to cook, stirring constantly and scraping the bottom of the pan to distribute the heat evenly and melt the foam back down into the mixture, about 5 minutes.

4. Once the foam subsides, boil over high heat (adjust the heat if the jam sputters) for another 3 to 5 minutes, stirring constantly. (Greengage plums make a thick preserve that sets quickly, so it is important to stir constantly and manage the heat carefully to prevent scorching. You may not be able to get the heat as high as with other jams, but this is fine.) To encourage the fruit to break down, mash the plums thoroughly with a potato masher, if necessary. Boil for another 5 to 10 minutes until the jam appears homogeneous with no pockets of liquid between pieces of fruit. As the jam cooks, gradually reduce the heat to medium-low if needed to prevent scorching, stirring constantly. The jam will very quickly appear homogeneous and

recipe continues

jammy—very close to what the end, cooled result will be. Remove from the heat and skim any foam from the surface.

5. Gently stir to evenly distribute the fruit within the syrup, and then test for doneness. The jam should pass the wrinkle test or sheet test and reach at least 200°F (100°C) on a candy thermometer (see page 21). If the jam still seems too loose, boil for another 3 to 5 minutes and check the set again. Once set, remove from the heat.

6. Pour the jam into the sterilized jars, leaving ¼ inch of headspace, and process by following the instructions on page 23. Arrange the hot jars about 1 inch apart in a cool place, and let sit undisturbed for at least 12 hours.

*You will need about 1.8 kg of whole plums. See **A NOTE ON MEASURING FRUIT** (page 19).

Dark Cherry, Plum, and Cocoa Jam

YIELD six 250 mL (8-ounce) jars

Somewhere between jam and chocolate spread, this fruity creation is pure decadence. We prefer dark, plump Bing cherries for this recipe, left whole so that they float within a sea of chocolatey, plummy goodness. Use a premium quality Dutch-processed cocoa powder to achieve a smooth, rich chocolate texture. Regular cocoa powder (also called natural) will yield a "powdery" mouthfeel and a less robust and fudgy chocolate flavour.

One of our favourite baking preserves, it is sure to elevate any jam-based dessert. Think chocolate cherry cruffins, jammy shortbread, twisted sweet breads, or as a drizzle over vanilla ice cream.

1 kg pitted and ½-inch diced black or red plums*
500 g stemmed and pitted dark sweet cherries*
690 g (3½ cups) granulated sugar
60 mL (¼ cup) lemon juice
60 g (¾ cup) Dutch-processed cocoa powder

1. **Macerate the fruit:** Combine the plums, cherries, sugar, and lemon juice in a large non-reactive container, and toss gently to evenly coat. Cover with a lid and macerate in the fridge overnight for at least 12 hours but no more than 24.

2. **The next day, make the jam:** Sterilize your jars and lids by following the instructions on page 23.

3. Remove the macerated fruit from the fridge. Scrape the fruit mixture and all the juices into your preserving pan. Bring to a boil over high heat, stirring constantly, until the juices run from the fruit and the sugar is dissolved. Once it boils, the mixture will begin to foam. Adjust the heat as needed to keep it as hot as possible without allowing the mixture to overflow or sputter. Continue to cook, stirring constantly and scraping the bottom of the pan to distribute the heat evenly and melt the foam back down into the mixture, about 5 minutes.

4. Once the foam subsides, sift the cocoa powder directly into the pot and stir to combine (this will help prevent clumping). Boil over high heat (adjust the heat if the jam sputters) for another 10 to 15 minutes, stirring frequently. The fruit will begin to soften and break down. If the plums are holding their shape, mash them thoroughly with a potato masher. Boil for another 10 to 15 minutes. As the jam cooks, gradually reduce the heat to medium-low if needed to prevent scorching, and stir constantly until it becomes thicker and slightly syrupy and the bubbles are smaller and evenly distributed across the surface. Because of its low sugar ratio, this jam will not firm up very much as it cools, so continue to cook until it is almost as thick as you want the

recipe continues

end product to be. Remove from the heat and skim any foam from the surface.

5. Gently stir to evenly distribute the fruit within the syrup, and then test for doneness. The jam should pass the wrinkle test or sheet test and reach at least 200°F (100°C) on a candy thermometer (see page 21). If the jam still seems too loose, boil for another 3 to 5 minutes and check the set again. Once set, remove from the heat.

6. Pour the jam into the sterilized jars, leaving ¼ inch of headspace, and process by following the instructions on page 23. Arrange the hot jars about 1 inch apart in a cool place, and let sit undisturbed for at least 12 hours.

*You will need about 1.2 kg of whole plums and 650 g of whole cherries. See **A NOTE ON MEASURING FRUIT** (page 19).

Tree Fruit

Pink Apple and Lilac Blossom Jelly

YIELD six 250 mL (8-ounce) jars

Floral, delicate, foraged, and inspired by a long-lost tradition. This recipe is a springtime ritual, with every step giving a certain satisfaction that only an age-old technique can offer.

Fresh lilac blossoms, which are one of the very first springtime blooms, are not available on a commercial scale. Thus, foraging is a must. Pluck your blossoms on a dry, sunny day when they are at their peak—full, bushy stems of firm, open blooms, so fragrant that you can smell them from a mile away, and before any petals are wilted or brown. It is tempting to allow them to live their full life on the stem, but don't wait, as their perfume will muddy as they age.

Don't throw out the apple mash. Store it to make Crab Apple, Sour Cherry, and Rosemary Jam (page 113).

75 g (3 cups) fresh lilac blossoms
1.5 kg pink-fleshed apples (such as wild pink crab apples, Geneva Crab, Pink Pearl, or Hidden Rose apples)

1.5 L (6 cups) water
60 mL (¼ cup) lemon juice
1 kg (5 cups) granulated sugar

1. Place the lilac blossoms in a large bowl or non-reactive container and place a metal mesh strainer on top. Set aside.

2. **Make the stock:** Cut the apples into 1-inch-thick wedges, including the cores and skins. Combine the apples and water in a Dutch oven or stainless steel maslin. Bring the mixture to a boil over high heat, uncovered, and then reduce the heat to a simmer. Cover with the lid slightly ajar, and cook for 30 minutes, stirring occasionally to prevent the fruit from sticking to the bottom of the pan.

3. After 30 minutes, remove the lid and continue to simmer over low heat for another 10 to 15 minutes, stirring occasionally, until the apples have softened and started to break down, and the liquid has darkened and has a slightly thickened, syrupy, and homogeneous consistency. Dip a spoon or spatula into the stock,

remove and allow it to cool slightly, and then touch the liquid with your finger. Sufficient pectin has been extracted if the liquid feels viscous and slippery when rubbed between two fingers. If it still feels watery, continue to simmer for another 5 minutes or so, pushing on the fruit with the spatula to encourage it to break down and release its pectin. Remove from the heat.

4. Immediately pour the stock through the strainer set up over the lilac blossoms. The apple stock will drip over the lilac blossoms to steep a floral concentrate. Cover the entire strainer setup with plastic wrap so you don't lose any volume to evaporation. Allow the stock to thoroughly drip out and the florals to infuse for a minimum of 4 hours at room temperature, or at least 12 hours but no more than 24 in the fridge.

recipe continues

5. When the stock has infused, make the jelly: Sterilize your jars and lids by following the instructions on page 23.

6. Unwrap the strainer setup. Discard or store the apple mash in an airtight container in the fridge for up to 1 week to use in other recipes. Rinse the strainer of apple particles, and then line the strainer with 2 layers of cheesecloth cut large enough to encase the lilac blossoms. Strain the floral apple stock through the strainer into your Dutch oven or stainless steel maslin (see Note). Bring the corners of the cheesecloth together and squeeze out every drop of infused liquid. Pour in the lemon juice, and then pour in the sugar in a slow, steady stream, stirring constantly to avoid clumping. Bring to a boil over high heat, stirring constantly, until the sugar is dissolved. Once it boils, the mixture may begin to foam minimally. Adjust the heat as needed to keep it as hot as possible without allowing the mixture to overflow or sputter. Continue to cook, stirring constantly and scraping the bottom of the pan as needed to distribute the heat evenly and melt the foam back down into the mixture, about 5 minutes.

7. Once the foam subsides, boil over high heat (adjust the heat if the jelly sputters) for 10 to 15 minutes, stirring occasionally. As the jelly cooks, gradually reduce the heat to medium-low if needed to prevent scorching, and stir constantly until it becomes deeper in colour and slightly syrupy and the bubbles are smaller and evenly distributed across the surface. Remove from the heat and skim any foam from the surface.

8. Gently stir to evenly distribute the heat, and then test for doneness. The jelly should pass the wrinkle test or sheet test and reach at least 200°F (100°C) on a candy thermometer (see page 21). If the jelly still seems too loose, boil for another 3 to 5 minutes and check the set again. Once set, remove from the heat.

9. Pour the jelly into the sterilized jars, leaving ¼ inch of headspace, and process by following the instructions on page 23. Arrange the hot jars about 1 inch apart in a cool place, and let sit undisturbed for at least 12 hours.

NOTE: If you are using a copper preserving pan, strain the stock into a large, non-reactive container. Pour in the lemon juice and sugar, and then transfer the mixture into your copper pan.

VARIATION: Pink-fleshed apples are rare, and if they are unavailable in your area, substitute for Pink Lady or any light-skinned red apple.

Apple, Rhubarb, and Onion Blossom Jam

YIELD six 250 mL (8-ounce) jars

With the perfect balance of sweet, tart, and savoury, this is the quintessential cheese board preserve. Rustic and full fruit, sprinkled throughout with bright white onion blossoms, it is as aesthetically pleasing as it is delicious, and will sit neatly atop your cheese and crackers without any pesky drips.

Onion blossoms are a lovely herb to have growing in your garden or window box. Easy to grow and bountiful, green onions can be freshly chopped as a delicious garnish for cheese scones, soft scrambled eggs, and puréed soups. In the early spring, at about the same time that rhubarb begins to appear, they explode with vibrant puff balls of white blossoms. With a delicate aromatic of onion and garlic, they are a particularly flavourful edible flower that will infuse your preserves with an exquisite savoury note without being overpowering. Like all fresh florals, stir into your jam at the very end of cooking off the heat for the freshest possible colour and flavour.

750 g topped and tailed rhubarb
750 g peeled, cored, and ¼-inch diced red
    apples* (such as Fuji, Gala, or Honeycrisp)

800 g (4 cups) granulated sugar
60 mL (¼ cup) lemon juice
52 g (¾ cup) fresh onion blossoms, or to taste

1. **Prepare the rhubarb:** Slice each stalk crosswise into ½-inch chunks. Individual rhubarb fibres may not break down during cooking, thus the length of each piece of fruit should not exceed the length of the bowl of a teaspoon to avoid an overly stringy preserve.

2. **Macerate the fruit:** Combine the rhubarb, apples, sugar, and lemon juice in a large non-reactive container, and toss gently to evenly coat. Cover with a lid and macerate at room temperature for at least 12 hours but no more than 24.

3. **The next day, make the jam:** Sterilize your jars and lids by following the instructions on page 23.

4. Remove the macerated fruit from the fridge. Scrape the fruit mixture and all the juices into your preserving pan. Bring to a boil over high heat, stirring constantly, until the juices run from the fruit and the sugar is dissolved. Once it boils, the mixture will begin to foam. Adjust the heat as needed to keep it as hot as possible without allowing the mixture to overflow or sputter. Continue to cook, stirring constantly and scraping the bottom of the pan to distribute the heat evenly and melt the foam back down into the mixture, about 5 minutes.

5. Once the foam subsides, boil over high heat (adjust the heat if the jam sputters) for another 10 minutes, stirring frequently. As the jam cooks, gradually reduce the heat to medium-low if needed to prevent scorching, and stir constantly until it becomes thicker and slightly syrupy and the bubbles are smaller and evenly distributed across the surface. Remove from the heat and skim any foam from the surface.

recipe continues

6. Gently stir to evenly distribute the fruit within the syrup, and then test for doneness. The jam should pass the wrinkle test or sheet test and reach at least 200°F (100°C) on a candy thermometer (see page 21). If the jam still seems too loose, boil for another 3 to 5 minutes and check the set again. Once set, remove from the heat. Immediately add the onion blossoms and stir to evenly distribute within the jam.

7. Pour the jam into the sterilized jars, leaving ¼ inch of headspace, and process by following the instructions on page 23. Arrange the hot jars about 1 inch apart in a cool place, and let sit undisturbed for at least 12 hours.

*You will need about 1.2 kg of whole apples. See **A NOTE ON MEASURING FRUIT** (page 19).

NOTES

Wild Apple and Spruce Jelly

YIELD six 250 mL (8-ounce) jars

This jelly takes a little bit of pre-planning, but we promise it is worth it. Compared to their red counterparts, wild white or green crab apples give this crystal-clear jelly a beautiful, tannic quality that makes it taste ever so slightly savoury. Spruce is a delightful pairing, its delicate evergreen sweetness enhancing the apple jelly's naturally herbaceous notes. Collect tender, light-green spruce or balsam fir tips in spring, and stash them away in your freezer or hang them to dry to use later.

Spruce is a hearty yet subtle herb, so you will need quite a bit for a flavourful jelly. For this recipe, we like to strain the hot apple stock directly over top of the foraged buds and steep it like tea for a strong infusion. For good measure, loosely fill a spice ball with more needles and allow them to infuse into the jelly throughout the entire cooking process. Save a couple of the prettiest sprigs to garnish your jars, and then put them aside for the holidays—these jars make for a gloriously festive homemade gift!

Don't throw out the apple mash. Store it to make Crab Apple, Sour Cherry, and Rosemary Jam (page 113).

120 g (2 cups) spruce tips, plus 6 more
    for garnish
2 L (8 cups) water

1.5 kg white or green crab apples (see Note)
1 kg (5 cups) granulated sugar
60 mL (¼ cup) lemon juice

1. Place 1 tablespoon of the spruce tips in a metal spice ball (the infuser should be about halfway full) and set aside. Place the remaining spruce tips in a large bowl or non-reactive container. Set a metal mesh strainer over the bowl. Set aside.

2. **Make the stock:** Pour the water into your Dutch oven or stainless steel maslin. White and green apples tend to oxidize more easily than their red counterparts, so chop the apples directly into the water. Cut small apples in half; cut large apples into 1-inch-thick wedges. Bring the mixture to a boil over high heat, uncovered, and then reduce the heat to a simmer. Cover with the lid slightly ajar, and cook for 20 minutes, stirring occasionally to prevent the fruit from sticking to the bottom of the pan.

3. Remove the lid and continue to simmer over low heat for another 10 to 15 minutes, stirring occasionally, until the apples have softened and started to break down, and the liquid has darkened and has a slightly thickened, syrupy, and homogeneous consistency. Dip a spoon or spatula into the stock, remove and allow it to cool slightly, and then touch the liquid with your finger. Sufficient pectin has been extracted if the liquid feels viscous and slippery when rubbed between two fingers. If it still feels watery, continue to simmer for another 5 minutes or so, pushing on the fruit with the spatula to encourage it to break down and release its pectin.

4. Immediately pour the stock into the prepared strainer. Cover the entire strainer

recipe continues

setup with plastic wrap so you don't lose any volume to evaporation. The apple stock will drip over the spruce tips to steep an herbaceous concentrate. Allow the stock to strain and infuse for a minimum of 4 hours at room temperature, or overnight for at least 12 hours but no more than 24 in the fridge.

5. **The next day, make the jelly:** Sterilize your jars and lids by following the instructions on page 23.

6. Unwrap the strainer setup. Discard or store the apple mash in an airtight container in the fridge for up to 1 week to use in other recipes. Rinse the strainer of apple particles, and then line the strainer with 2 layers of cheesecloth cut large enough to encase the spruce tips. Strain the infused apple stock through the strainer into your Dutch oven or stainless steel maslin (see Note). Bring the cheesecloth corners together and squeeze out every drop of infused liquid. Pour in the sugar and lemon juice in a slow, steady stream, stirring constantly to avoid clumping.

7. Submerge the metal spice ball filled with spruce tips into the mixture. Bring to a boil over high heat, stirring constantly, until the sugar is dissolved. Once it boils, the mixture may begin to foam minimally. Adjust the heat as needed to keep it as hot as possible without allowing the mixture to overflow or sputter. Continue to cook, stirring constantly and scraping the bottom of the pan as needed to distribute the heat evenly and melt the foam back down into the mixture, about 5 minutes.

8. Once the foam subsides, boil over high heat (adjust the heat if the jelly sputters) for another 10 to 15 minutes, stirring occasionally. As the jelly cooks, gradually reduce the heat to medium-low if needed to prevent scorching, and stir constantly until it becomes deeper in colour and slightly syrupy and the bubbles are smaller and evenly distributed across the surface. Remove from the heat and skim any foam from the surface. Remove the spice ball, allowing the flavourful jelly to drain back into the pot.

9. Gently stir to evenly distribute the heat, and then test for doneness. The jelly should pass the wrinkle test or sheet test and reach at least 200°F (100°C) on a candy thermometer (see page 21). If the jelly still seems too loose, boil for another 3 to 5 minutes and check the set again. Once set, remove from the heat.

10. Pour the jelly into the sterilized jars, leaving ¼ inch of headspace. Using a clean butter knife or chopstick, submerge 1 reserved fresh spruce tip into the centre of each jar of jelly. If the spruce tip floats above the fill line, allow the jelly to cool in the jars for about 5 minutes, and then try again. Process by following the instructions on page 23. Arrange the hot jars about 1 inch apart in a cool place, and let sit undisturbed for at least 12 hours.

NOTE: Wild green crab apples (especially when picked underripe) are very dry and starchy, and they soak up a lot of water, which is why we use more water to make the stock than in the red apple jelly recipes in this book. If you are using commercially available green apples instead or if your green crab apples are juicy and ripe/overripe, reduce the water in the stock to 1.5 L (6 cups).

If you are using a copper preserving pan, strain the stock into a large, non-reactive container. Pour in the lemon juice and sugar, and then transfer the mixture into your copper pan.

Crab Apple and Pie Spice Jelly

YIELD six 250 mL (8-ounce) jars

Crab apples are abundant in our northern climate and come in a plethora of shapes, sizes, flavours, and varieties. From tiny, cherry-looking orbs to the green garden variety, crab apple trees can be found studding parks, adorning lawns, and lining neighbourhood streets. Though most varieties are too tart and tannic to be palatable raw, this is also what makes them one of the most perfect fruits for jelly making.

Jelly, as opposed to jam, does not include any fruit solids. So, the jam maker must rely on the Pectin:Sugar:Acid Ratio (page 9) for a balanced and, most importantly, firmly set preserve. With crab apples, their naturally acidic flavour allows for enough sugar to be added for a firm set without being overly sweet, and a super-high pectin content results in an astonishingly fast cook time for that bright and well-balanced flavour that makes crab apple jellies so prized.

Don't throw out the apple mash. Store it to make Crab Apple, Sour Cherry, and Rosemary Jam (page 113).

1.5 kg crab apples
1.5 L (6 cups) water
60 mL (¼ cup) lemon juice
1 teaspoon ground cinnamon
1 teaspoon ground cardamom
½ teaspoon ground nutmeg
¼ teaspoon ground allspice
1 kg (5 cups) granulated sugar

1. Place a metal mesh strainer over a large bowl or non-reactive container. Set aside.

2. **Make the stock:** Cut small apples in half and large apples into 1-inch-thick wedges, including cores and skins. Combine the apples and water in a Dutch oven or stainless steel maslin. Bring the mixture to a boil over high heat, uncovered, and then reduce the heat to a simmer. Cover with the lid slightly ajar, and cook for 20 minutes, stirring occasionally to prevent the fruit from sticking to the bottom of the pan.

3. Remove the lid and continue to simmer over low heat for another 10 to 15 minutes, stirring occasionally, until the apples have softened and started to break down, and the liquid has darkened and has a slightly thickened, syrupy, and homogeneous consistency. Dip a spoon or spatula into the stock, remove and allow it to cool slightly, and then touch the liquid with your finger. Sufficient pectin has been extracted if the liquid feels viscous and slippery when rubbed between two fingers. If it still feels watery, continue to simmer for another 5 minutes or so, pushing on the fruit with the spatula to encourage it to break down

recipe continues

and release its pectin. Remove from the heat. Immediately pour the stock through the strainer. Wrap the entire strainer setup with plastic wrap so you don't lose any volume to evaporation. Allow the stock to thoroughly drip out for at least 4 hours at room temperature, or overnight for at least 12 hours but no more than 24 in the fridge.

4. **Make the jelly:** Sterilize your jars and lids by following the instructions on page 23.

5. Unwrap the strainer setup. Discard or store the apple mash in an airtight container in the fridge for up to 1 week to use in other recipes. Rinse the strainer of apple particles and strain the stock once again back into your Dutch oven or stainless steel maslin (see Note). Pour in the lemon juice. Add the cinnamon, cardamom, nutmeg, and allspice, then pour in the sugar in a slow, steady stream, stirring constantly to avoid clumping. Bring to a boil over high heat, stirring constantly, until the sugar is dissolved. Once it boils, the mixture may begin to foam minimally. Adjust the heat as needed to keep it as hot as possible without allowing the mixture to overflow or sputter. Continue to stir and scrape the bottom of the pan to distribute the heat evenly and melt the foam back down into the mixture, about 5 minutes.

6. Once the foam subsides, boil over high heat (adjust the heat if the jelly sputters) for another 10 to 15 minutes, stirring occasionally. As the jelly cooks, gradually reduce the heat to medium-low if needed to prevent scorching, and stir constantly until it becomes deeper in colour and slightly syrupy and the bubbles are smaller and evenly distributed across the surface. Remove from the heat and skim any foam from the surface.

7. Gently stir to evenly distribute the heat, and then test for doneness. The jelly should pass the wrinkle test or sheet test and reach at least 200°F (100°C) on a candy thermometer (see page 21). If the jelly still seems too loose, boil for another 3 to 5 minutes and check the set again. Once set, remove from the heat.

8. Pour the jelly into the sterilized jars, leaving ¼ inch of headspace, and process by following the instructions on page 23. Arrange the hot jars about 1 inch apart in a cool place, and let sit undisturbed for at least 12 hours.

NOTE: If you are using a copper preserving pan, strain the stock into a large, non-reactive container. Pour in the lemon juice and sugar, and then transfer the mixture into your copper pan.

NOTES

_____

_____

_____

_____

_____

_____

_____

_____

Crab Apple, Sour Cherry, and Rosemary Jam

YIELD six 250 mL (8-ounce) jars

What to do with your crab apple mash after making your annual batch of jelly? Crab apple jam, of course! This recipe is a delight—in flavour, but also because it makes use of what would otherwise be extremely flavourful waste from jelly making. Pulp from any apples will work, as the addition of sour cherries will dye any brownish purée a lovely red colour.

To make the crab apple purée from your reserved apple mash, pass the mash through a food mill into a large bowl to separate the seeds and skins from the pulp. Push the pulp through a fine-mesh strainer using a ladle or the back of a spoon. The result will be a silky smooth, barely gritty purée that is still bursting with tart crab apple flavour.

Feel free to use your favourite variety of cherry, fresh or frozen, without altering the recipe—our preference is bright-red sour cherries, which intensify the tart, fruity profile. A final infusion of rosemary lends an herbaceous, wintery note. We recommend this jam as a cranberry sauce substitute, slathered on roasted poultry or pork, or atop your favourite sharp cheeses.

500 g crab apple purée (reserved apple mash from Pink Apple and Lilac Blossom Jelly, page 101, Crab Apple and Pie Spice Jelly, page 109, or Wild Apple and Spruce Jelly, page 107)

900 g stemmed and pitted sour cherries*
125 mL (½ cup) fresh-pressed apple cider
1 kg (5 cups) granulated sugar
60 mL (¼ cup) lemon juice
3 sprigs fresh rosemary

1. **Macerate the fruit:** Combine the crab apple purée, pitted cherries, apple cider, sugar, and lemon juice in a large non-reactive container, and toss gently to evenly coat. Cover with a lid and macerate in the fridge overnight for at least 12 hours but no more than 24.

2. **The next day, make the jam:** Sterilize your jars and lids by following the instructions on page 23.

3. Remove the macerated fruit from the fridge. Scrape the fruit mixture and all the juices into your preserving pan. Bring to a boil over high heat, stirring constantly, until the juices run from the fruit and the sugar is dissolved. Once it boils, the mixture will begin to foam. Adjust the heat as needed to keep it as hot as possible without allowing the mixture to overflow or sputter. Continue to cook, stirring constantly and scraping the bottom of the pan as needed to distribute the heat evenly and melt the foam back down into the mixture, about 5 minutes.

4. Once the foam subsides, boil over high heat (adjust the heat if the jam sputters) for another 15 to 20 minutes, stirring frequently. As the jam cooks, reduce the heat to medium-low if needed to prevent scorching, and stir constantly until it becomes thicker and slightly syrupy and the bubbles are smaller and evenly distributed across the surface. Remove from the heat and skim any foam from the surface.

recipe continues

5. Gently stir to evenly distribute the fruit within the syrup, and then test for doneness. The jam should pass the wrinkle test or sheet test and reach at least 200°F (100°C) on a candy thermometer (see page 21). If the jam still seems too loose, boil for another 3 to 5 minutes and check the set again. Once set, remove from the heat.

6. Submerge the rosemary sprigs into the jam and steep for 5 minutes. Using tongs, remove the sprigs and transfer to a heat-proof plate. Use a spatula to press the leaves and scrape away as much jam as possible back into the pot. Stir thoroughly to evenly distribute the flavour. Discard the rosemary sprigs.

7. Pour the jam into the sterilized jars, leaving ¼ inch of headspace, and process by following the instructions on page 23. Arrange the hot jars about 1 inch apart in a cool place, and let sit undisturbed for at least 12 hours.

*You will need about 1.2 kg of whole cherries. See **A NOTE ON MEASURING FRUIT** (page 19).

Baked Apple and Brown Sugar Jam

YIELD five 250 mL (8-ounce) jars

Inspired by the rustic, homespun treat, apples are roasted to caramelized perfection and then paired with brown sugar, apple cider, and a hint of cinnamon for a warm, comforting preserve reminiscent of its namesake.

What makes this apple jam truly special is the texture—rather than a cooked down, puréed apple-butter-style preserve, this jam boasts a clarified, firm set apple base with apple chunks floating within. The key is in the high starting sugar ratio, which allows the jam to be cooked hot and fast, resulting in a fresh apple flavour. The high natural pectin content of the apples and quick cooking time make for barely any evaporation or reduction, and thus a resulting sweetness that is exceptionally well balanced. For more about perceived sweetness, see Sugar Concentration (page 10).

1 kg red apples* (such as Fuji, Gala, or Honeycrisp)
300 g (1½ cups, packed) brown sugar, divided
1 teaspoon ground cinnamon
½ teaspoon ground nutmeg
¼ teaspoon ground cloves
550 mL (2¼ cups) water

750 mL (3 cups) fresh-pressed apple cider, divided
250 g peeled, cored, and ¼-inch diced red apples* (such as Fuji, Gala, or Honeycrisp)
750 g (3¾ cups) granulated sugar
125 mL (½ cup) lemon juice

1. **Prepare the baked apples:** Preheat the oven to 375°F (190°C). Cut the 1 kg of whole apples (skin-on with cores intact) in half. Arrange the apple halves, cut side up, in a medium baking dish. Sprinkle the tops with 100 g (½ cup) of the brown sugar, cinnamon, nutmeg, and cloves. Bake for 45 minutes or until the apples are soft and caramelized.

2. **Make the jam:** Sterilize your jars and lids by following the instructions on page 23.

3. Scrape the baked apples and their juices into your Dutch oven or stainless steel maslin. Pour in the water and 500 mL (2 cups) of the apple cider and bring to a boil over medium heat. Then, reduce the heat to medium-low and cook, uncovered, maintaining a rapid simmer for 25 minutes, stirring occasionally, until the apples are broken down and the mixture is homogeneous. Remove from the heat.

4. Pass the fruit mixture through a food mill into a large bowl or non-reactive container to remove the seeds and skins. Transfer the pulp mixture back into your preserving pan. Discard the seeds and skins.

5. Add the 250 g diced apple, granulated sugar, the remaining 200 g (1 cup) brown sugar, the remaining 250 mL (1 cup) apple cider, and lemon juice, and stir to combine. Cook over high heat, stirring constantly, until the sugar is dissolved. Once it boils, adjust the heat as needed to keep it as hot

recipe continues

as possible without allowing the mixture to overflow or sputter. Boil for 15 to 20 minutes, stirring frequently. If the diced apple is floating, use your spatula to stir and push it back down into the jam. As the jam cooks, gradually reduce the heat to medium-low if needed to prevent scorching, and stir constantly until it becomes thicker and slightly syrupy and the bubbles are smaller and evenly distributed across the surface.

6. Gently stir to evenly distribute the fruit within the syrup, and then test for doneness. The jam should pass the wrinkle test or sheet test and reach at least 200°F (100°C) on a candy thermometer (see page 21). If the jam still seems too loose, boil for another 3 to 5 minutes and check the set again. Once set, remove from the heat. Let sit for 1 to 2 minutes, and then stir again to re-incorporate any apple pieces that have floated to the top. For this recipe, you will notice that once the jam is off the heat, a matte skin will quickly form on the surface.

7. Pour the jam into the sterilized jars, leaving ¼ inch of headspace, and process by following the instructions on page 23. Arrange the hot jars about 1 inch apart in a cool place, and let sit undisturbed for at least 12 hours.

*You will need about 1.4 kg of whole apples (total combined weight needed for the whole and diced apples). See **A NOTE ON MEASURING FRUIT** (page 19).

NOTES

_____

_____

_____

_____

_____

_____

_____

_____

_____

Persimmon, Cardamom, and Rose Jam

YIELD six 250 mL (8-ounce) jars

Inspired by an aromatic Persian palate, this preserve is delicately scented with green cardamom and wisps of rose. Persimmon is an elegant canvas for such a romantic blend of ingredients, with a naturally rich cinnamon-honey sweetness and velvety texture. Use only Fuyu persimmons for this recipe—the squatter, tomato-shaped variety—and allow them to fully ripen until they are completely soft and mushy for the most decadent preserve. You will practically be able to squeeze the ripened flesh from its skin.

A beautiful and unique baking preserve, it truly shines when blended with caramelized sugar, custard sauces, and soft, yeasty doughs. Find it sandwiched between layers of freshly baked bread, cardamom, and sugar in our Spiced Persimmon Pull-Apart Bread (page 267), best fresh out of the oven when the spices and floral notes fill the air.

1.5 kg peeled, pitted, and diced Fuyu persimmons*
900 g (4½ cups) granulated sugar
60 mL (¼ cup) lemon juice
2 teaspoons ground cardamom
10 g (¼ cup) dried culinary rose petals, or to taste

1. **Macerate the fruit:** Combine the persimmons, sugar, lemon juice, and cardamom in a large non-reactive container, and toss gently to evenly coat. Cover with a lid and macerate in the fridge overnight for at least 12 hours but no more than 24.

2. **The next day, make the jam:** Sterilize your jars and lids by following the instructions on page 23.

3. Remove the macerated fruit from the fridge. Scrape the fruit mixture and all the juices into your preserving pan. Bring to a boil over high heat, stirring constantly, until the juices run from the fruit and the sugar is dissolved.

4. Scoop a small amount of the warm syrup into a small bowl. Drop in the dried rose petals and soak them in the syrup to saturate them with liquid until ready to use.

When the rose petals are rehydrated and heavy with syrup, they will sink and suspend within your jam, rather than float to the top. Set aside.

5. Once it boils, the mixture will begin to foam dramatically. Adjust the heat as needed to keep it as hot as possible without allowing the mixture to overflow or sputter. Continue to cook, stirring constantly and scraping the bottom of the pan to distribute the heat evenly and melt the foam back down into the mixture, about 5 minutes.

6. Once the foam subsides, boil over high heat (adjust the heat if the jam sputters) for another 15 to 20 minutes, stirring frequently. The persimmons will begin to break down and become transparent, and the jam will appear homogeneous with

recipe continues

no pockets of liquid between pieces of fruit. As the jam cooks, gradually reduce the heat to medium-low if needed to prevent scorching, and stir constantly until it becomes thicker and slightly syrupy and the bubbles are smaller and evenly distributed across the surface. Remove from the heat and skim any foam from the surface.

7. Gently stir to evenly distribute the fruit within the syrup, and then test for doneness. The jam should pass the wrinkle test or sheet test and reach at least 200°F (100°C) on a candy thermometer (see page 21). If the jam still seems too loose, boil for another 3 to 5 minutes and check the set again. Once set, remove from the heat. Immediately add the syrup-saturated rose petals and stir vigorously to incorporate evenly throughout the jam.

8. Pour the jam into the sterilized jars, leaving ¼ inch of headspace, and process by following the instructions on page 23. Arrange the hot jars about 1 inch apart in a cool place, and let sit undisturbed for at least 12 hours.

*You will need about 2.25 kg of whole persimmons. See **A NOTE ON MEASURING FRUIT** (page 19).

Pear, Maple, and Scotch Jam

YIELD six 250 mL (8-ounce) jars

Flavourful Bosc pears are blended with a splash of scotch and a heavy-handed addition of pure, dark maple syrup. A midwinter favourite, the result is a decadent preserve with notes of butterscotch and caramel.

Pear is a notoriously difficult fruit to set, and the key to successful pear preserves is to use a blend of ripe and underripe pears. The softer fruit will break down under heat, while the firm pears will add much needed pectin and maintain their shape, softening slightly and adding texture to the final product. This recipe relies heavily on evaporation to thicken the jam, so it is important to achieve as much reduction in the first half of the boiling process as possible to avoid having to spend too much time stirring as the jam thickens. Boil it fast and hard while the fruit is still floating, as it will make for easier work toward the end.

Choose a bold, peaty scotch to allow the rich booziness to shine through. To bump the scotch into the foreground, we like to add a splash of strongly steeped Lapsang souchong, Chinese smoked tea, to this recipe.

1.5 kg peeled, pitted, and diced Bosc pears*
660 g (3⅓ cups) granulated sugar
90 mL (¼ cup + 2 tablespoons) pure maple syrup
125 mL (½ cup) lemon juice
1 teaspoon loose-leaf Lapsang souchong tea (optional)
60 mL (¼ cup) boiling water
2 tablespoons scotch

1. **Macerate the fruit:** Combine the pears, sugar, maple syrup, and lemon juice in a large non-reactive container, and gently toss to evenly coat. Cover with a lid and macerate in the fridge overnight for at least 12 hours but no more than 24.

2. **The next day, make the tea concentrate, if using:** Steep the tea in the boiling water, covered, for 8 to 10 minutes. You will notice that there is quite a bit of tea for a small amount of water. This is to increase the strength of the concentrate without making it taste overly extracted and bitter by extending the steep time. Strain the tea through a fine-mesh strainer into a cup, pushing firmly on the leaves to squeeze out every drop of concentrate to yield about 1 teaspoon of liquid. Set aside.

3. **Make the jam:** Sterilize your jars and lids by following the instructions on page 23.

4. Remove the macerated fruit from the fridge. Scrape the fruit mixture and all the juices into your preserving pan. Bring to a boil over high heat, stirring constantly, until the juices run from the fruit and the sugar is dissolved. Once it boils, the mixture will begin to foam. Adjust the heat as needed to keep it as hot as possible

recipe continues

without allowing the mixture to overflow or sputter. Continue to cook, stirring constantly and scraping the bottom of the pan to distribute the heat evenly and melt the foam back down into the mixture, about 5 minutes.

5. Once the foam subsides, boil over high heat (adjust the heat if the jam sputters) for another 30 to 40 minutes, stirring frequently. The pears will begin to soften and become transparent, and the jam will appear homogeneous with no pockets of liquid between pieces of fruit. As the jam cooks, gradually reduce the heat to medium-low if needed to prevent scorching, and stir constantly until it becomes thicker and slightly syrupy and the bubbles are smaller and evenly distributed across the surface. Remove from the heat and skim any foam from the surface.

6. Gently stir to evenly distribute the fruit within the syrup, and then test for doneness. The jam should pass the wrinkle test or sheet test and reach at least 200°F (100°C) on a candy thermometer (see page 21). You'll be adding additional water content in the form of tea concentrate, so you need to be sure you have achieved enough reduction. If the jam still seems too loose, boil for another 3 to 5 minutes and check the set again. Once set, remove from the heat. Immediately pour in the tea concentrate and scotch, and stir vigorously to incorporate the flavour and encourage evaporation. (Make sure your head is not over the pot, as the alcohol vapour has a very strong smell.)

7. Pour the jam into the sterilized jars, leaving ¼ inch of headspace, and process by following the instructions on page 23.

Arrange the hot jars about 1 inch apart in a cool place, and let sit undisturbed for at least 12 hours.

*You will need about 2.25 kg of whole pears. See A NOTE ON MEASURING FRUIT (page 19).

NOTES

Pear and Mulled Wine Jam

YIELD five to six 250 mL (8-ounce) jars, plus extra mulled wine for sipping

This festive preserve is perfect for sweet and savoury applications, and is our favourite jam for baked brie or camembert topped with candied walnuts. Boozy and spiced, made with a dose of homemade mulled wine, the trick to this preserve is adding a handful of fresh cranberries for a dose of pectin and lovely red colour.

We typically recommend adding liquors at the middle or end of the cooking process, but for this recipe we add the mulled wine into the maceration liquid. This helps the wine to absorb fully into the pears, lending a richer, more cohesive flavour profile and deeper burgundy colour to the final preserve. Because of the sheer volume of mulled wine added, expect to cook this preserve a little longer than usual to allow all the liquid to evaporate. This also helps to concentrate all the flavours for a deeply caramelized, spiced profile.

Mulled Wine

750 mL (one 26-ounce bottle) Merlot or your favourite rich red wine
115 g (½ cup + 1 tablespoon) granulated sugar
Zest and juice of 1 orange (use a vegetable peeler to zest the orange in strips)
2 cinnamon sticks
1 star anise
3 whole cloves
½ whole nutmeg, crushed
7 green cardamom pods
2 allspice berries
5 pink peppercorns
5 black peppercorns
1 bay leaf
1 black cardamom pod (optional)

Jam

500 mL (2 cups) mulled wine (recipe at left)
175 g fresh cranberries
1 kg peeled, cored, and diced Bartlett pears*
660 g (3⅓ cups) granulated sugar
125 mL (½ cup) lemon juice

1. Make the mulled wine: Combine the red wine, sugar, orange zest and juice, cinnamon sticks, star anise, cloves, nutmeg, green cardamom pods, allspice berries, pink peppercorns, black peppercorns, bay leaf, and black cardamom pod (if using) in a medium saucepan. Bring to a simmer over medium-low heat, stirring gently until the sugar is dissolved. Reduce the heat to low so that the wine is steaming but not boiling, cover with the lid slightly ajar, and infuse for at least 1 hour or until sufficiently flavourful. Remove from the heat.

2. After 1 hour, make the cranberry purée: Strain the warm wine through a fine-mesh strainer into a large bowl or pitcher. Discard the spice and citrus mixture. Pour 500 mL (2 cups) of the mulled wine back into the saucepan. Add the cranberries. Bring back to a simmer over medium heat and cook for about 5 minutes, until the cranberries burst and break down completely, stirring frequently to avoid scorching. Remove from the heat.

recipe continues

3. Strain the warm wine once again through a fine-mesh strainer into a large non-reactive container. Use the back of a large spoon or ladle to push the cranberries through the strainer to remove the skins and make a purée. Scrape the bottom of the strainer, as purée likes to cling to it.

4. **Macerate the fruit:** Add the pears, sugar, and lemon juice to the warm wine and cranberry purée and toss gently to evenly coat. Cover with a lid slightly ajar to allow residual heat to escape, and macerate in the fridge overnight for at least 12 hours but no more than 24.

5. **The next day, make the jam:** Sterilize your jars and lids by following the instructions on page 23.

6. Remove the macerated fruit from the fridge. Scrape the fruit mixture and all the juices into your preserving pan. Bring to a boil over high heat, stirring constantly, until the juices run from the fruit and all the sugar is dissolved. Once it boils, the mixture will begin to foam. Adjust the heat as needed to keep it as hot as possible without allowing the mixture to overflow or sputter. Continue to cook, stirring constantly and scraping the bottom of the pan to distribute the heat evenly and melt the foam back down into the mixture, about 5 minutes.

7. Once the foam subsides, boil over high heat (adjust the heat if the jam sputters) for 40 to 45 minutes, stirring frequently. The pears will begin to soften and become transparent, and the jam will appear homogeneous with no pockets of liquid between pieces of fruit. Since we added a lot of liquid at the beginning of the cooking process in the form of mulled wine, it needs to be evaporated to a flavourful reduction. As the jam cooks, gradually reduce the heat to medium-low if needed to prevent scorching, and stir constantly until it becomes thicker and slightly syrupy and the bubbles are smaller and evenly distributed across the surface. Remove from the heat and skim any foam from the surface.

8. Gently stir to evenly distribute the fruit within the syrup, and then test for doneness. The jam should pass the wrinkle test or sheet test and reach at least 200°F (100°C) on a candy thermometer (see page 21). If the jam still seems too loose, boil for another 3 to 5 minutes and check the set again. Once set, remove from the heat.

9. Pour the jam into the sterilized jars, leaving ¼ inch of headspace, and process by following the instructions on page 23. Arrange the hot jars about 1 inch apart in a cool place, and let sit undisturbed for at least 12 hours.

*You will need about 1.5 kg of whole pears. See **A NOTE ON MEASURING FRUIT** (page 19).

Sundried Fig, Apple, and Brandy Jam

YIELD six 250 mL (8-ounce) jars

Fig preserves are one of the most traditional and coveted for jam connoisseurs, fetching high prices at fromageries and specialty grocers. You can't get a more perfect or historic pairing for cheese than fig jams, and this preserve is no exception. Instead of using fresh figs, we like to use high-quality sundried figs for this recipe, which are easy to acquire in any season and yield consistent results. You can use any white or brown skinned fig for this recipe, such as Smyrna or Turkish figs.

Dried fig conserves tend to be overly dense and seedy, but the addition of fresh-pressed apple cider gives the figs room to breathe in this delicate fig creation. To continue with the theme of traditional pairings, a splash of brandy lends a fruit-cake-like depth of flavour.

250 g stemmed and diced sundried white or brown figs

300 mL (1¼ cups) fresh-pressed apple cider

300 g green apples*

250 mL (1 cup) water

700 g peeled, cored, and ¼-inch diced green apple*

1 kg (5 cups) granulated sugar

125 mL (½ cup) lemon juice

60 mL (¼ cup) brandy

1. **Prepare the figs:** Place the diced figs in a small, flat-bottomed non-reactive container. Set aside.

2. In a small saucepan, heat the apple cider over high heat until just boiling. Remove from the heat, and pour over the diced figs. Let cool for 1 hour or until the mixture is at room temperature, and then cover with a lid and refrigerate for 12 to 24 hours. Wipe the pan.

3. **The same day, make the apple purée and macerate:** Cut the 300 g of whole apples into 1-inch-thick wedges, including the cores and skins. In the same saucepan, combine the apple wedges and water. Bring the mixture to a boil over high heat, uncovered, and then reduce the heat to a simmer. Cover with the lid slightly ajar, and cook for about 15 minutes, stirring occasionally to prevent the fruit from sticking to the bottom of the pan. Once the apples are soft and can be easily mashed, pass the apples and their cooking liquid through a food mill into a large non-reactive container. (Alternatively, you can use a potato masher to completely break down the apples, and then push the purée through a strainer to remove the skins and seeds.)

4. **Macerate the fruit:** Add the 700 g diced apples, sugar, and lemon juice to the apple purée, and toss gently to evenly coat. Cover with a lid and macerate in the fridge overnight for at least 12 hours but no more than 24.

recipe continues

5. The next day, make the jam: Sterilize your jars and lids by following the instructions on page 23.

6. Remove the macerated apples and soaked figs from the fridge. Using a potato masher, mash the figs in their liquid until they are broken down and the mixture is homogeneous. Transfer both the apple mixture and the mashed figs to your preserving pan. Bring to a boil over high heat, stirring constantly, until the juices run from the fruit and all the sugar is dissolved. Once it boils, the mixture will begin to foam. Adjust the heat as needed to keep it as hot as possible without allowing the mixture to overflow or sputter. Continue to cook, stirring constantly and scraping the bottom of the pan to distribute the heat evenly and melt the foam back down into the mixture, about 5 minutes.

7. Once the foam subsides, boil over high heat (adjust the heat if the jam sputters) for 15 to 20 minutes, stirring frequently. The apple pieces will begin to soften and turn transparent. Once the apples are no longer opaque, the jam should be close to set and the fruit will suspend in the preserve. Gradually reduce the heat to medium-low if needed to prevent scorching, and stir constantly until it becomes thicker and slightly syrupy and the bubbles are smaller and evenly distributed across the surface. Remove from the heat and skim any foam from the surface.

8. Gently stir to evenly distribute the fruit within the syrup, and then test for doneness. The jam should pass the wrinkle test or sheet test and reach at least 200°F (100°C) on a candy thermometer (see page 21). If the jam still seems too loose, boil for another 3 to 5 minutes and check the set again. Once set, remove from the heat. Immediately pour in the brandy and stir vigorously to incorporate the flavour and allow any alcohol to burn off. (Make sure your head is not over the pot, as the alcohol vapour has a very strong smell.)

9. Pour the jam into the sterilized jars, leaving ¼ inch of headspace, and process by following the instructions on page 23. Arrange the hot jars about 1 inch apart in a cool place, and let sit undisturbed for at least 12 hours.

*You will need about 1.35 kg of whole apples (total combined weight needed for the whole and diced apples). See A NOTE ON MEASURING FRUIT (page 19).

Citrus

Sweet Orange and Honeyed Whisky Marmalade

YIELD six to seven 250 mL (8-ounce) jars

An updated, elegant twist on classic Irish marmalade, this preserve is made with hand-cut, sweet Navel oranges and honey-flavoured whisky for a rich, rounded profile without hiding any of the traditional bite.

Marmalade is a quintessential teatime treat that is unique from jam as it is made with the peel of citrus fruits boiled with sugar and water. Without having the flesh of whole fruits to lean on, we must achieve the perfect balance of pectin:sugar:acid (page 9), combined with reduction, for a perfectly set and brightly coloured marmalade. Our favourite way to achieve this was popularized by Rachel Saunders in her iconic jam cookbook *The Blue Chair Fruit Cookbook*— start by boiling lemon halves in water until they are completely broken down for a rich stock that will add an extra boost of pectin to help your marmalade set quickly.

900 g firm lemons, cut lengthwise into 1-inch-thick wedges (including any juices and seeds)

3 L (12 cups) water, divided

900 g thinly sliced Navel oranges,* plus any seeds, pith, and scraps reserved

60 mL (¼ cup) lemon juice

1.5 kg (7¾ cups) granulated sugar

60 mL (¼ cup) honey-flavoured whisky (optional)

1. Soak the lemon wedges: Place the lemon wedges, and any juices or seeds from your cutting board, in a large non-reactive container, and cover with 1.5 L (6 cups) of the water. The fruit should bob freely. Cover with a lid and soak at room temperature for at least 12 hours but no more than 24. This begins to soften the zest and removes unwanted bitterness.

2. At the same time, soak the orange slices: Place the orange slices in a separate large non-reactive container and cover with the remaining 1.5 L (6 cups) water. (These will be the strips of zest in your finished marmalade.) Any reserved seeds, pith, and scraps from your cutting board may be added to the container with the lemon wedges for an extra hit of pectin (see Step 1). Cover with a lid and soak at room temperature for at least 12 hours but no more than 24. This begins to soften the zest and removes unwanted bitterness.

3. The next day, make the lemon stock: Place a metal mesh strainer over a large bowl or non-reactive container. Set aside.

4. Pour the soaked lemon wedges and their soaking liquid into your Dutch oven or stainless steel maslin (see Note). Bring to a boil, uncovered, over high heat, and then reduce to a simmer. Cover with the lid slightly ajar, and cook for 1 hour, stirring occasionally to ensure the fruit does not stick to the bottom of the pan. The lemons will have started to soften but will still be in intact wedges in the surrounding liquid.

recipe continues

5. After 1 hour, remove the lid and continue to simmer over low heat for another 30 minutes, stirring frequently, until the lemons have broken down and the liquid has darkened and has a slightly thickened, syrupy, and homogeneous consistency. Dip a spoon or spatula into the stock, remove and allow it to cool slightly, and then touch the liquid with your finger. Sufficient pectin has been extracted if the liquid feels viscous and slippery when rubbed between two fingers. If it still feels watery, continue to simmer for another 5 minutes or so, pushing on the fruit with the spatula to encourage it to break down and release its pectin.

6. Immediately pour the stock through the prepared strainer. Cover the entire strainer setup with plastic wrap so you don't lose any volume to evaporation. Allow the stock to thoroughly drip out while you prepare the oranges.

7. Poach the orange slices: Wash your pan thoroughly of any lemon residue. Pour the soaked orange slices and their soaking liquid into your Dutch oven or stainless steel maslin. Bring the mixture to a boil, uncovered, over high heat, and then reduce to a simmer. Cover with the lid slightly ajar and cook for 45 minutes, stirring occasionally to ensure no fruit sticks to the bottom of the pot. At this stage, the cooking liquid should have reduced enough so that the orange slices are no longer floating, and the mixture appears homogeneous. The orange slices will firm up when the sugar is added, so the goal during this step is to poach them until they are tender enough to bite through easily. Remove an orange slice with a spoon or spatula, allow to cool, and

squish it between two fingers. If it breaks apart easily, the slices are done. If they still feel too firm, simmer for another 5 minutes and test the texture again. Remove from the heat.

8. Make the marmalade: Sterilize your jars and lids by following the instructions on page 23.

9. Unwrap the strainer setup and discard the lemon wedges. Combine the strained lemon stock, orange slices, and fresh lemon juice in your Dutch oven or stainless steel maslin. Pour in the sugar in a slow, steady stream, stirring constantly to avoid clumping. Stir to combine. Bring to a boil over high heat, stirring constantly, until the sugar is dissolved. Once it boils, the mixture may begin to foam minimally. Adjust the heat as needed to keep it as hot as possible without allowing the mixture to overflow or sputter. Continue to cook, stirring constantly and scraping the bottom of the pan to distribute the heat evenly and melt the foam back down into the mixture, about 5 minutes.

10. Once the foam subsides, boil over high heat (adjust the heat if the marmalade sputters) for another 10 minutes, stirring frequently, until the marmalade becomes deeper in colour and slightly syrupy and the bubbles are smaller and evenly distributed across the surface. Remove from the heat and skim any foam from the surface.

11. Gently stir to evenly distribute the fruit within the syrup, and then test for doneness. The marmalade should pass the wrinkle test or sheet test and reach at least 200°F (100°C) on a candy thermometer (see page 21). If the marmalade still seems too loose, boil for another 3 to 5 minutes and check the set again. Once set, remove from the heat. Immediately pour in the whisky (if using) and stir vigorously to allow any alcohol to burn off. (Make sure your head is not over the pot, as the alcohol vapour has a very strong smell.)

12. Pour the marmalade into the steril-ized jars, leaving ¼ inch of headspace, and process by following the instructions on page 23. Arrange the hot jars about 1 inch apart in a cool place, and let sit undisturbed for at least 12 hours.

NOTE: If you are using a copper preserving pan, it is best to cook the lemon stock and orange slices in a stainless steel saucepan or Dutch oven. Then, combine all of the ingredients with the sugar in a large non-reactive container before transferring the mixture into the copper pan.

*You will need about 910 g of whole oranges. See **A NOTE ON MEASURING FRUIT** (page 19). For preparation instructions, see the chart **UNIQUE FRUIT PREPARATION** (page 19).

Raspberry and Pink Grapefruit Jamalade

YIELD six 250 mL (8-ounce) jars

A sparkling cocktail-inspired combination, the red berry sweetness of raspberries bounces perfectly off the pink lemonade-like tartness of pink grapefruit. Grapefruits tend to impart a heavy dose of bitterness when preserved, and though this jamalade does have a hint of maturity from the addition of zest and grapefruit flesh, it is refreshingly delicate. To reduce bitterness and allow the grapefruit flavour to shine, we recommend using a sharp vegetable peeler to shave only the very outermost layer of zest with as little white pith as possible. Additionally, giving your zest a good soak in fresh water overnight and a quick blanch will further reduce unwanted bitterness.

A true jamalade, this preserve includes the flesh of the grapefruit. The juicy segments, also called supremes, are carefully cut from the membranes and then macerated with sugar and their own juices overnight. This process helps to lightly candy the fruit and lend some structural stability so the segments stay as intact as possible in the pot. Although the temptation is real, try to stir the jamalade minimally throughout the quick boiling process. There is nothing more delightful than spooning a nice chunk of grapefruit onto your scone.

600 g pink grapefruits* (about 2 grapefruits)
90 mL (6 tablespoons) grapefruit juice (from above grapefruits)
1.2 kg (scant 6¼ cups) granulated sugar, divided
1.25 kg raspberries

1. **Prepare the grapefruits:** Wash your grapefruits well, scrubbing each fruit with mild soap and hot water. Using a sharp vegetable peeler, shave just the exterior skin, avoiding as much white pith as possible. Julienne each piece of zest crosswise into short, thin strips, no thicker than ⅛ inch. Place 50 g of zest in a small bowl, and cover with fresh water. Cover with a lid and soak at room temperature for at least 12 hours but no more than 24. This begins to soften the zest and removes unwanted bitterness.

2. At the same time, using a very sharp kitchen knife, slice off the stem and blossom ends of the grapefruit so that the flesh is revealed. Set each grapefruit upright on your cutting board on one of the flat cut ends. Working vertically, carefully slice off the white pith in sections, rotating the grapefruit as you work. You will now have a completely bare grapefruit. Discard the pith.

3. Set a mesh strainer over a medium bowl. Cradle the bare grapefruit in your non-dominant hand over the strainer. You will see the thin white membrane between each section of flesh. Using a sharp knife, carefully cut along the membrane on one side of each segment, and then the other side, allowing each segment of fruit (as well as lots of juice!) to slide out into the strainer. Once you have removed all segments from the pith, give the innards a good squeeze over top of the strainer to reserve as much

recipe continues

juice as possible, and then discard. Continue until you have 200 g of grapefruit segments, being sure to pick out and discard any seeds. Place the segments and 90 mL (6 tablespoons) of grapefruit juice in a small non-reactive container. Blanket with 200 g (scant 1¼ cups) of the sugar without stirring. Macerate in the fridge overnight for at least 12 hours but no more than 24.

4. **The next day, blanch the grapefruit zest:** Remove the soaked grapefruit zest from the fridge. Pour the zest and its soaking liquid into a small saucepan. Bring the mixture to a boil, uncovered, over high heat, then reduce to a simmer. Cook for 5 minutes. Remove from the heat and pour the mixture through a strainer over your sink. Discard the liquid. Return the zest back into the saucepan and cover with fresh water. Bring the mixture to a boil, uncovered, over high heat, and then reduce to a simmer. Cover with the lid slightly ajar and cook for 10 to 15 minutes, stirring occasionally to ensure no fruit sticks to the bottom of the pan. The grapefruit zest will firm up when the sugar is added, so the goal during this step is to poach them until they are tender enough to bite through easily. Remove a strip with a spoon or spatula, allow to cool, and try to bite it with your teeth. If you are able to bite through easily, the strips are done. If they still feel too firm, simmer for another 5 minutes and test the texture again. Once the slices are sufficiently softened, strain once more and discard the liquid.

5. **Make the jamalade:** Sterilize your jars and lids by following the instructions on page 23.

6. Combine the raspberries with the remaining 1 kg (5 cups) sugar in your preserving pan. Heat the mixture over low heat, stirring constantly, gradually increasing the heat as the juices run from the berries, the sugar dissolves, the fruit is floating, and you reach medium-high heat. Add the blanched grapefruit zest, macerated grapefruit segments, and their liquid, and stir gently to combine. Once it boils, the mixture may begin to foam minimally. Adjust the heat as needed to keep it as hot as possible without allowing the mixture to overflow or sputter. Continue to cook, stirring occasionally and scraping the bottom of the pan to distribute the heat evenly and melt the foam back down into the mixture, about 5 minutes.

7. Once the foam subsides, continue to boil over high heat (adjust the heat if the jamalade sputters) for another 10 minutes, occasionally scraping the bottom of the pan to prevent scorching, until the jam becomes thicker, slightly syrupy, and the bubbles are smaller and evenly distributed across the surface. For this recipe, this is a very good sign that your jamalade is reduced to the proper consistency. Remove from the heat and skim any foam from the surface.

8. Gently stir to evenly distribute the fruit within the syrup, and then test for doneness. The jamalade should pass the wrinkle test or sheet test and reach at least 200°F (100°C) on a candy thermometer (see page 21). If the jamalade still seems too loose, boil for another 3 to 5 minutes and check the set again. Once set, remove from the heat.

9. Pour the jamalade into the sterilized jars, leaving ¼ inch of headspace, and process by following the instructions on page 23. Arrange the hot jars about 1 inch apart in a cool place, and let sit undisturbed for at least 12 hours.

*You will need about 600 g of whole grapefruits. See **A NOTE ON MEASURING FRUIT** (page 19).

Blood Orange and Papaya Jamalade

YIELD six 250 mL (8-ounce) jars

Half marmalade and half jam, this ruby red preserve boasts all of the traditional pithiness of marmalade paired with the musky, tropical sweetness of papaya and a soft-set, velvety texture with wisps of citrus zest floating within.

Jamalades are a wonderful introduction to the world of marmalade making. Blending citrus zest with a fleshy fruit allows you to relax and not worry so much about the science of set while enjoying the marmalade making process and citrus flavours. Blood oranges and papayas, though a seemingly summery pairing, both come into season in the middle of our Canadian winter, making this jamalade a lovely little tropical escape while snow covers the ground.

750 g thinly sliced blood oranges*
1 L (4 cups) water
750 g peeled, seeded, and diced papaya*
1 kg (5 cups) granulated sugar
60 mL (¼ cup) lemon juice

1. Soak the orange slices: Place the orange slices into a large non-reactive container, and cover with the water. Cover with a lid and soak at room temperature for at least 12 hours but no more than 24.

2. At the same time, macerate the papaya: Combine the papaya, sugar, and lemon juice in a separate large non-reactive container, and toss gently to coat evenly. Cover with a lid and macerate in the fridge overnight for at least 12 hours but no more than 24.

3. The next day, poach the orange slices: Pour the soaked orange slices and their soaking liquid into your Dutch oven or stainless steel maslin. Bring the mixture to a boil, uncovered, over high heat, and then reduce to a simmer. Cover with the lid slightly ajar, and cook for 20 to 30 minutes, stirring occasionally to ensure no fruit sticks to the bottom of the pot.

At this stage, the cooking liquid should have reduced so that the orange slices are no longer floating, and the mixture appears homogeneous. The orange slices will firm up when the sugar is added, so the goal during this step is to poach them until they are tender enough to bite through easily. Remove an orange slice with a spoon or spatula, allow to cool, and squish it between two fingers. If it breaks apart easily, the slices are done. If they still feel too firm, simmer for another 5 minutes and test the texture again. Remove from the heat.

4. Make the jamalade: Sterilize your jars and lids by following the instructions on page 23.

5. Add the papaya mixture and all the juices to the pan with the warm orange slices. Stir well to combine all the ingredients. Bring to a boil over high heat, stirring

recipe continues

constantly, until the juices run from the fruit and the sugar is dissolved. Once it boils, the mixture will begin to foam. Adjust the heat as needed to keep it as hot as possible without allowing the mixture to overflow or sputter. Continue to cook, stirring constantly and scraping the bottom of the pan to distribute the heat evenly and melt the foam back down into the mixture, about 5 minutes.

6. Once the foam subsides, boil over high heat (adjust the heat if the jamalade sputters) for another 15 to 20 minutes, stirring frequently. The papaya will begin to soften and become transparent, and the jamalade will appear homogeneous with no pockets of liquid between pieces of fruit. As the jamalade cooks, gradually reduce the heat to medium-low if needed to prevent scorching, and stir constantly until it becomes thicker and slightly syrupy and the bubbles are smaller and evenly distributed across the surface. Remove from the heat and skim any foam from the surface.

7. Gently stir to evenly distribute the fruit within the syrup, and then test for doneness. The jamalade should pass the wrinkle test or sheet test and reach at least 200°F (100°C) on a candy thermometer (see page 21). If the jamalade still seems too loose, boil for another 3 to 5 minutes and check the set again. Once set, remove from the heat.

8. Pour the jamalade into the sterilized jars, leaving ¼ inch of headspace, and process by following the instructions on page 23. Arrange the hot jars about 1 inch apart in a cool place, and let sit undisturbed for at least 12 hours.

*You will need about 760 g of whole oranges and 1.2 kg of whole papaya. See **A NOTE ON MEASURING FRUIT** (page 19). For preparation instructions, see the chart **UNIQUE FRUIT PREPARATION** (page 19).

NOTES

Blueberry and French Bergamot Jamalade

YIELD six 250 mL (8-ounce) jars

Bold, dark, and immensely flavourful, blueberry jam always welcomes a fruit friend to break up its natural richness. Bright and airy pairings work particularly well to lighten things up—think lavender, mint, or citrus. For this recipe, we chose the elegant French bergamot. Often confused with the Italian bergamot—the citrus fruit used to flavour Earl Grey tea—French bergamots are also known as sweet limes or sweet lemons and boast a highly perfumed citronella-like zest and sweet, juicy flesh.

Blanching the wisps of zest before adding to your blueberry base will remove any bitterness from their thin skin, as well as soften the bite. Note that the result will not be a traditional marmalade, but rather a classic jam with the addition of tender juliennes of candied citrus to decorate your toast and add delicate texture and perfume.

400 g thinly sliced French bergamots*
1.1 kg blueberries
900 g (4½ cups) granulated sugar
60 mL (¼ cup) lemon juice

1. **Soak the bergamot slices:** Place the bergamot slices in a large non-reactive container, and cover with water. Cover with a lid and soak at room temperature for at least 12 hours but no more than 24. This begins to soften the zest and removes unwanted bitterness.

2. **The next day, blanch the bergamot slices:** Pour the soaked bergamot slices and their soaking liquid into a small saucepan. Bring the mixture to a boil, uncovered, over high heat, and then reduce to a simmer. Cook for 5 minutes. Remove from the heat and pour the mixture through a strainer back into the large soaking container. Discard the liquid. Return the slices back into the saucepan and cover with fresh water. Bring the mixture to a boil, uncovered, over high heat, and then reduce to a simmer. Cover with the lid slightly ajar and cook for 10 to

15 minutes, stirring occasionally to ensure no fruit sticks to the bottom of the pan. The bergamot slices will firm up when the sugar is added, so the goal during this step is to poach them until they are tender enough to bite through easily. Remove a bergamot slice with a spoon or spatula, allow to cool, and squish it between two fingers. If it breaks apart easily, the slices are done. If they still feel too firm, simmer for another 5 minutes and test their texture again. Once the slices are sufficiently softened, remove from the heat, strain once more and discard the liquid.

3. **Make the jamalade:** Sterilize your jars and lids by following the instructions on page 23.

4. Combine the blueberries, sugar, and lemon juice in your preserving pan. Heat

recipe continues

the mixture over low heat, stirring constantly, gradually increasing the heat as the juices run from the berries, the sugar dissolves, the fruit is floating, and you reach medium-high heat. Add the blanched bergamot slices and stir gently to combine. Once it boils, the mixture may begin to foam minimally. Adjust the heat as needed to keep it as hot as possible without allowing the mixture to overflow or sputter. Continue to cook, stirring constantly and scraping the bottom of the pan to distribute the heat evenly and melt the foam back down into the mixture, about 5 minutes.

5. Once the foam subsides, continue to boil over high heat (adjust the heat if the jamalade sputters) for another 10 minutes, stirring frequently, until the jamalade becomes thicker and slightly syrupy and the bubbles are smaller and evenly distributed across the surface. For this recipe, this is a very good sign that your jamalade is reduced to the proper consistency. Remove from the heat and skim any foam from the surface.

6. Gently stir to evenly distribute the fruit within the syrup, and then test for doneness. The jamalade should pass the wrinkle test or sheet test and reach at least 200°F (100°C) on a candy thermometer (see page 21). If the jamalade still seems too loose, boil for an additional 3 to 5 minutes and check the set again. Once set, remove from the heat.

7. Pour the jamalade into the sterilized jars, leaving ¼ inch of headspace, and process by following the instructions on page 23. Arrange the hot jars about 1 inch apart in a cool place, and let sit undisturbed for at least 12 hours.

VARIATION: If French bergamots are unavailable, substitute with Meyer or conventional lemons.

*You will need about 410 g of whole bergamots. See **A NOTE ON MEASURING FRUIT** (page 19). For preparation instructions, see the chart **UNIQUE FRUIT PREPARATION** (page 19).

NOTES

Lemon Cream Marmalade

YIELD six 250 mL (8-ounce) jars

It is tempting to pair lemon with floral, bright, or acidic flavours such as lavender, mint, and ginger. However, lemon is delightful made into something sweet and creamy. This marmalade is inspired by some of our favourite citrus cream desserts—think lemon meringue, lemon curd tartlets, buttery lemon shortbread, and citrus creamsicles. The vanilla note is such a contrast to the pithy tang of lemon and zest yet rounds out the flavour for a vintage-y dessert profile.

As in our Strawberry, Raspberry, and Cream Jam (page 35), we opt for a high-quality vanilla flavour or vanilla/whipped cream/birthday cake flavoured vodka for this recipe to achieve that pastry-like flavour note. If you prefer a more classic vanilla bean flavour, simply swap the vanilla flavour for pure vanilla extract.

2.05 kg lemons,* divided (1.15 kg cut lengthwise into 1-inch-thick wedges,
    including any seeds and juices; 900 g thinly sliced)
3.25 L (13 cups) water, divided
60 mL (¼ cup) lemon juice
1.9 kg (9½ cups) granulated sugar
1 tablespoon natural vanilla flavouring or extract

1. **Soak the lemon wedges:** Place the 1.15 kg lemon wedges, and any juices or seeds from your cutting board, into a large non-reactive container, and cover with 1.75 L (7 cups) of the water. The fruit should bob freely. Cover with a lid and soak at room temperature for at least 12 hours but no more than 24. This begins to soften the zest and removes unwanted bitterness.

2. **At the same time, soak the lemon slices:** Place the 900 g lemon slices into a separate large non-reactive container and cover with the remaining 1.5 L (6 cups) water. (These will be the strips of zest in your finished marmalade.) Any reserved seeds, pith, and scraps from your cutting board may be added to the container with the lemon wedges for an extra hit of pectin (see Step 1). Cover with a lid and soak at room temperature for at least

12 hours but no more than 24. This begins to soften the zest and removes unwanted bitterness.

3. **The next day, make the lemon stock:** Place a metal mesh strainer over a large bowl or non-reactive container. Set aside.

4. Pour the soaked lemon wedges and their soaking liquid into your Dutch oven or stainless steel maslin (see Note). Bring the mixture to a boil uncovered, over high heat, and then reduce to a simmer. Cover with the lid slightly ajar, and cook for 1 hour, stirring occasionally to ensure the fruit does not stick to the bottom of the pan. The lemons will have started to soften but will still be in intact wedges in the surrounding liquid.

5. After 1 hour, remove the lid and continue to simmer over low heat for another

recipe continues

30 minutes, stirring frequently, until the lemons have broken down and the liquid has darkened and has a slightly thickened, syrupy, and homogeneous consistency. Dip a spoon or spatula into the stock, remove and allow it to cool slightly, and then touch the liquid with your finger. Sufficient pectin has been extracted if the liquid feels viscous and slippery when rubbed between two fingers. If it still feels watery, continue to simmer for another 5 minutes or so, pushing on the fruit with the spatula to encourage it to break down and release its pectin.

6. Immediately pour the stock through the prepared strainer. Cover the entire strainer setup with plastic wrap so you don't lose any volume to evaporation. Allow the stock to thoroughly drip out while you prepare the lemon slices. Wash the pan thoroughly of any lemon residue.

7. **Poach the lemon slices:** Pour the soaked lemon slices and their soaking liquid into your Dutch oven or stainless steel maslin. Bring the mixture to a boil, uncovered, over high heat, and then reduce to a simmer. Cover with the lid slightly ajar and cook for 45 minutes, stirring occasionally to ensure no fruit sticks to the bottom of the pot. At this stage, the cooking liquid should have reduced enough so that the lemon slices are no longer floating, and the mixture appears homogeneous. The lemon slices will firm up when the sugar is added, so the goal during this step is to poach them until they are tender enough to bite through easily. Remove a lemon slice with a spoon or spatula, allow to cool, and squish it between two fingers. If it breaks apart easily, the slices are done. If they still feel too firm,

simmer for another 5 minutes and test the texture again. Remove from the heat.

8. **Make the marmalade:** Sterilize your jars and lids by following the instructions on page 23.

9. Unwrap the strainer setup and discard the lemon wedges. Combine the strained lemon stock, lemon slices, and fresh lemon juice in your Dutch oven or stainless steel maslin. Pour in the sugar in a slow, steady stream, stirring constantly to avoid clumping. Stir to combine. Bring to a boil over high heat, stirring constantly, until the sugar is dissolved. Once it boils, the mixture may begin to foam minimally. Adjust the heat as needed to keep it as hot as possible without allowing the mixture to overflow or sputter. Continue to cook, stirring constantly and scraping the bottom of the pan to distribute the heat evenly and melt the foam back down into the mixture, about 5 minutes.

10. Once the foam subsides, boil over high heat (adjust the heat if the marmalade sputters) for another 10 minutes, stirring frequently, until the marmalade becomes deeper in colour and slightly syrupy and the bubbles are smaller and evenly distributed across the surface. Remove from the heat and skim any foam from the surface.

11. Gently stir to evenly distribute the fruit within the syrup, and then test for doneness. The marmalade should pass the wrinkle test or sheet test and reach at least 200°F (100°C) on a candy thermometer (see page 21). If the marmalade still seems too loose, boil for another 3 to 5 minutes and check the set again. Once set, remove from the heat. Immediately pour in the vanilla and stir vigorously to incorporate.

12. Pour the marmalade into the sterilized jars, leaving ¼ inch of headspace, and
process by following the instructions on
page 23. Arrange the hot jars about 1 inch
apart in a cool place, and let sit undisturbed
for at least 12 hours.

VARIATION: You can substitute the vanilla
flavouring with 60 mL (¼ cup) vanilla,
birthday cake, or whipped cream flavoured
vodka. Add the vodka toward the end
of cooking when the marmalade is 3 to
5 minutes from being set. Stir vigorously
to allow any alcohol to burn off. (Make sure
your head is not over the pot, as the alcohol
vapour has a very strong smell.)

NOTE: If you are using a copper preserving
pan, you must cook the lemon stock and
lemon slices in a stainless steel saucepan
or Dutch oven. Then, combine all the
ingredients with the sugar in a large non-
reactive container before transferring the
mixture into the copper pan.

*You will need about 2.1 kg of whole
lemons (total combined weight needed
for the wedged and sliced lemons). See
A NOTE ON MEASURING FRUIT (page 19).
For preparation instructions, see the chart
UNIQUE FRUIT PREPARATION (page 19).

Meyer Lemon and Chamomile Marmalade

YIELD six 250 mL (8-ounce) jars

There are few flavour pairings as perfect as lemon and chamomile, and this marmalade is no exception. The addition of steeped chamomile blossoms into this traditional Meyer lemon marmalade is so delicate that you may only notice the ever so slight floral infusion at the very fringes of your palate, and only by paying very close attention. Meyer lemons are one of our very favourite citrus fruits, as they make a practically foolproof marmalade and have a beautifully complex lemon-candy flavour. This recipe is sure to delight even the most traditional marmalade lover who may not prefer extra ingredients in their lemon preserves.

Perfect for practically any application from afternoon tea with scones and marmalade, baked into your favourite jammy pastries, or swirled into hot tea for a hint of citrusy sweetness.

2.05 kg Meyer lemons,* divided (1.15 kg cut lengthwise into 1-inch-thick wedges including any juices and seeds; 900 g thinly sliced)
3.25 L (13 cups) water, divided
90 g (1 cup) dried chamomile blossoms
60 mL (¼ cup) lemon juice
1.9 kg (9½ cups) granulated sugar

1. **Soak the lemon wedges:** Place the 1.15 kg lemon wedges, and any juices or seeds from your cutting board, into a large non-reactive container and cover with 1.75 L (7 cups) of the water. The fruit should bob freely. Cover with a lid and soak at room temperature for at least 12 hours but no more than 24. This begins to soften the zest and removes unwanted bitterness.

2. **At the same time, soak the lemon slices:** Place the 900 g lemon slices in a separate large non-reactive container, and cover with the remaining 1.5 L (6 cups) water. (These will be the strips of zest in your finished marmalade.) Any reserved seeds, pith, or scraps from your cutting board can be added to the container with the lemon wedges for an extra hit of pectin (see Step 1). Cover with a lid and soak at room temperature for at least 12 hours but no more than 24. This begins to soften the zest and removes unwanted bitterness.

3. **The next day, make the lemon stock:** Place the chamomile blossoms in a large bowl or non-reactive container, and place a metal mesh strainer on top. Set aside.

4. Pour the soaked lemon wedges and their soaking liquid into your Dutch oven or stainless steel maslin (see Note). Bring to a boil, uncovered, over high heat, and then reduce to a simmer. Cover with the lid slightly ajar, and cook for 1 hour, stirring occasionally to ensure the fruit does not stick to the bottom of the pan. The lemons will have started to soften but will still be in intact wedges in the surrounding liquid.

recipe continues

5. After 1 hour, remove the lid and continue to simmer over low heat for another 30 minutes, stirring frequently, until the lemons have broken down and the liquid has darkened and has a slightly thickened, syrupy, and homogeneous consistency. Dip a spoon or spatula into the stock, remove and allow it to cool slightly, and then touch the liquid with your finger. Sufficient pectin has been extracted if the liquid feels viscous and slippery when rubbed between two fingers. If it still feels watery, continue to simmer for another 5 minutes or so, pushing on the fruit with the spatula to encourage it to break down and release its pectin.

6. Immediately pour the stock through the prepared strainer. The lemon stock will drip out on top of the chamomile blossoms to steep a floral concentrate. Cover the entire strainer setup with plastic wrap so you don't lose any volume to evaporation. Allow the stock to thoroughly drip out and the florals to infuse while you are preparing the lemon slices.

7. **Poach the lemon slices:** Wash your pan thoroughly of any lemon residue. Pour the soaked lemon slices and their soaking liquid into your Dutch oven or stainless steel maslin. Bring the mixture to a boil, uncovered, over high heat, and then reduce to a simmer. Cover with the lid slightly ajar and cook for 20 to 30 minutes, stirring occasionally to ensure no fruit sticks to the bottom of the pan. At this stage, the cooking liquid should have reduced enough so that the lemon slices are no longer floating and the mixture appears homogeneous. The lemon slices will firm up when the sugar is added, so the goal during this step is to poach them until they are tender enough to bite

through easily. Remove a lemon slice with a spoon or spatula, allow it to cool, and squish it between two fingers. If it breaks apart easily, the slices are done. If they still feel too firm, simmer for another 5 minutes and test their texture again. Remove from the heat.

8. **Make the marmalade:** Sterilize your jars and lids by following the instructions on page 23.

9. Unwrap the strainer setup and discard the lemon wedges. Rinse the strainer of lemon particles, and line with 2 layers of cheesecloth cut large enough to encase the chamomile. Strain the floral lemon stock through the sieve into a medium bowl, and then bring the cheesecloth corners together and squeeze out every drop of infused liquid. Discard the chamomile and set the stock aside.

10. Combine the infused lemon stock, lemon slices, and fresh lemon juice in your Dutch oven or stainless steel maslin. Pour in the sugar in a slow, steady stream, stirring constantly to avoid clumping. Stir to combine. Bring to a boil over high heat, stirring constantly, until the sugar is dissolved. Once it boils, the mixture may begin to foam minimally. Adjust the heat as needed to keep it as hot as possible without allowing the mixture to overflow or sputter. Continue to cook, stirring constantly and scraping the bottom of the pan to distribute the heat evenly and melt the foam back down into the mixture, about 5 minutes.

11. Once the foam subsides, boil over high heat (adjust the heat if the marmalade sputters) for another 10 minutes, stirring frequently, until the marmalade becomes deeper in colour and slightly syrupy and

the bubbles are smaller and evenly distributed across the surface. Remove from the heat and skim any foam from the surface.

12. Gently stir to evenly distribute the fruit within the syrup, and then test for doneness. The marmalade should pass the wrinkle test or sheet test and reach 200°F (100°C) on a candy thermometer (see page 21). If the marmalade still seems too loose, boil for another 3 to 5 minutes and check the set again. Once set, remove from the heat.

13. Pour the marmalade into the sterilized jars, leaving ¼ inch of headspace, and process by following the instructions on page 23. Arrange the hot jars about 1 inch apart in a cool place, and let sit undisturbed for at least 12 hours.

NOTE: If you are using a copper preserving pan, you must cook the lemon stock and slices in a stainless steel saucepan or Dutch oven. Then, combine all of the ingredients with the sugar in a large non-reactive container before transferring the mixture into the copper pan.

*You will need about 2.1 kg of whole lemons (total combined weight needed for the wedged and sliced lemons). See **A NOTE ON MEASURING FRUIT** (page 19). For preparation instructions, see the chart **UNIQUE FRUIT PREPARATION** (page 19).

Seville Orange, Rum, and Hibiscus Marmalade

YIELD six 250 mL (8-ounce) jars

Seville oranges are some of the most (if not *the* most) prized and coveted citrus fruits for classic marmalade making, as their extra-thick pith creates silky ribbons within a crystal-clear jelly. For this traditional preserve, we paired the bitter oranges with white rum and steeped hibiscus flowers, which lends a tart, tea-like infusion and intensifies the electric orange-red colour.

Complex and cocktail-like, this is a traditionalist marmalade—bitter, with a hint of sweetness and an ever so slightly boozy note. Enjoy slathered on buttermilk scones or crusty toast and lots of butter or dissolved into your favourite marmalade cocktails.

1.15 kg lemons, cut lengthwise into 1-inch-thick wedges (including any juice and seeds)

4.75 L (19 cups) water, divided

900 g thinly sliced Seville oranges* (plus any seeds, pith, and scraps reserved)

50 g (½ cup) dried hibiscus flowers

90 mL (6 tablespoons) lemon juice

1.9 kg (9½ cups) granulated sugar

45 mL (¼ cup) white rum

1. **Soak the lemon wedges:** Place the lemon wedges, and any juices or seeds from your cutting board, into a large non-reactive container, and cover with 1.75 L (7 cups) of the water. The fruit should bob freely. Cover with a lid and soak at room temperature for at least 12 hours but no more than 24. This begins to soften the zest and removes unwanted bitterness.

2. **At the same time, soak the orange slices:** Place the orange slices in a separate large non-reactive container, and cover with 1.5 L (6 cups) of the water. (These will be the strips of zest in your finished marmalade.) Any reserved seeds, pith, or scraps you have collected from your cutting board may be added to the container with the lemon wedges for an extra hit of pectin (see Step 1). Cover with a lid and soak at room temperature for at least 12 hours but no more than 24. This begins to soften the zest and removes unwanted bitterness.

3. **The next day, make the lemon stock:** Place a metal mesh strainer over a large bowl or non-reactive container. Set aside.

4. Pour the soaked lemon wedges and their soaking liquid into your Dutch oven or stainless steel maslin (see Note). Bring to a boil, uncovered, over high heat, and then reduce to a simmer. Cover with the lid slightly ajar, and cook for 1 hour, stirring occasionally to ensure the fruit does not stick to the bottom of the pan. The lemons will have started to soften but will still be in intact wedges in the surrounding liquid.

5. After 1 hour, remove the lid and continue to simmer over low heat for another 10 minutes, stirring frequently, until the

recipe continues

lemons have broken down, and the liquid has darkened and has a slightly thickened, syrupy, and homogeneous consistency. Dip a spoon or spatula into the stock, remove and allow to cool slightly, and then touch the liquid with your finger. Sufficient pectin has been extracted if the liquid feels viscous and slippery when rubbed between two fingers. If it still feels watery, continue to simmer for another 5 minutes or so, pushing on the fruit with the spatula to encourage it to break down and release its pectin.

6. Immediately pour the stock through the prepared strainer. Cover the entire strainer setup with plastic wrap so you don't lose any volume to evaporation. Allow the stock to thoroughly drip out while you prepare the oranges.

7. **Blanch the orange slices:** Wash your pan thoroughly of any lemon residue. Pour the soaked orange slices and their soaking liquid into your Dutch oven or stainless steel maslin. Bring the mixture to a boil, uncovered, over high heat, and then reduce to a simmer. Cook for 5 minutes. Remove from the heat and pour the mixture through a strainer back into its large soaking container. Discard the liquid. Return the orange slices back into the pan and cover with the remaining 1.5 L (6 cups) water. Bring the mixture to a boil, uncovered, over high heat, and then reduce to a simmer. Cover with the lid slightly ajar and cook for 30 to 45 minutes, stirring occasionally to ensure no fruit sticks to the bottom of the pan. At this stage, the cooking liquid should have reduced enough so that the orange slices are no longer floating, and the mixture appears homogeneous. The orange slices will firm

up when the sugar is added, so the goal during this step is to poach them until they are tender enough to bite through easily. Remove an orange slice with a spoon or spatula, allow to cool, and squish it between two fingers. If it breaks apart easily, the slices are done. If they still feel too firm, simmer for another 20 to 30 minutes, testing their texture every 10 minutes. (Note: This may take up to 2 hours total if your oranges are very fresh.) Once sufficiently softened, remove from the heat.

8. **Meanwhile, prepare the hibiscus flowers:** Place the hibiscus in a small bowl, and cover with plenty of boiling water. The hibiscus will rehydrate and bloom. Agitate the flowers with a spoon to encourage them to open, and allow to steep for 10 minutes. Pour through a heatproof strainer and discard the liquid. Rinse the flowers well under cool water, rubbing them with your fingertips—hibiscus can be sandy depending on how it was harvested, so be sure to wash away any sand or dirt. If your hibiscus flowers are full and intact, tear them apart into thin, visually appealing strips. If they are already broken up into the size of pieces you would like floating in your marmalade, leave them as they are. Set aside.

9. **Make the marmalade:** Sterilize your jars and lids by following the instructions on page 23.

10. Unwrap the strainer setup and discard the lemon wedges. Combine the strained lemon stock, orange slices, hibiscus pieces, and lemon juice in your Dutch oven or stainless steel maslin. Pour in the sugar in a slow, steady stream, stirring constantly to avoid clumping. Stir to combine. Bring to a boil over high heat, stirring constantly,

until the sugar is dissolved. Once it boils, the mixture may begin to foam minimally. Adjust the heat as needed to keep it as hot as possible without allowing the mixture to overflow or sputter. Continue to cook, stirring constantly and scraping the bottom of the pan to distribute the heat evenly and melt the foam back down into the mixture, about 5 minutes.

11. Once the foam subsides, boil over high heat (adjust the heat if the marmalade sputters) for another 10 minutes, stirring frequently, until the marmalade becomes deeper in colour and slightly syrupy and the bubbles are smaller and evenly distributed across the surface. Remove from the heat and skim any foam from the surface.

12. Gently stir to evenly distribute the fruit within the syrup, and then test for doneness. The marmalade should pass the wrinkle test or sheet test and reach at least 200°F (100°C) on a candy thermometer (see page 21). If the marmalade still seems too loose, boil for another 3 to 5 minutes and check the set again. Once set, remove from the heat. Immediately pour in the white rum and stir vigorously to allow any alcohol to burn off. (Make sure your head is not over the pot, as the alcohol vapour has a very strong smell.)

13. Pour the marmalade into the sterilized jars, leaving ¼ inch of headspace, and process by following the instructions on page 23. Arrange the hot jars about 1 inch apart in a cool place, and let sit undisturbed for at least 12 hours.

NOTE: If you are using a copper preserving pan, you must cook the lemon stock and orange slices in a stainless steel saucepan or Dutch oven. Then, combine all of the ingredients with the sugar in a large non-reactive container before transferring the mixture into the copper pan.

*You will need about 910 g of whole oranges. See **A NOTE ON MEASURING FRUIT** (page 19). For preparation instructions, see the chart **UNIQUE FRUIT PREPARATION** (page 19).

NOTES

Preserved Meyer Lemon and Saffron Marmalade

YIELD six 250 mL (8-ounce) jars

An elegant culinary delight, this gorgeous golden-coloured preserve with its unique preparation boasts a complex flavour—sweet and sour, salty and savoury, with aromatic notes of saffron. The true lover of sour flavours will enjoy this preserve on crusty toast with butter, though it is equally fun as a glaze for tangy chicken wings, roasted carrots, or as a base for a salad vinaigrette.

This recipe includes the preparation of preserved lemons, which is an intensely satisfying culinary experience. In a pinch, feel free to use regular lemons instead of Meyer lemons. Alternatively, to cut down the preparation time (by about a month!), feel free to substitute with good-quality jarred preserved lemons from your local specialty grocer. Try to find a brand with the fewest preservatives and added flavourings.

Preserved Meyer Lemons

1 kg (2¼ pounds) Meyer lemons
216 g (1½ cups) Diamond Crystal kosher salt
125 mL (½ cup) Meyer lemon juice

Marmalade

1.5 kg lemons, cut lengthwise into 1-inch thick
    wedges (including any juice and seeds)
2 L (8 cups) water
1 teaspoon saffron threads
900 g thinly sliced preserved Meyer lemons*
    (recipe at left)
60 mL (¼ cup) lemon juice
1.75 kg (8¾ cups) granulated sugar

1. Make the preserved Meyer lemons: Wash your Meyer lemons well, scrubbing each lemon with mild soap and hot water. Dry thoroughly with a clean kitchen towel. Slice each lemon twice, lengthwise, to make a deep cross in the top of the fruit, stopping about an inch from the bottom to keep the lemon intact.

2. Sprinkle about 1 tablespoon of the salt in the bottom of a clean 1 L (4-cup) mason jar. Working over a wide bowl, pack each lemon generously with salt and place in the mason jar. Sprinkle another tablespoon or so of salt between each layer of lemon, and continue to pack each salted fruit into the

jar tightly, pressing down with your fingers or the back of a large spoon as you work. You will notice the juices running from the lemons.

3. Once your jar is completely full, pour the additional Meyer lemon juice into the jar to cover the fruit. Note that depending on the jar, you may have some salt and lemon juice left over—simply use enough to fill and pack your jar. Seal the jar and shake well to combine and evenly distribute the salt and juice throughout. Let sit at room temperature for 48 hours, shaking the jar each day.

recipe continues

4. On the third day, place the jar in the fridge for 3 weeks, shaking the jar every few days to continue dissolving the salt and evenly distribute the brine. After the 3-week preservation, your Meyer lemons will be soft to the touch, and the pith will break down easily between your fingertips. Once your preserved lemons are sufficiently softened, you are ready to make the marmalade.

5. Once the Meyer lemons are preserved, prepare the fresh lemon wedges: Place the wedges, and any juices or seeds from your cutting board, into a large non-reactive container and cover with the water. The fruit should bob freely. Cover with a lid and soak at room temperature for at least 12 hours but no more than 24. This begins to soften the zest and removes unwanted bitterness.

6. The next day, make the lemon stock: Place the saffron in a large bowl or non-reactive container, and place a metal mesh strainer on top. Set aside.

7. Pour the soaked lemon wedges and their soaking liquid into your Dutch oven or stainless steel maslin (see Note). Bring to a boil, uncovered, over high heat, and then reduce to a simmer. Cover with the lid slightly ajar, and cook for 1 hour, stirring occasionally to ensure the fruit does not stick to the bottom of the pan. The lemons will have begun to soften but will still be in intact wedges in the surrounding liquid.

8. After 1 hour, remove the lid from the lemon stock and continue to simmer over low heat for another 30 minutes, stirring frequently, until the lemons have broken down and the liquid has darkened and has a slightly thickened, syrupy, and homogeneous consistency. Dip a spoon or spatula

into the stock, remove and allow it to cool slightly, and then touch the liquid with your finger. Sufficient pectin has been extracted if the liquid feels viscous and slippery when rubbed between two fingers. If it still feels watery, continue to simmer for another 5 minutes or so, pushing on the fruit with the spatula to encourage it to break down and release its pectin.

9. Immediately pour the stock through the strainer setup. The lemon stock will drip over the saffron to steep a floral concentrate. Cover the entire strainer setup with plastic wrap so you don't lose any volume to evaporation. Allow the stock to thoroughly drip out and the florals to infuse while you prepare the preserved lemon slices.

10. Make the marmalade: Sterilize your jars and lids by following the instructions on page 23.

11. Remove the preserved Meyer lemons from their brine and rinse under cool running water. Break each lemon into quarters, and gently remove the seeds and discard. Slice each lemon quarter crosswise into thin triangle-shaped slices no more than ⅛ inch thick. Weigh the lemon slices; you need 900 g.

12. Unwrap the strainer setup and discard the lemon wedges. Combine the strained lemon stock, Meyer lemon slices, and fresh lemon juice in your Dutch oven or stainless steel maslin. Pour in the sugar in a slow, steady stream, stirring constantly to avoid clumping. Stir to combine.

13. Bring to a boil over high heat, stirring constantly, until the sugar is dissolved. Once it boils, the mixture may begin to foam minimally. Adjust the heat as needed to keep it as hot as possible without allowing the mixture to overflow or sputter. Continue to cook, stirring and scraping the bottom of the pan to distribute the heat evenly and melt the foam back down into the mixture, about 5 minutes.

14. Once the foam subsides, boil over high heat (adjust the heat if the marmalade sputters) for another 10 minutes, stirring frequently, until the marmalade becomes deeper in colour and slightly syrupy and the bubbles are smaller and evenly distributed across the surface. Remove from the heat and skim any foam from the surface.

15. Gently stir to evenly distribute the fruit within the syrup, and then test for doneness. The marmalade should pass the wrinkle test or sheet test and reach at least

200°F (100°C) on a candy thermometer (see page 21). If the marmalade still seems too loose, boil for another 3 to 5 minutes and check the set again. Once set, remove from the heat.

16. Pour the marmalade into the sterilized jars, leaving ¼ inch of headspace, and process by following the instructions on page 23. Arrange the hot jars about 1 inch apart in a cool place, and let sit undisturbed for at least 12 hours.

NOTE: If you are using a copper preserving pan, you must cook the lemon stock in a stainless steel saucepan or Dutch oven. Then, combine all of the ingredients with the sugar in a large non-reactive container before transferring the mixture into the copper pan.

*You will need about 910 g of whole preserved lemons. See A NOTE ON MEASURING FRUIT (page 19). For preparation instructions, see the chart UNIQUE FRUIT PREPARATION (page 19).

Tropical, Vine, and Other

Pink Pluot, Guava, and Lime Leaf Jam

YIELD six 250 mL (8-ounce) jars

A true showstopper—what makes this preserve stand apart is its creamy texture and bold tropical flavour. Use fresh, extra ripe white guavas for this Popsicle-like jam. If you have never smelled a ripe guava fruit, look out! They release a noticeably pungent, musky aroma. We like to ripen them in resealable food storage bags, which will inflate substantially as the fruit ripens. Release them outside when the guavas are no longer green and are soft to the touch—this is when the flesh is at its sweetest and most flavourful.

Pink pluots are a lovely canvas for the guava, as they are typically high in water content and not overly flavourful on their own. However, they will allow the guava to shine, add body to the texture, and lend their lovely rosy colour. Use fruit in a variety of stages of ripening, which will add texture to the jam. The addition of lime leaves adds layered complexity to the sweet, tropical profile.

500 g peeled white guavas*
375 mL (1½ cups) water
1 kg pitted and diced pink pluots*
1 kg (5 cups) granulated sugar
60 mL (¼ cup) lime juice
10 to 12 fresh lime leaves
1 lime

1. **Prepare the guavas:** Place the peeled guavas in a small saucepan. Pour in the water, ensuring the fruit is completely covered. (If the water does not cover the fruit, use a smaller saucepan.) Bring to a simmer over low heat, cover with a lid, and cook for 5 to 10 minutes until the guavas are tender and easily pierced with a fork.

2. Set a wire-mesh strainer over a medium bowl. Pour the guava mixture through the strainer. Using the back of a large spoon, mash the guavas and push them through the strainer to separate the seeds from the fruit pulp. Be sure to scrape the bottom of the strainer into the bowl, as fruit pulp tends to cling to it. Discard the seeds.

3. **Macerate the fruit:** Combine the guava purée, diced pluots, sugar, and lime juice in a large non-reactive container, and toss gently to evenly coat. Cover with a lid and macerate overnight in the fridge for at least 12 hours but no more than 24.

4. **The next day, make the jam:** Sterilize your jars and lids by following the instructions on page 23.

5. Remove the macerated fruit from the fridge. Scrape the fruit mixture and all the juices into your preserving pan. Bring to a boil over high heat, stirring constantly, until the juices run from the fruit and the sugar is dissolved. Once it boils, the mixture

recipe continues

will begin to foam. Adjust the heat as needed to keep it as hot as possible without allowing the mixture to overflow or sputter. Continue to cook, stirring constantly and scraping the bottom of the pan to distribute the heat evenly and melt the foam back down into the mixture, about 5 minutes.

6. Once the foam subsides, boil over high heat (adjust the heat if the jam sputters) for another 20 minutes, stirring frequently. The pluots will begin to break down and become transparent, and the guava purée will take on a thickened, pudding-like texture. This will make the jam appear to be more set than it is; the texture will not change much once the jam is cool. As the jam cooks, gradually reduce the heat to medium-low if needed to prevent scorching, and stir constantly until the jam becomes thicker and darkens. Remove from the heat and skim any foam from the surface.

7. Gently stir to evenly distribute the fruit within the syrup, and then test for doneness. The jam should pass the wrinkle test or sheet test and reach at least 200°F (100°C) on a candy thermometer (see page 21). If the jam still seems too loose, boil for another 3 to 5 minutes and check the set again. Once set, remove from the heat. Using tongs, submerge the whole lime leaves directly into the jam. Steep for 5 minutes, remove the leaves from the jam, and transfer them to a heatproof plate. Use a spatula to press and scrape away any jam from the leaves back into the pot. Zest the lime over the pan, and then cut the lime in half and squeeze the juice into the jam. Stir thoroughly to evenly distribute the flavour. Discard the lime leaves.

8. Pour the jam into the sterilized jars, leaving ¼ inch of headspace, and process by following the instructions on page 23. Arrange the hot jars about 1 inch apart in a cool place, and let sit undisturbed for at least 12 hours.

*You will need about 750 g of whole guavas and 1.2 kg of whole pluots. See **A NOTE ON MEASURING FRUIT** (page 19).

NOTES

Apricot, Mango, and Passion Fruit Jam

YIELD six 250 mL (8-ounce) jars

Ripe mango mingles beautifully with apricot in this rich, golden preserve. The two fruits have such a similar texture and colour that when cooked, you almost can't tell where one ends and the next begins. The addition of fresh passion fruit lends its tartness, seedy crunch, and recognizable perfume.

For this recipe, we prefer to use Ataulfo or Champagne mangoes—the smaller, golden-yellow, bean-shaped variety. Sweet and buttery with notes of honey, their flesh is not fibrous, as compared to their larger red-and-green-blushed cousins most often seen at the grocer. Ataulfo mangoes begin to come into season around late March and stick around throughout the summer months. Use mangoes of a variety of ripeness for added texture.

675 g pitted and diced apricots*
675 g pitted, peeled, and diced Ataulfo mango*
150 g pulp and seeds of fresh passion fruit (about 6 to 8 passion fruits)
1 kg (5 cups) granulated sugar
60 mL (¼ cup) lemon juice

1. **Macerate the fruit:** Combine the apricots, mango, passion fruit, sugar, and lemon juice in a large non-reactive container, and toss gently to evenly coat. Cover with a lid and macerate in the fridge overnight for at least 12 hours but no more than 24.

2. **The next day, make the jam:** Sterilize your jars and lids by following the instructions on page 23.

3. Remove the macerated fruit from the fridge. Scrape the fruit mixture and all the juices into your preserving pan. Bring to a boil over high heat, stirring constantly, until the juices run from the fruit and the sugar is dissolved. Once it boils, the mixture will begin to foam. Adjust the heat as needed to keep it as hot as possible without allowing the mixture to overflow or sputter. Continue to cook, stirring constantly and scraping the bottom of the pan to distribute the heat evenly and melt the foam back down into the mixture, about 5 minutes.

4. Once the foam has subsided, boil over high heat (adjust the heat if the jam sputters) for another 10 to 15 minutes, stirring frequently. The apricots will begin to soften and break down, and the jam will appear homogeneous with no pockets of liquid between pieces of fruit. As the jam cooks, gradually reduce the heat to medium-low if needed to avoid scorching, and stir constantly until the jam becomes thicker, slightly syrupy, and the bubbles are smaller and evenly distributed across the surface. Remove from the heat and skim any foam from the surface.

5. Gently stir to evenly distribute the fruit within the syrup, and then test for

recipe continues

doneness. The jam should pass the wrinkle test or sheet test and reach at least 200°F (100°C) on a candy thermometer (see page 21). If the jam still seems too loose, boil for another 3 to 5 minutes and check the set again. Once set, remove from the heat.

6. Pour the jam into the sterilized jars, leaving ¼ inch of headspace, and process by following the instructions on page 23. Arrange the hot jars about 1 inch apart in a cool place, and let sit undisturbed for at least 12 hours.

*You will need about 800 g of whole apricots and 1 kg of whole mangoes. See A NOTE ON MEASURING FRUIT (page 19).

Golden Papaya and Strawberry Jam

YIELD four to five 250 mL (8-ounce) jars

Papaya is one of our favourite fruits for preserving, though underused in our Canadian culinary tradition. We fell in love with papaya jam after receiving a special gift of Ontario's very first crop of papayas in 2018—a tiny basket of six golden-yellow treasures. Papayas are starting to be greenhouse cultivated in the Niagara region by pioneering farmers, and we look forward to more non-native fruit varieties becoming available locally in the coming years.

Easy to prepare and high yielding, papayas make a lovely preserve on their own or as a flavourful base for several fruit pairings, such as our Blood Orange and Papaya Jamalade (page 141). In this recipe, we added a handful of springtime strawberries for a fruity, smoothie-inspired blend. Try blending a spoonful with milk, yogurt, and fresh banana for a sippable tutti-frutti breakfast or dilute with water and freeze in ice-pop moulds for a refreshing summertime treat (see Strawberry Daiquiri Poptail, page 305).

750 g peeled, seeded, and diced papaya*
750 g hulled strawberries
750 g (3¾ cups) granulated sugar
125 mL (½ cup) lemon juice
Zest of 1 orange (optional)

1. **Macerate the fruit:** Combine the papaya, strawberries, sugar, and lemon juice in a large non-reactive container, and toss gently to evenly coat. Cover with a lid and macerate in the fridge overnight for at least 12 hours but no more than 24.

2. **The next day, make the jam:** Sterilize your jars and lids by following the instructions on page 23.

3. Remove the macerated fruit from the fridge. Scrape the fruit mixture and all the juices into your preserving pan. Bring to a boil over high heat, stirring constantly, until the juices run from the fruit and the sugar is dissolved. Once it boils, the mixture will begin to foam. Adjust the heat as needed to keep it as hot as possible without allowing the mixture to overflow or sputter.

Continue to cook, stirring constantly and scraping the bottom of the pan to distribute the heat evenly and melt the foam back down into the mixture, about 5 minutes.

4. Once the foam subsides, boil over high heat (adjust the heat if the jam sputters) for another 20 to 25 minutes, stirring frequently. The fruit will begin to soften and become transparent, and the jam will become noticeably darker. As the jam cooks, gradually reduce the heat to medium-low if needed to prevent scorching, and stir constantly until the jam becomes thicker and slightly syrupy and the bubbles are smaller and evenly distributed across the surface. Remove from the heat and skim any foam from the surface.

recipe continues

5. Gently stir to evenly distribute the fruit within the syrup, and then test for doneness. The jam should pass the wrinkle test or sheet test and reach at least 200°F (100°C) on a candy thermometer (see page 21). If the jam still seems too loose, boil for another 3 to 5 minutes and check the set again. Once set, remove from the heat.

6. Zest the orange (if using) over the pan. Stir thoroughly to evenly distribute the flavour.

7. Pour the jam into the sterilized jars, leaving ¼ inch of headspace, and process by following the instructions on page 23. Arrange the hot jars about 1 inch apart in a cool place, and let sit undisturbed for at least 12 hours.

*You will need about 1.2 kg of whole papaya. See **A NOTE ON MEASURING FRUIT** (page 19).

NOTES

Kiwi and Soursop Jam

YIELD four to five 250 mL (8-ounce) jars

With its adorably fuzzy brown skin and green flesh, kiwi is an unassuming option for preserving, but its jam is positively delightful. Bright green with a sweet, almost tropical, pineapple-like flavour, kiwis have a naturally high pectin content, which makes for a bright, fresh, and tart preserve with a quick cooking time. Even its tiny seeds add a signature and unobtrusive crunch.

Soursop is a natural pairing for kiwi, with a similar pineapple-like, perfumed aroma, and complex flavour that moves through your taste buds from intensely tangy to sweet to sour. Its creamy texture is an unexpected and stark contrast to its sharp and fruity flavour, reminiscent of a fibrous mango or very ripe banana. Its ivory flesh doesn't muddle the green of the kiwi and gives a bit of breathing room between the chunks of fruit and seeds.

Soursop fruits are available year-round, with peak seasons in the late autumn and early winter, and ripen to a blushed yellow skin and slight give when pressed with a finger. Feel free to use frozen purée soursop in a 1:1 ratio, which can be found at specialty grocers or Caribbean markets.

1.1 kg peeled and diced kiwis*
400 g peeled, seeded, and roughly chopped soursop*
800 g (4 cups) granulated sugar
60 mL (¼ cup) lemon juice

1. **Macerate the fruit:** Combine the kiwi, soursop, sugar, and lemon juice in a large non-reactive container, and toss gently to evenly coat. Cover with a lid and macerate in the fridge overnight for at least 12 hours but no more than 24.

2. **The next day, make the jam:** Sterilize your jars and lids by following the instructions on page 23.

3. Remove the macerated fruit from the fridge. Scrape the fruit mixture and all the juices into your preserving pan. Bring to boil over high heat, stirring constantly, until the juices run from the fruit and the sugar is dissolved. Once it boils, the mixture will begin to foam. Adjust the heat as needed to keep it as hot as possible without allowing the mixture to overflow or sputter.

Continue to cook, stirring constantly and scraping the bottom of the pan to distribute the heat evenly and melt the foam back down into the mixture, about 5 minutes.

4. Once the foam has subsided, boil over high heat (adjust the heat if the jam sputters) for another 15 minutes, stirring frequently. The kiwi will begin to soften and become transparent. Use a potato masher to encourage the kiwi to break down, and the jam will instantly thicken.

5. Boil for another 5 to 10 minutes until the jam appears homogeneous with no pockets of liquid between pieces of fruit. As the jam cooks, gradually reduce the heat to medium-low if needed to prevent

recipe continues

scorching, and stir constantly until it becomes thicker and slightly syrupy and the bubbles are smaller and evenly distributed across the surface. Remove from the heat and skim any foam from the surface.

6. Gently stir to evenly distribute the fruit within the syrup, and then test for doneness. The jam should pass the wrinkle test or sheet test and reach at least 200°F (100°C) on a candy thermometer (see page 21). If the jam still seems too loose, boil for another 3 to 5 minutes and check the set again. Once set, remove from the heat.

7. Pour the jam into the sterilized jars, leaving ¼ inch of headspace, and process by following the instructions on page 23. Arrange the hot jars about 1 inch apart in a cool place, and let sit undisturbed for at least 12 hours.

*You will need about 1.3 kg of whole kiwis and 800 g of whole soursop. See **A NOTE ON MEASURING FRUIT** (page 19).

Banana, Bourbon, and Vanilla Bean Jam

YIELD six 250 mL (8-ounce) jars

This was one of the very first jams we made as Kitten and the Bear, and it remains one of our most loved flavours. The warmth of vanilla bean and notes of bourbon pair perfectly with bananas for a preserve that is dessert-like, yet unexpectedly bright and subtly tart. Think banana bread, bananas foster, and banana splits—rather than a tropical vibe most often associated with banana-flavoured treats.

An immense amount of lemon juice and sugar is needed to keep this preserve bright in colour and flavour. This ratio allows for an extremely quick cooking time to achieve that warm yellow banana colour. Additionally, we recommend buying your bananas green and keeping a close eye as they ripen in your kitchen. The moment they are just ripe (yellow, with a green stem and no brown spots), make your banana jam.

2 cups (500 mL) lemon juice
1.5 kg peeled ripe bananas*
1.75 kg (8¾ cups) granulated sugar
1 vanilla pod, split lengthwise and seeds scraped
2 tablespoons bourbon

1. **Prepare the bananas and macerate:** Place a large non-reactive container on a kitchen scale. Pour in the lemon juice and tare the scale to zero. Slice the bananas directly into the lemon juice, tossing every so often to prevent browning. This will help maintain a bright colour. Once you have exactly 1.5 kg of sliced bananas, toss once again in the lemon juice to evenly coat, and then blanket the mixture with the sugar without stirring so that no air can reach the fruit. Cover with a lid and macerate in the fridge overnight for at least 12 hours but no more than 24.

2. **The next day, make the jam:** Sterilize your jars and lids by following the instructions on page 23.

3. Remove the macerated fruit from the fridge. Scrape the fruit mixture and all the juices into your preserving pan. Bring to a boil over high heat, stirring constantly, until the juices run from the fruit and the sugar is dissolved. Once it boils, the mixture will begin to foam dramatically. Adjust the heat as needed to keep it as hot as possible without allowing the mixture to overflow or sputter. Continue to cook, stirring constantly and scraping the bottom of the pan to distribute the heat evenly and melt the foam back down into the mixture, about 5 minutes.

4. Once the foam subsides, remove from the heat and thoroughly skim the foam from the surface of the jam using a large spoon. Collect all the foam in a medium bowl or heatproof container and set aside.

5. Add the vanilla seeds to the jam, and then submerge the pod for extra vanilla

recipe continues

flavour. Increase the heat back to medium-high (as high as possible without the mixture sputtering) and continue to boil for another 7 to 10 minutes, stirring frequently. As the jam cooks, gradually reduce the heat to medium-low if needed to prevent scorching, and stir constantly until the jam becomes thicker and slightly syrupy and the bubbles are smaller and evenly distributed across the surface. Remove from the heat and skim any foam from the surface into the container of reserved foam. At this point, the foam you have set aside will have settled, and you will notice that syrup has sunk to the bottom of the container. Use a spoon to move the foam to one side of the container, and then pour as much of the clear syrup as possible back into the jam.

6. Gently stir to evenly distribute the fruit within the syrup, and then test for doneness. The jam should pass the wrinkle test or sheet test and reach at least 200°F (100°C) on a candy thermometer (see page 21). If the jam still seems too loose, boil for another 2 to 3 minutes and check the set again. Once set, remove from the heat. Immediately pour in the bourbon and stir vigorously to allow any alcohol to burn off. (Make sure your head is not over the pot, as the alcohol vapour has a very strong smell.)

7. Pour the jam into the sterilized jars, leaving ¼ inch of headspace, and process by following the instructions on page 23. Arrange the hot jars about 1 inch apart in a cool place, and let sit undisturbed for at least 12 hours.

NOTE: This jam can have many colour variations that are dependent on the length of cooking and ripeness of the bananas. If this jam is made with starchy bananas, or is ever-so-slightly overcooked, it may turn a rosy pink shade. If your bananas are underripe, it will turn a more vibrant yellow. This is normal and the jam is perfectly safe to consume no matter the resulting colour.

*You will need about 2.4 kg of whole bananas. See A NOTE ON MEASURING FRUIT (page 19).

NOTES

_____

_____

_____

_____

_____

_____

_____

Roasted Concord Grape Jam

YIELD six 250 mL (8-ounce) jars

Any preservationist knows that true Concord jam is a delicacy. Just getting your hands on local, freshly picked Concord grapes is a treat these days, as many growers are switching their crop to the more popular seedless blue or Coronation variety. Though Coronation grapes are beautiful, there is nothing that quite compares to that robust Concord flavour and aroma.

To ease the laborious process of separating the seeds from the flesh of the grapes, many recipes for Concord preserves encourage a jelly or part-jelly process, where the grapes are boiled in water to soften the flesh, and then pressed through a strainer or food mill to remove the seeds. In our version, we roast the grapes whole just until the juices run—this softens the grape enough to easily remove the seeds, without the addition of any water content or loss of flesh or skin. The result is a full fruit jam with a deep, undiluted Concord flavour for an elevated take on this childhood classic.

1.75 kg stemmed Concord grapes
1 kg (5 cups) granulated sugar
60 mL (¼ cup) lemon juice

1. **Prepare the grapes:** Preheat the oven to 400°F (200°C).

2. Place the grapes in a large baking dish or roasting pan. The grapes do not have to be in a single layer, but no more than 2 or 3 grapes should be piled on top of each other to allow for even heat distribution. Bake for 5 to 10 minutes or until the skins look shrivelled, juice has started to run from the fruit, and the colour of the grapes has changed from blue to mauve-purple.

3. Pass the roasted grapes and any juices through a food mill into a medium-large bowl or heatproof container. Milling the grapes separates the seeds and creates a rich purée.

4. **Make the jam:** Sterilize your jars and lids by following the instructions on page 23.

5. Add the sugar and lemon juice to the warm grape purée and mix to combine. Scrape the mixture into your preserving pan, and bring to a boil over high heat, stirring constantly, until the sugar is dissolved. Once it boils, adjust the heat as needed to keep it as hot as possible without allowing the mixture to overflow or sputter. Continue to cook for 10 minutes, stirring constantly and scraping the bottom of the pan as needed to distribute the heat evenly. As the jam cooks, gradually reduce the heat to medium-low if needed to prevent scorching, and stir constantly until the jam becomes thicker, slightly syrupy, and the bubbles are smaller and evenly distributed across the surface. Remove from the heat and skim any foam from the surface.

recipe continues

6. Gently stir to evenly distribute the fruit within the syrup, and then test for doneness. The jam should pass the wrinkle test or sheet test and reach at least 200°F (100°C) on a candy thermometer (see page 21). If the jam still seems too loose, boil for another 3 to 5 minutes and check the set again. Once set, remove from the heat.

7. Pour the jam into the sterilized jars, leaving ¼ inch of headspace, and process by following the instructions on page 23. Arrange the hot jars about 1 inch apart in a cool place, and let sit undisturbed for at least 12 hours.

Spiced Tomato and Tawny Port Jam

YIELD five 250 mL (8-ounce) jars

Did you know tomatoes are actually a fruit? This recipe brings out all the delicious and fruity qualities of the tomato, perfectly paired with a complex, toasty spice blend. A dose of aged tawny port adds warmth and depth to this complex preserve.

For this style of preserve, we prefer large, firm, meaty tomatoes, such as hot house or beefsteak, that have dense flesh, fewer seeds, and more mild flavour than vine-ripened or heirloom varieties. Your tomatoes should be slightly underripe, close to the texture of an apple, which will create beautiful, candied cubes rather than tomato-sauce-like purée.

Though we typically aim for the shortest cooking process possible to maintain the bright freshness of fruit, the trick to this unique and special preserve is a long, extended cooking process. Continue to cook the mixture and stir, stir, stir until any liquid remaining has a thick, syrupy consistency and the tomatoes have a rich, caramelized aroma. You will know it when you see it!

3 kg tomatoes
1.1 kg (5½ cups) granulated sugar
175 mL (¾ cup) tawny port
60 mL (¼ cup) lemon juice
7 whole cloves
5 black peppercorns
5 green cardamom pods
3 allspice berries

3 juniper berries
3 star anise
1 black cardamom pod
½ whole nutmeg, crushed
1 bay leaf
1 cinnamon stick
¼ teaspoon cayenne pepper, or to taste (optional)

1. **Prepare the tomatoes:** Bring a large, wide rondeau or stock pot of water to a boil. Hull the tomatoes. Slice an X into the skin on the bottom, which will help the boiling water lift the skin from the flesh. Working in batches of about 3 tomatoes, gently submerge the tomatoes into the water for 1 minute or until the skin begins to crack and peel. Using a slotted spoon, remove the tomatoes from the water and place on a large baking sheet to cool.

2. Peel the skins off the blanched tomatoes and discard. Dice the tomatoes into ½-inch cubes. Scale out your prepared tomatoes to 2.5 kg, including any juice and seeds.

3. Combine the tomatoes, sugar, port, and lemon juice in a large non-reactive container and stir well. Cover with a lid and macerate in the fridge overnight for at least 12 hours but no more than 24.

4. **The next day, make the jam:** Sterilize your jars and lids by following the instructions on page 23.

5. Remove the macerated tomatoes from the fridge. Scrape the tomato mixture and all the juices into your Dutch oven or stainless steel maslin (see Note).

6. Place the black peppercorns, green cardamom pods, allspice berries, juniper berries,

recipe continues

star anise, black cardamom pod, and nutmeg in a metal mesh spice ball or muslin pouch and submerge in the mixture. Add the bay leaf, cinnamon stick, and cayenne pepper (if using) and allow to float freely. Bring to a boil over high heat, stirring constantly, until the sugar is dissolved. Once it boils, the mixture will begin to foam. Adjust the heat as needed to keep it as hot as possible without allowing the mixture to overflow or sputter. Continue to cook, stirring constantly and scraping the bottom of the pan to distribute the heat evenly and melt the foam back down into the mixture, about 5 minutes.

7. Once the foam subsides, reduce the heat to medium and simmer for another 40 to 50 minutes, stirring frequently. As the jam cooks, gradually reduce the heat to medium-low if needed to prevent scorching, and stir frequently until the jam becomes remarkably thickened. Cook the jam until it is about as thick as you will want the end product to be—thick enough that you get a clean line on the bottom of the pan for a moment when you scrape with your spatula. Remove from the heat. Scoop out the spices and spice ball, allowing any syrup to completely drip back into the jam. Skim any foam from the surface.

8. Gently stir to evenly distribute the fruit within the syrup, and then test for doneness. The jam should pass the wrinkle test or sheet test and reach at least 200°F (100°C) on a candy thermometer (see page 21). If the jam still seems too loose, boil for another 3 to 5 minutes and check the set again. Once set, remove from the heat.

9. Pour the jam into the sterilized jars, leaving ¼ inch of headspace, and process by following the instructions on page 23. Arrange the hot jars about 1 inch apart in a cool place, and let sit undisturbed for at least 12 hours.

NOTE: Because of the low-sugar nature of this jam, we do not recommend using a copper preserving pan for this recipe. Use a double-bottomed stainless steel pot, maslin pan, or Dutch oven.

NOTES

_____

_____

_____

_____

_____

_____

_____

_____

Roasted Red Pepper and Apricot Jam

YIELD five to six 250 mL (8-ounce) jars

In our fruity spin on classic red pepper jelly, red bell peppers are charred until their skin blisters and then chopped into a classic apricot jam base for a full-bodied and vibrantly flavoured preserve. A splash of sriracha sauce and gochugaru (Korean red chili flakes) marries the flavours into a sweet and tangy condiment with just the right amount of spice.

Delicious in place of chutney and red pepper spreads—think cheese boards, grilled cheese sandwiches, roasted meats, and barbecues.

1 kg pitted and halved apricots*
900 g (4½ cups) granulated sugar, divided
175 mL (¾ cup) rice wine vinegar, divided
2 tablespoons sriracha sauce
1 teaspoon gochugaru
1 teaspoon onion powder (optional)
5 large red bell peppers

1. **Macerate the fruit:** Combine the apricots, 450 g (2¼ cups) of the sugar, 125 mL (½ cup) of the rice wine vinegar, sriracha sauce, gochugaru, and onion powder (if using) in a large non-reactive container, and toss gently to evenly coat. Cover with a lid and macerate in the fridge overnight for at least 12 hours but no more than 24.

2. **The next day, roast the red peppers:** Preheat the oven to 450°F (230°C). Line a baking sheet with parchment paper.

3. Cut the red peppers in half lengthwise and place cut side down on the lined baking sheet. Roast for 20 to 25 minutes, until the skin is charred and blistered. Remove from the oven and let sit until cool enough to handle.

4. Cut out the stem and core so the pepper is a flat fillet. Place the pepper on a cutting board and scrape off the charred skin with the back side of a kitchen knife. Rinse thoroughly under cool running water to remove any remaining seeds, pieces of char, and skin. Cut into small cubes, about ¼ inch, until you have 500 g of prepared peppers.

5. **Make the jam:** Sterilize your jars and lids by following the instructions on page 23.

6. Remove the macerated fruit from the fridge. Combine the roasted red peppers, the remaining 450 g (2¼ cups) sugar, and the remaining 60 mL (¼ cup) rice wine vinegar in your preserving pan and bring to a simmer over medium-low heat until the sugar is dissolved and you have steamed off some of the liquid from the peppers, about 10 minutes. Add the apricot mixture and all the juices, and stir well to combine. Bring to a boil over high heat,

recipe continues

stirring constantly, until the juices run from the fruit and the sugar is dissolved. Once it boils, the mixture will begin to foam. Adjust the heat as needed to keep it as hot as possible without allowing the mixture to overflow or sputter. Continue to cook, stirring constantly and scraping the bottom of the pan to distribute the heat evenly and melt the foam back down into the mixture, about 5 minutes.

7. Once the foam subsides, boil over high heat (adjust the heat if the jam sputters) for another 20 to 25 minutes, stirring frequently. The apricots will begin to soften and break down, and the jam will appear homogeneous with no pockets of liquid between pieces of fruit. As the jam cooks, gradually reduce the heat to medium-low if needed to prevent scorching, and stir constantly until it becomes thicker and slightly syrupy and the bubbles are smaller and evenly distributed across the surface. Remove from the heat and skim any foam from the surface.

8. Gently stir to evenly distribute the fruit within the syrup, and then test for doneness. The jam should pass the wrinkle test or sheet test and reach at least 200°F (100°C) on a candy thermometer (see page 21).
If the jam still seems too loose, boil for another 3 to 5 minutes and check the set again. Once set, remove from the heat.

9. Pour the jam into the sterilized jars, leaving ¼ inch of headspace, and process by following the instructions on page 23. Arrange the hot jars about 1 inch apart in a cool place, and let sit undisturbed for at least 12 hours.

*You will need about 1.2 kg of whole apricots. See A NOTE ON MEASURING FRUIT (page 19).

NOTES

Date, Caramelized Onion, and Plum Jam

YIELD five 250 mL (8-ounce) jars

Richly flavoured and rustic, this onion preserve is bursting with savoury, umami flavours, making it the perfect accompaniment for egg scrambles, sandwiches, summertime barbecues, and burgers (veggie or meat). The addition of dates and a stout reduction adds an elegant and comforting profile of dried fruits and malt.

Many onion jams are not technically jams, but rather are relishes! Traditional jam is made with a fruit base, which brings the sugar and acidity needed for safe preservation. We have used a base of Empress plums, which are a delightful and plentiful plum with an earthy flavour and rich, meaty texture. Find them at the market at the end of the summer, in late August to early September. Their dense flesh makes for a full-bodied canvas for the onions to shine, while the skins add a delightful pop of acidity.

550 g Empress or Italian blue plums*
800 g (4 cups) granulated sugar
100 g (½ cup packed) brown sugar
90 mL (6 tablespoons) apple cider vinegar
90 mL (6 tablespoons) white balsamic vinegar
100 g (⅔ cup) pitted and diced dried Medjool dates*

250 mL (1 cup) stout
1 tablespoon olive oil
1.5 kg sweet onions, roughly chopped (12 cups)
250 g shallots, roughly chopped (2 cups)
½ teaspoon dried thyme

1. **Macerate the fruit:** Combine the plums, granulated sugar, brown sugar, apple cider vinegar, and white balsamic vinegar in a large non-reactive container, and toss gently to evenly coat. Cover with a lid and macerate in the fridge overnight for at least 12 hours but no more than 24.

2. At the same time, combine the dates and stout in a small bowl. Cover with a lid or plastic wrap and soak in the fridge overnight for at least 12 hours but no more than 24.

3. **The next day, prepare the onions:** Heat the olive oil in a large saucepan over medium-low heat. Add the onions and shallots and cook, stirring frequently, until the onions are well softened and golden brown, about

30 minutes. Add the thyme and cook for another 10 minutes, stirring constantly. If the onions start to stick to the bottom of the pan, reduce the heat to low.

4. **Make the jam:** Sterilize your jars and lids by following the instructions on page 23.

5. Remove the macerated fruit and soaked dates from the fridge. Using a fork, mash the dates until they are completely broken down.

6. Combine the plum and date mixture with the caramelized onions in your preserving pan. Bring to a boil over high heat, stirring constantly, until the juices run from the fruit and the sugar is dissolved. Once it boils, the mixture will begin to foam.

recipe continues

Adjust the heat as needed to keep it as hot as possible without allowing the mixture to overflow or sputter. Continue to cook, stirring constantly and scraping the bottom of the pan as needed to distribute the heat evenly and melt the foam back down into the mixture, about 5 minutes.

7. Once the foam subsides, boil over high heat (adjust the heat if the jam sputters) for another 15 to 20 minutes, stirring frequently. The plums will begin to soften and break down, and the jam will appear homogeneous with no pockets of liquid between pieces of fruit. As the jam cooks, gradually reduce the heat to medium-low if needed to prevent scorching, and stir constantly until it becomes thicker and slightly syrupy and the bubbles are smaller and evenly distributed across the surface. Remove from the heat and skim any foam from the surface.

8. Gently stir to evenly distribute the fruit within the syrup, and then test for doneness. The jam should pass the wrinkle test or sheet test and reach at least 200°F (100°C) on a candy thermometer (see page 21). If the jam still seems too loose, boil for another 3 to 5 minutes and check the set again. Once set, remove from the heat.

9. Pour the jam into the sterilized jars, leaving ¼ inch of headspace, and process by following the instructions on page 23. Arrange the hot jars about 1 inch apart in a cool place, and let sit undisturbed for at least 12 hours.

*You will need about 660 g of whole plums and 120 g of whole dried dates. See **A NOTE ON MEASURING FRUIT** (page 19).

PART TWO

Scones, Sweets, Savoury Delights, and Drinks

Scones and Traditional Spreads

Signature Buttermilk Scones

YIELD 16 scones

We started Kitten and the Bear committed to jam making and preserving, but when we opened our first shop, we needed the perfect canvas to showcase our spreads. Scones were a traditional choice, and over the years they have taken on a life of their own. Now, our scones are as much a part of the world of Kitten and the Bear as our jams. Multiple recipe tweaks, from ingredient proportions to methodology, have given our scones a unique character all their own—layered and flaky like a biscuit, yet fluffy and soft inside, with that beautiful creamy bite from cultured buttermilk and lots (and lots) of butter.

Scones

574 g (3¾ cups + 1 tablespoon) all-purpose flour

38 g (3 tablespoons) granulated sugar, plus more for garnish

4½ teaspoons baking powder

1½ teaspoons baking soda

½ teaspoon Diamond Crystal kosher salt

340 g (¾ pound) cold unsalted butter, cut into cubes

375 mL (1½ cups) buttermilk

Egg Wash

1 egg

1 tablespoon water

For serving

Clotted Cream (page 239)

Your favourite preserve

1. **Make the scones:** In a large bowl, whisk together the flour, sugar, baking powder, baking soda, and salt to combine. Drop in the butter and rub into the flour mixture by rolling each cube of butter between your thumb and index finger until mostly incorporated, about 7 minutes. It will have a fine, fluffy texture but should hold together when squeezed. (Alternatively, you can use a stand mixer fitted with the paddle attachment and mix on low speed for 5 to 10 minutes. Scrape the flour mixture into a large bowl.)

2. Create a well in the centre of the flour mixture. Pour the buttermilk into the well and stir quickly with a fork until a shaggy dough forms, 30 to 60 seconds. The buttermilk should be fully incorporated, and there may still be some dry, crumbly bits in the bottom of the bowl.

3. Dust a work surface generously with flour. Stack the shaggy dough, a handful at a time, onto the work surface to form a layered mound. On the final handful, press the dough into any dry mix in the bottom of the bowl to push as much as possible into

the dough. Press down on the dough with your hands to shape it into a rough 10-inch circle, about 1¼ inches thick. (The circle doesn't have to be perfect.) Cut the dough in half, and then place one half top side down on the other half. Press down on the dough again to form it into an 11 to 12-inch circle, about ¾ inches thick. (The stacking and cutting process will create layers within the scones.)

4. Use a 2½-inch round cookie cutter to punch out rounds, cutting them as close together as possible to maximize the yield. Gather the scraps and press them together (don't knead or reroll) and punch out more rounds. Transfer the scones to a container in a single layer and chill in the freezer for 4 hours. If you plan to bake the scones later, allow them to freeze, and store them in a resealable plastic bag or airtight container in the freezer for up to 1 month. Bake from frozen.

5. **Prepare the egg wash and bake the scones:** Preheat the oven to 325°F (160°C). Line a baking sheet with parchment paper.

6. Remove the scones from the freezer and arrange on the lined baking sheet 2 to 3 inches apart. In a small bowl, whisk together the egg and water. Using a pastry brush, brush the tops of the scones evenly with the egg wash. Sprinkle with sugar for a sweet, crunchy top. Bake for 35 minutes, or until golden brown, rotating the pan after 25 minutes. Remove from the oven and transfer the scones to a wire rack. Let cool until warm but not piping hot, 5 to 10 minutes.

7. Enjoy warm or at room temperature with clotted cream and your favourite preserve. Store the scones in a vented plastic container at room temperature for up to 2 days.

step-by-step photos continue

Raspberry and Rose Scones

YIELD 10 scones

Red berry scones are always a crowd pleaser, and our raspberry and rose variety are no exception. Fresh raspberries add a pop of bright fruit flavour, and a delicate dusting of pink icing sugar, made by blending dragon fruit powder and rose petals into icing sugar, gives an ethereal look to these pretty pastries. Don't forget an extra sprinkle of rose petals, which add a lovely contrast to the blush-pink palate. We love to make these rose-scented lovelies around Valentine's Day—a delicious substitute for a dozen roses!

Scones

574 g (3¾ cups + 1 tablespoon) all-purpose
    flour
38 g (3 tablespoons) granulated sugar
4½ teaspoons baking powder
1½ teaspoons baking soda
½ teaspoon Diamond Crystal kosher salt
340 g (¾ pound) cold unsalted butter,
    cut into cubes
125 g (1 cup) fresh raspberries
335 mL (1¼ cups + 2½ tablespoons) buttermilk
1½ tablespoons rose water

Rose Sugar

2 tablespoons granulated sugar
1 tablespoon dried rose petals, plus more
    for garnish
1 tablespoon icing sugar
½ teaspoon freeze-dried dragon fruit
    (pitaya) powder (optional, for a more
    vibrant colour)

1. **Make the scones:** In a large bowl, whisk together the flour, sugar, baking powder, baking soda, and salt to combine. Drop in the butter and rub into the flour mixture by rolling each cube of butter between your thumb and index finger until mostly incorporated, about 7 minutes. It will have a fine, fluffy texture but should hold together when squeezed. (Alternatively, you can use a stand mixer fitted with the paddle attachment and mix on low speed for 5 to 10 minutes. Scrape the flour mixture into a large bowl.)

2. Add the raspberries and toss gently to evenly distribute them throughout the flour mixture. In a measuring cup, stir together the buttermilk and rose water to combine. Create a well in the centre of the flour mixture. Pour the buttermilk mixture into the well and stir quickly with a fork until a shaggy dough forms, 30 to 60 seconds. The buttermilk should be fully incorporated, and there may still be some dry, crumbly bits in the bottom of the bowl.

3. Dust a work surface generously with flour. Stack the shaggy dough, a handful at a time, onto the work surface to form a layered mound. On the final handful, press the dough into any dry mix in the bottom of the bowl to push as much as possible into

recipe continues

the dough. Press down on the dough with your hands to shape it into a rough 10-inch circle, about 1¼ inches thick. (The circle doesn't have to be perfect.) Cut the dough in half, and then place one half top side down on the other half. Press down on the dough again to form it into another 10 to 11-inch circle, about 1 inch thick. (The stacking and cutting process will create layers within the scones.)

4. Use a 4-inch triangle cookie cutter to punch out the scones, cutting them as close together as possible to maximize the yield. Gather the scraps and press them together (don't knead or reroll) and punch out more triangles. Transfer the scones to a container in a single layer and chill in the freezer for 6 hours. If you plan to bake the scones later, allow them to freeze, and store them in a resealable plastic bag or airtight container in the freezer for up to 1 month. Bake from frozen.

5. **Bake the scones:** Preheat the oven to 325°F (160°C). Line a baking sheet with parchment paper.

6. Remove the scones from the freezer, and arrange on the lined baking sheet 2 to 3 inches apart. Bake for 40 minutes, or until golden brown, rotating the pan after 30 minutes. Remove from the oven and transfer the scones to a wire rack to cool completely.

7. **Meanwhile, prepare the rose sugar:** In a small blender, combine the dried rose petals and granulated sugar and blend until the rose petals are fully broken down into a fine powder. Then, sift the rose sugar through a fine-mesh sieve into a small bowl. Add the icing sugar and dragon fruit powder, if using. Stir well to combine.

8. **Finish the scones:** Using a fine-mesh sieve or sifter, dust the scones with the pink rose sugar and top with rose petals. Store the scones in a vented plastic container at room temperature for up to 2 days.

VARIATION: If you prefer a stronger rose flavour, feel free to add up to 2 tablespoons of rose water, and remove the corresponding amount of liquid by adding only 330 mL (1¼ cups + 2 tablespoons) buttermilk.

NOTES

_____

_____

_____

_____

_____

_____

_____

_____

Lemon and Lavender Scones

YIELD 10 scones

Ever-so-slightly floral with a hint of sunshine from the zest of a single lemon, these light and airy scones are a favourite in springtime when the crocus are just beginning to poke through the snow. Be sure to use dried culinary lavender buds that have no added fragrance to ensure the floral note is delicate and authentic. Use a mortar and pestle to grind the lavender into a fine powder to release all its fragrance and so the lavender evenly distributes throughout your dry ingredients and doesn't add any unwanted floral bits in your otherwise fluffy and pristine scone.

Scones

574 g (3¾ cups + 1 tablespoon) all-purpose flour

38 g (3 tablespoons) granulated sugar

4½ teaspoons baking powder

1½ teaspoons baking soda

½ teaspoon Diamond Crystal kosher salt

2 teaspoons dried culinary lavender blossoms, ground to a fine powder, plus more whole buds for garnish (see Tip)

Zest of 1 lemon

340 g (¾ pound) cold unsalted butter, cut into cubes

375 g (1½ cups) buttermilk

Egg Wash

1 egg

1 tablespoon water

Lemon Glaze

110 g (1 cup) icing sugar

1½ tablespoons whole milk, plus more if needed

1 teaspoon lemon juice

1. **Make the scones:** In a large bowl, whisk together the flour, sugar, baking powder, baking soda, salt, lavender powder, and lemon zest to combine. Drop in the butter and rub into the flour mixture by rolling each cube of butter between your thumb and index finger until mostly incorporated, about 7 minutes. It will have a fine, fluffy texture but should hold together when squeezed. (Alternatively, you can use a stand mixer fitted with the paddle attachment and mix on low speed for 5 to 10 minutes. Scrape the flour mixture into a large bowl.)

2. Create a well in the centre of the flour mixture. Pour the buttermilk into the well and stir quickly with a fork until a shaggy dough forms, 30 to 60 seconds.

The buttermilk should be fully incorporated, and there may still be some dry, crumbly bits in the bottom of the bowl.

3. Dust a work surface generously with flour. Stack the shaggy dough, a handful at a time, onto the work surface to form a layered mound. On the final handful, press the dough into any dry mix in the bottom of the bowl to push as much as possible into the dough. Press down on the dough with your hands to shape it into a rough 10-inch circle, about 1¼ inches thick. (The circle doesn't have to be perfect.) Cut the dough in half, and then place one half top side down on the other half.

recipe continues

Press down on the dough again to form it into another 10 to 11-inch circle, about 1 inch thick. (The stacking and cutting process will create layers within the scones.)

4. Use a 4-inch triangle cookie cutter to punch out the scones, cutting them as close together as possible to maximize the yield. Gather the scraps and press them together (don't knead or reroll) and punch out more triangles. Transfer the scones to a container in a single layer and chill in the freezer for 6 hours. If you plan to bake the scones later, allow them to freeze, and store them in a resealable plastic bag or airtight container in the freezer for up to 1 month. Bake from frozen.

5. **Prepare the egg wash and bake the scones:** Preheat the oven to 325°F (160°C). Line a baking sheet with parchment paper.

6. Remove the scones from the freezer and arrange on the lined baking sheet, 2 to 3 inches apart. In a small bowl, whisk together the egg and water. Using a pastry brush, brush the tops of the scones evenly with the egg wash. Bake for 40 minutes, or until golden brown, rotating the pan after 30 minutes. Remove from the oven and transfer the scones to a wire rack set over a baking sheet. Let cool until warm but not piping hot, 5 to 10 minutes.

7. **Meanwhile, prepare the lemon glaze:** Place the icing sugar in a small bowl. Mix in the milk and lemon juice and stir until no lumps remain. Add a touch more milk if needed for a smooth, liquidy texture.

8. **Finish the scones:** Spoon the glaze over the warm scones, spreading it out to completely cover the tops and allowing it to drip over the sides. (Glazing the scones warm allows for a light yet opaque coating that is not overly sweet.) While the glaze is still wet, sprinkle the scones with a few whole lavender buds for garnish. Let sit for 5 to 10 minutes for the glaze to set and harden. Store the scones in a vented plastic container at room temperature for up to 2 days.

TIP: Dried culinary lavender buds can vary greatly in potency depending on brand and age. You may adjust the amount of lavender to your liking without altering the rest of the recipe.

NOTES

Peaches and Cream Scones

YIELD 6 scones

Fresh diced peaches float in these creamy scones, made even richer with the inclusion of heavy cream and vanilla. Adding fruits that contain a lot of moisture, such as strawberries or peaches, can be a bit tricky, as the extra weight of the fruit plus additional humidity in the oven while baking can make your scones fall flat. To keep these scones light and airy, we used a drop scone technique—meaning that the batter is made quickly with heavy (35%) cream instead of butter, and then scooped and dropped onto your baking sheet. This means there is no rolling, layering, or cutting, which greatly reduces the amount of gluten worked from the flour, yielding a tender, fluffy cloud speckled with vanilla bean and chunks of juicy peach.

280 g (1¾ cups + 2 tablespoons) all-purpose flour
67 g (⅓ cup) granulated sugar
2 teaspoons baking powder
½ teaspoon Diamond Crystal kosher salt
150 g (1 cup) peeled, pitted, and diced frozen or underripe peaches*

325 mL (1⅓ cups) heavy (35%) cream
1 tablespoon pure vanilla extract
1 vanilla pod, split lengthwise and seeds scraped (optional)
Coarse sugar, for garnish

1. Preheat the oven to 350°F (180°C). Line a baking sheet with parchment paper.

2. In a large bowl, whisk together the flour, granulated sugar, baking powder, and salt to combine. Add the diced peaches and mix to combine and coat with the flour mixture. (If you are using frozen peaches, do not defrost; simply dice and add them to the mixture still frozen.)

3. In a large measuring cup, stir together the cream, vanilla extract, and vanilla bean seeds, if using.

4. Create a well in the centre of the flour mixture. Pour the cream mixture into the well and stir quickly with a fork until no dry patches remain, being careful not to overmix. The dough will be thick, moist, and sticky.

5. Using 2 spoons, the first to scoop, the second to release the dough, drop 6 equal portions of dough onto the lined baking sheet, evenly spaced. Sprinkle the tops generously with coarse sugar. Bake for 20 to 30 minutes or until golden brown, rotating the pan halfway through. Remove from the oven and transfer the scones to a wire rack until cool enough to handle. Store the scones in a vented plastic container at room temperature for up to 2 days.

NOTE: You can freeze the batter and bake the scones later. Freeze the formed dough on the baking sheet for 6 hours. Once frozen, store them in a resealable plastic bag or airtight container in the freezer for up to 1 month. Bake from frozen in a 350°F (180°C) oven for 30 to 40 minutes.

*You will need about 225 g of whole peaches. See A NOTE ON MEASURING FRUIT (page 19).

Pear, Oat, and Honey Scones

YIELD 6 scones

This delightful scone is inspired by traditional Scottish oat scones, enriched with rolled oats and honey for an oatmeal-cookie-like warmth. Oats have been an important staple in the Scottish diet for their belly-filling ability and as a hearty source of nutrition. In our cream drop version, we substitute a portion of the cream for wildflower honey, which lends a sweet, cozy flavour. Use nice, firm pears so the fruit remains intact with some bite after baking, giving the scone a fruit-filled texture.

225 g (1½ cups) all-purpose flour
135 g (1½ cups) rolled oats
67 g (⅓ cup) granulated sugar
2 teaspoons baking powder
½ teaspoon Diamond Crystal kosher salt

175 g (1 cup) peeled, cored, and diced underripe pears*
250 mL (1 cup) heavy (35%) cream
75 mL (⅓ cup) liquid honey
1 teaspoon pure vanilla extract
Coarse sugar, for garnish

1. Preheat the oven to 375°F (190°C). Line a baking sheet with parchment paper.

2. In a large bowl, whisk together the flour, rolled oats, granulated sugar, baking powder, and salt to combine. Add the diced pears and mix to evenly coat.

3. In a large measuring cup, combine the cream, honey, and vanilla and stir well to dissolve the honey into the mixture.

4. Create a well in the centre of the flour mixture. Pour the cream mixture into the well and stir quickly with a fork until no dry patches remain, being careful not to overmix. The dough will be thick, moist, and sticky.

5. Using 2 spoons, the first to scoop, the second to release the dough, drop 6 equal portions of dough onto the lined baking sheet, evenly spaced. Sprinkle the tops generously with coarse sugar. Bake for 18 to 20 minutes or until golden brown, rotating the pan halfway through. Remove from the oven and transfer the scones to a wire rack to cool completely. Store the scones in a vented plastic container at room temperature for up to 2 days.

NOTE: You can freeze the batter and bake the scones later. Freeze the formed dough on the baking sheet for 6 hours. Once frozen, store them in a resealable plastic bag or airtight container in the freezer for up to 1 month. Bake from frozen in a 350°F (180°C) oven for 30 to 40 minutes.

*You will need about 245 g of whole pears. See A NOTE ON MEASURING FRUIT (page 19).

Blueberry Crumble Scones

YIELD 9 scones

With sweet, ooey-gooey pockets of fruity goodness studded throughout, blueberry scones are forever a classic. Use ripe, juicy blueberries, as their warm, purple juice saturating the dough is an integral part of the blueberry scone experience. We love pairing blueberries with warm and comforting flavours, and you can't get more comforting than streusel crumb topping. A spoonful of sour cream mixed into the buttermilk ensures a dense, cake-like crumb, and the tiniest pinch of cinnamon adds a certain magic, making these fruity scones a year-round favourite.

Cinnamon Streusel

150 g (1 cup) all-purpose flour

75 g (⅓ cup + 1 teaspoon) granulated sugar

½ teaspoon ground cinnamon

118 g (½ cup) cold unsalted butter, cut into cubes

Scones

574 g (3¾ cups + 1 tablespoon) all-purpose flour

38 g (3 tablespoons) granulated sugar

4½ teaspoons baking powder

1½ teaspoons baking soda

½ teaspoon salt

340 g (¾ pound) cold unsalted butter, cut into cubes

250 mL (1 cup) buttermilk

125 mL (½ cup) sour cream

150 g (1 cup) blueberries

Icing sugar, for garnish

1. **Make the cinnamon streusel:** In the bowl of a stand mixer fitted with the paddle attachment (or in a medium bowl if mixing by hand) combine the flour, sugar, and cinnamon, and gently mix on low speed until the ingredients are evenly distributed. (If mixing by hand, use a fork.)

2. With the mixer running on low speed, gradually drop in the cold butter, one cube at a time. Once all the butter is incorporated, increase the speed to medium-low. The mixture will look dry and sandy. After 11 or 12 minutes, you will see the crumbs coming together. Stop the mixer and scrape down the sides of the bowl. Increase the speed to medium-high and mix for another 4 to 6 minutes until marble-size pieces begin to form. Be sure not to overmix; you do not want to form a dough. (If you are mixing by hand, rub the butter into the flour mixture until the desired texture is achieved, similar to making scones or pastry.) Cover with a lid or plastic wrap and set aside in the fridge.

3. **Make the scones:** In a large bowl, whisk together the flour, sugar, baking powder, baking soda, and salt to combine. Drop in the butter and rub into the flour mixture by rolling each cube of butter between your thumb and index finger until mostly incorporated, about 7 minutes. It will have a fine, fluffy texture but should hold together when squeezed. (Alternatively, you can use a stand mixer fitted with the paddle attachment and mix on low speed

recipe continues

for 5 to 10 minutes. Scrape the flour mixture into a large bowl.)

4. In a large measuring cup, combine the buttermilk and sour cream. Stir well with a fork to fully dissolve the sour cream until no lumps remain. Create a well in the centre of the flour mixture. Pour the buttermilk mixture into the well and stir quickly with a fork until a shaggy dough forms, 30 to 60 seconds. The buttermilk mixture should be fully incorporated, and there may still be some dry, crumbly bits in the bottom of the bowl.

5. Dust a work surface generously with flour. Stack the shaggy dough, a handful at a time, onto the work surface to form a layered mound. After each handful, scatter a portion of the blueberries on top of the dough and press them into the dough before adding the next handful of dough on top. On the final handful, press the dough into any dry mix in the bottom of the bowl to push as much as possible into the dough. Press down on the dough with your hands to shape it into a rough 10-inch circle, about 1¼ inches thick. (The circle doesn't have to be perfect.) Cut the dough in half, and then place one half top side down on the other half. Press down on the dough again and form it into a 9-inch square, about 1 inch thick. (The stacking and cutting process will create layers within the scones.)

6. Cut the square of dough with a kitchen knife twice in each direction to make a 3 by 3 grid. Transfer the scones to a container in a single layer and chill in the freezer for 6 hours. If you plan to bake the scones later, allow them to freeze, and store them in a resealable plastic bag or airtight container in the freezer for up to 1 month. Bake from frozen.

7. **Bake the scones:** Preheat the oven to 325°F (160°C). Line a baking sheet with parchment paper. Remove the cinnamon streusel from the fridge.

8. Remove the scones from the freezer and arrange on the lined baking sheet 2 to 3 inches apart. Use cupped hands to pack as much streusel as possible on top of each scone, pressing it together so it stays in place. Bake for 45 minutes, or until golden brown, rotating the pan after 35 minutes. Remove from the oven and transfer the scones to a wire rack to cool completely.

9. Using a fine-mesh sieve or sifter, dust the scones with the icing sugar. Store the scones in a vented plastic container at room temperature for up to 2 days.

Birthday Cake Scones

YIELD 8 scones

Perhaps our most fun and whimsical pastry, these birthday cake scones call for celebration! Easy to whip together and perfect for a birthday tea party, these adorable pie-cut scones are sure to delight your inner (or actual!) child. To make these taste exactly like birthday cake, we substitute a portion of the flour with store-bought vanilla cake mix—there is some sort of magic about the nostalgic flavour of cake mix that just can't be replicated.

Originally made for our daughter who is allergic to eggs, we have paired them with a classic American-style buttercream, which is a sweet and festive topping for these celebratory pastries.

Scones

450 g (3 cups) all-purpose flour

144 g (1 cup) vanilla cake mix

2 tablespoons granulated sugar

4 teaspoons baking powder

1½ teaspoons baking soda

½ teaspoon Diamond Crystal kosher salt

340 g (¾ pound) cold unsalted butter, cut into cubes

75 g (½ cup) small round rainbow sprinkles, plus more for garnish

375 mL (1½ cups) buttermilk, plus more for brushing

Buttercream

113 g (¼ pound) unsalted butter, room temperature

220 g (2 cups) icing sugar, plus more for garnish

1½ tablespoons whole milk, room temperature

½ teaspoon pure vanilla extract

Pinch of Diamond Crystal kosher salt

1. **Make the scones:** In a large bowl, whisk together the flour, cake mix, sugar, baking powder, baking soda, and salt to combine. Drop in the butter and rub into the flour mixture by rolling each cube of butter between your thumb and index finger until mostly incorporated, about 7 minutes. It will have a fine, fluffy texture but should hold together when squeezed. (Alternatively, you can use a stand mixer fitted with the paddle attachment and mix on low speed for 5 to 10 minutes. Scrape the flour mixture into a large bowl.)

2. Add the rainbow sprinkles and toss gently within the flour mixture to evenly distribute them throughout.

3. Create a well in the centre of the flour mixture. Pour the buttermilk into the well and stir quickly with a fork until a shaggy dough forms, 30 to 60 seconds. The buttermilk should be fully incorporated, and there may still be some dry, crumbly bits in the bottom of the bowl.

recipe continues

4. Dust a work surface generously with flour. Stack the shaggy dough, a handful at a time, onto the work surface to form a layered mound. On the final handful, press the dough into any dry mix in the bottom of the bowl to push as much as possible into the dough. Press down on the dough with your hands to shape it into a rough 10-inch circle, about 1¼ inches thick. (The circle doesn't have to be perfect.) Cut the dough in half, and then place one half top side down on the other half. Press down on the dough again to form it into a 9-inch circle, about 1¼ inches thick. (The stacking and cutting process will create layers within the scones.)

5. Cut the round of dough into 8 equal pie wedges. Transfer the scones to a container in a single layer and chill in the freezer for 6 hours. If you plan to bake the scones later, allow them to freeze, and store them in a resealable plastic bag or airtight container in the freezer for up to 1 month. Bake from frozen.

6. Bake the scones: Preheat the oven to 325°F (160°C). Line a baking sheet with parchment paper.

7. Remove the scones from the freezer and arrange on the lined baking sheet 2 to 3 inches apart. Using a pastry brush, brush the tops of the scones with a small amount of buttermilk for sheen once baked. Bake for 45 minutes, or until golden brown, rotating the pan after 35 minutes. Remove from the oven and transfer the scones to a wire rack to cool completely.

8. Meanwhile, prepare the buttercream: In a stand mixer fitted with the whisk attachment, combine the butter, icing sugar, milk, vanilla, and salt and beat, starting on low and increasing the speed to high as the buttercream comes together, until fluffy, light in colour, and smooth when rubbed between your fingers. Add a splash of additional milk if needed to achieve a silky, smooth texture. Set aside at room temperature.

9. Finish the scones: For a fun birthday cake aesthetic, fill a piping bag or resealable food storage bag with the tip cut off, fitted with a large star tip. Pipe large rosettes of icing on the outer edge of the scones, and sprinkle with rainbow sprinkles. Alternatively, for a more rustic look, simply slather the tops of the scones with frosting and sprinkle with rainbow sprinkles. Using a fine-mesh sieve or sifter, dust the scones with icing sugar. Serve with any extra frosting on the side. Store the scones in a vented plastic container at room temperature for up to 2 days.

Morning Glory Scones

YIELD 11 scones

Inspired by the infamous Morning Glory muffin, created by Chef Pamela McKinstry for her eponymous Nantucket café in the late 1970s, these hearty scones bring all the magic of the original recipe in scone form. Whole wheat flour, grated carrots, pineapple, coconut, cinnamon, and brown sugar come together for an iconic and wholesome blend that has become a modern American classic.

The perfect breakfast scone, the healthful and energizing ingredients in these flavourful biscuits will fill you up and keep you going all day long. We like to keep them frozen and bake one or two in the morning to enjoy fresh and warm slathered in cultured butter.

Scones

300 g (2 cups) all-purpose flour

240 g (2 cups) whole wheat flour

38 g (3 tablespoons) granulated sugar

25 g (3 tablespoons) brown sugar

4½ teaspoons baking powder

1½ teaspoons baking soda

1½ teaspoons ground cinnamon

½ teaspoon ground ginger

½ teaspoon Diamond Crystal kosher salt

340 g (¾ pound) cold unsalted butter, cut into cubes

112 g (⅔ cup) dried black currants

30 g (3 tablespoons) sunflower seeds

30 g (¼ cup) pumpkin seeds

30 g (⅓ cup) sweetened shredded coconut

50 g (¼ cup) diced candied pineapple

140 g (1½ cups) peeled, grated, and loosely packed carrots

425 mL (1¾ cups) buttermilk

Egg Wash

1 egg

1 tablespoon water

Coarse sugar, for garnish

1. **Make the scones:** In a large bowl, whisk together the all-purpose flour, whole wheat flour, granulated sugar, brown sugar, baking powder, baking soda, cinnamon, ginger, and salt to combine. Drop in the butter and rub into the flour mixture by rolling each cube of butter between your thumb and index finger until mostly incorporated, about 7 minutes. It will have a fine, fluffy texture but should hold together when squeezed. (Alternatively, you can use a stand mixer fitted with the paddle attachment and mix on low speed for 5 to 10 minutes. Scrape the flour mixture into a large bowl.)

2. Add the currants, sunflower seeds, pumpkin seeds, coconut, candied pineapple, and carrots and toss gently to evenly distribute them throughout the flour mixture.

3. Create a well in the centre of the flour mixture. Pour the buttermilk into the well and stir quickly with a fork until a shaggy dough forms, 30 to 60 seconds. The buttermilk should be fully incorporated, and

recipe continues

there may still be some dry, crumbly bits in the bottom of the bowl.

4. Dust a work surface generously with flour. Stack the shaggy dough, a handful at a time, onto the work surface to form a layered mound. On the final handful, press the dough into any dry mix in the bottom of the bowl to push as much as possible into the dough. Press down on the dough with your hands to shape it into a rough 10-inch circle, about 1¼ inches thick. (The circle doesn't have to be perfect.) Cut the dough in half, and then place one half top side down on the other half. Press down on the dough again to form into another 10 to 11-inch circle, about 1 inch thick. (The stacking and cutting process will create layers within the scones.)

5. Use a 4-inch triangle cookie cutter to punch out the scones, cutting them as close together as possible to maximize the yield. Gather the scraps and press them together (don't knead or reroll) and punch out more triangles. Transfer the scones to a container in a single layer and chill in the freezer for 6 hours. If you plan to bake the scones later, allow them to freeze, and store them in a resealable plastic bag or airtight container in the freezer for up to 1 month. Bake from frozen.

6. **Prepare the egg wash and bake the scones:** Preheat the oven to 325°F (160°C). Line a baking sheet with parchment paper.

7. Remove the scones from the freezer and arrange on the lined baking sheet 2 to 3 inches apart. In a small bowl, whisk together the egg and water. Using a pastry brush, brush the tops of the scones evenly with the egg wash. Sprinkle with coarse sugar for a sweet, crunchy top. Bake for 40 minutes, or until golden brown, rotating the pan after 30 minutes. Remove from the oven and transfer the scones to a wire rack and let sit until cool enough to handle. Store the scones in a vented plastic container at room temperature for up to 2 days.

NOTES

_____

_____

_____

_____

_____

_____

_____

_____

Goat Cheese and Onion Blossom Scones

YIELD 9 scones

As cheese scones go, goat cheese is always a favourite, as it pairs well with a vast array of herbs—think lemon thyme, rosemary, or herbs de Provence. However, we absolutely adore them with fresh onion or chive flowers, which adds a bit of whimsy to an otherwise traditional scone. Green onion is such a delightful herb, adding a fresh and dainty onion flavour without being overly savoury. Be sure to save a few flowers to decorate the tops for an adorable pressed-flower look.

Use cold, soft unripened goat cheese for this recipe and add to your mixture in teaspoon-size chunks after the butter is incorporated. This will ensure the goat cheese stays intact after baking, leaving pockets of cheesy goodness, instead of melting into the surrounding dough.

Scones

574 g (3¾ cups + 1 tablespoon)
    all-purpose flour
38 g (3 tablespoons) granulated sugar
4½ teaspoons baking powder
1½ teaspoons baking soda
1 teaspoon garlic powder
1 teaspoon onion powder
½ teaspoon Diamond Crystal kosher salt
340 g (¾ pound) cold unsalted butter,
    cut into cubes

35 g (½ cup) fresh onion or chive blossoms,
    or to taste, plus more for garnish
115 g (1 cup) 1-inch pieces cold unripened
    goat cheese (store in the fridge until
    ready to use)
375 g (1½ cups) buttermilk

Egg Wash

1 egg
1 tablespoon water

Pretzel or flaky sea salt, for garnish

1. **Make the scones:** In a large bowl, whisk together the flour, sugar, baking powder, baking soda, garlic powder, onion powder, and salt to combine. Drop in the butter and rub into the flour mixture by rolling each cube of butter between your thumb and index finger until mostly incorporated, about 7 minutes. It will have a fine, fluffy texture but should hold together when squeezed. (Alternatively, you can use a stand mixer fitted with the paddle attachment and mix on low speed for 5 to 10 minutes. Scrape the flour mixture into a large bowl.)

2. Add the fresh onion or chive blossoms to the flour mixture, and toss gently to evenly distribute them throughout. Remove the goat cheese from the fridge and toss the pieces of cheese throughout the mixture.

3. Create a well in the centre of the flour mixture. Pour the buttermilk into the well and stir quickly with a fork until a shaggy dough forms, 30 to 60 seconds. The buttermilk should be fully incorporated, and there may still be some dry, crumbly bits in the bottom of the bowl.

4. Dust a work surface generously with flour. Stack the shaggy dough, a handful at a time, onto the work surface to form

recipe continues

a layered mound. On the final handful, press the dough into any dry mix in the bottom of the bowl to push as much as possible into the dough. Press down on the dough with your hands to shape it into a rough 10-inch circle, about 1¼ inches thick. (The circle doesn't have to be perfect.) Cut the dough in half, and then place one half top side down on the other half. Press down on the dough again and form it into a 9-inch square, about 1 inch thick. (The stacking and cutting process will create layers within the scones.)

5. Cut the square of dough with a kitchen knife twice in each direction to make a 3 by 3 grid. Press one onion or chive blossom flat onto the centre of each scone for garnish. Transfer the scones to a container in a single layer and chill in the freezer for 6 hours. If you plan to bake the scones later, allow them to freeze, and store them in a resealable plastic bag or airtight container in the freezer for up to 1 month. Bake from frozen.

6. **Prepare the egg wash and bake the scones:** Preheat the oven to 325°F (160°C). Line a baking sheet with parchment paper.

7. Remove the scones from the freezer and arrange on the lined baking sheet, 2 to 3 inches apart. In a small bowl, whisk together the egg and water. Using a pastry brush, brush the tops of the scones evenly with the egg wash. Sprinkle the tops with pretzel or flaky sea salt. Bake for 45 minutes, or until golden brown, rotating the pan after 35 minutes. Remove from the oven and transfer the scones to a wire rack until cool enough to handle.

8. Enjoy warm or at room temperature with your favourite savoury preserve. Store the scones in a vented plastic container at room temperature for up to 2 days.

VARIATIONS: If you can't find fresh onion or chive blossoms, feel free to substitute for 60 mL (¼ cup) finely chopped chives.

If you prefer cheddar scones, you can substitute the goat cheese for an equal weight of aged cheddar cheese. Grate the cheddar on the large holes of a box grater and add to the flour mixture just before the buttermilk.

NOTES

Apple Fritter Scones

YIELD 9 scones

Inspired by an apple fritter doughnut, this nostalgic scone is a ode to its dessert-y counterpart. Give this traditional apple scone a fritter makeover by scoring the top of the raw dough in a crosshatch pattern, which puffs apart during baking, and adding an all-over poured maple glaze to get into all of those nooks and crannies.

Scones

574 g (3¾ cups + 1 tablespoon) all-purpose flour

38 g (3 tablespoons) granulated sugar

30 g (3½ tablespoons) brown sugar

4½ teaspoons baking powder

1½ teaspoons baking soda

1½ teaspoons ground cinnamon

1 teaspoon ground cardamom

½ teaspoon ground nutmeg

½ teaspoon Diamond Crystal kosher salt

340 g (¾ pound) cold unsalted butter, cut into cubes

150 g (1¼ cups) cored and diced red apples* (Fuji, Gala, or Honeycrisp)

250 mL (1 cup) buttermilk

125 mL (½ cup) unsweetened applesauce

Egg Wash

1 egg

1 tablespoon water

Maple Glaze

110 g (1 cup) icing sugar

75 mL (⅓ cup) pure maple syrup, plus more as needed

1. **Make the scones:** In a large bowl, whisk together the flour, granulated sugar, brown sugar, baking powder, baking soda, cinnamon, cardamom, nutmeg, and salt to combine. Drop in the butter and rub into the flour mixture by rolling each cube of butter between your thumb and index finger until mostly incorporated, about 7 minutes. It will have a fine, fluffy texture but should hold together when squeezed. (Alternatively, you can use a stand mixer fitted with the paddle attachment and mix on low speed for 5 to 10 minutes. Scrape the flour mixture into a large bowl.)

2. Add the diced apples and toss gently to evenly distribute them throughout the flour mixture. In a large measuring cup, stir together the buttermilk and applesauce to combine. Create a well in the centre of the flour mixture. Pour the buttermilk mixture into the well and stir quickly with a fork until a shaggy dough forms, 30 to 60 seconds. The buttermilk mixture should be fully incorporated, and there may still be some dry, crumbly bits in the bottom of the bowl.

3. Dust a work surface generously with flour. Stack the shaggy dough, a handful at a time, onto the work surface to form a layered mound. On the final handful, press the dough into any dry mix in the bottom

recipe continues

of the bowl to push as much as possible into the dough. Press down on the dough with your hands to shape it into a rough 10-inch circle, about 1¼ inches thick. (The circle doesn't have to be perfect.) Cut the dough in half, and then place one half top side down on the other half. Press down on the dough again and form it into a 9-inch square, about 1 inch thick. (The stacking and cutting process will create layers within the scones.)

4. Cut the square of dough with a kitchen knife twice in each direction to make a 3 by 3 grid. Then, using a sharp kitchen knife, score a crosshatch pattern into the top of each scone, cutting 2 diagonal cuts across in each direction (like tic-tac-toe), about ¼ inch deep. This pattern will puff during baking, creating an apple fritter–like shape. Transfer the scones to a container in a single layer and chill in the freezer for 6 hours. If you plan to bake the scones later, allow them to freeze, and store them in a resealable plastic bag or airtight container in the freezer for up to 1 month. Bake from frozen.

5. **Prepare the egg wash and bake the scones:** Preheat the oven to 325°F (160°C). Line a baking sheet with parchment paper.

6. Remove the scones from the freezer and arrange on the lined baking sheet 2 to 3 inches apart. In a small bowl, whisk together the egg and water. Using a pastry brush, brush the tops of the scones evenly with the egg wash. Bake for 45 minutes, or until golden brown, rotating the pan after 35 minutes. Remove from the oven and transfer the scones to a wire rack set over a baking sheet. Let cool until warm but not piping hot, 5 to 10 minutes.

7. **Meanwhile, prepare the maple glaze:** Place the icing sugar in a small bowl. Mix in the maple syrup and stir until no lumps remain. Add a touch more maple syrup if needed for a smooth, liquidy texture.

8. **Finish the scones:** Spoon the glaze over the warm scones, spreading it out to completely cover the top and allowing it to drip over the sides. Glazing the scones warm allows for a light yet opaque coating that is not overly sweet. Let sit for 5 to 10 minutes for the glaze to set and harden. Store the scones in a vented plastic container at room temperature for up to 2 days.

*You will need about 225 g of whole apples. See **A NOTE ON MEASURING FRUIT** (page 19).

NOTES

Pumpkin Spice Scones

YIELD 10 scones

Practically a season unto itself, pumpkin spice is a fun and fitting start to autumn. Perfectly paired with your coziest sweater and a good book, the trick to these seasonal scones is using sweetened pumpkin pie filling, which lends an authentic flavour and less fibrous texture than simply pumpkin purée. It's paired with a splash of fancy molasses and a heavy-handed scoop of our house-made pumpkin spice blend, and topped with candied pecans. A new Thanksgiving morning tradition unlocked!

Candied Pecans

25 g (3 tablespoons) brown sugar

½ teaspoon ground cinnamon

1 tablespoon water

¼ teaspoon Diamond Crystal kosher salt

120 g (1 cup) pecan halves

Scones

574 g (3¾ cups + 1 tablespoon) all-purpose flour

38 g (3 tablespoons) granulated sugar

4½ teaspoons baking powder

1½ teaspoons baking soda

1 teaspoon ground cinnamon

½ teaspoon ground cardamom

½ teaspoon ground nutmeg

¼ teaspoon ground allspice

¼ teaspoon ground cloves

¼ teaspoon ground ginger

½ teaspoon Diamond Crystal kosher salt

340 g (¾ pound) cold unsalted butter, cut into cubes

210 mL (¾ cup + 2 tablespoons) buttermilk

125 mL (½ cup) pumpkin pie filling

45 mL (3 tablespoons) fancy molasses

1 teaspoon pure vanilla extract

Egg Wash

1 egg

1 tablespoon water

Milk Glaze

110 g (1 cup) icing sugar

1½ tablespoons whole milk, plus more if needed

1 teaspoon pure vanilla extract

1. **Make the candied pecans:** Line a baking sheet with parchment paper and set aside. In a small skillet, combine the brown sugar, cinnamon, water, and salt over medium heat. Cook, stirring constantly, for about 1 minute or until the sugar is melted into a bubbling sauce. Add the pecans and toss to completely coat with the syrup. Continue to cook for another 2 to 3 minutes or until the pecans are shiny and aromatic.

2. Scrape the candied pecans onto the lined baking sheet and spread in a single layer and let cool and harden at room temperature, about 30 minutes. Once cooled, using your hands, break up the nuts. The candied pecans can be stored in an airtight container at room temperature for up to 3 weeks.

recipe continues

3. **Make the scones:** In a large bowl, whisk together the flour, sugar, baking powder, baking soda, cinnamon, cardamom, nutmeg, allspice, cloves, ginger, and salt to combine. Drop in the butter and rub into the flour mixture by rolling each cube of butter between your thumb and index finger until mostly incorporated, about 7 minutes. It will have a fine, fluffy texture but should hold together when squeezed. (Alternatively, you can use a stand mixer fitted with the paddle attachment and mix on low speed for 5 to 10 minutes. Scrape the flour mixture into a large bowl.)

4. In a large measuring cup, combine the buttermilk, pumpkin pie filling, molasses, and vanilla. Stir well with a fork to fully dissolve and break down the pumpkin pie filling so no lumps remain. Create a well in the centre of the flour mixture. Pour the buttermilk mixture into the well and stir quickly with a fork until a shaggy dough forms, 30 to 60 seconds. The buttermilk mixture should be fully incorporated, and there may still be some dry, crumbly bits in the bottom of the bowl.

5. Dust a work surface generously with flour. Stack the shaggy dough, a handful at a time, onto the work surface to form a layered mound. On the final handful, press the dough into any dry mix in the bottom of the bowl to push as much as possible into the dough. Press down on the dough with your hands to shape it into a rough 10-inch circle, about 1¼ inches thick. (The circle doesn't have to be perfect.) Cut the dough in half, and then place one half top side down on the other half. Press down on the dough again to form it into another 10 to 11-inch circle, about 1 inch thick.

(The stacking and cutting process will create layers within the scones.)

6. Use a 4-inch triangle cookie cutter to punch out the scones, cutting them as close together as possible to maximize the yield. Gather the scraps and press them together (don't knead or reroll) and punch out more triangles. Transfer the scones to a container in a single layer and chill in the freezer for 6 hours. If you plan to bake the scones later, allow them to freeze, and store them in a resealable plastic bag or airtight container in the freezer for up to 1 month. Bake from frozen.

7. **Prepare the egg wash and bake the scones:** Preheat the oven to 325°F (160°C). Line a baking sheet with parchment paper.

8. Remove the scones from the freezer and arrange on the lined baking sheet 2 to 3 inches apart. In a small bowl, whisk together the egg and water. Using a pastry brush, brush the tops of the scones evenly with the egg wash. Bake for 40 minutes, or until golden brown, rotating the pan after 30 minutes. Remove from the oven and transfer the scones to a wire rack to cool completely.

9. **Meanwhile, prepare the milk glaze:** Place the icing sugar in a small mixing bowl. Mix in the milk and vanilla, stirring until no lumps remain. Set aside.

10. **Finish the scones:** Place the candied pecans on a cutting board. Using a sharp knife, chop the pecans until they are pea size.

11. Using a spoon, generously drizzle the milk glaze on top of the scones. Sprinkle with candied pecans while the glaze is wet. Let sit to harden for 5 to 10 minutes. Store the scones in a vented plastic container at room temperature for up to 2 days.

Brie and Black Currant Scones

YIELD 8 scones

Inspired by sweet and savoury baked brie, this fancy take on a traditional cheese scone is studded with gobs of melty, aromatic triple crème brie, which melts right into the surrounding dough. A sprinkling of dried black currants is a natural choice—currant scones are perhaps the most traditional variety and currants add delicate texture and a hint of dried fruit sweetness.

Scones

574 g (3¾ cups + 1 tablespoon) all-purpose flour

38 g (3 tablespoons) granulated sugar

4½ teaspoons baking powder

1½ teaspoons baking soda

1 teaspoon garlic powder

1 teaspoon onion powder

½ teaspoon Diamond Crystal kosher salt

340 g (¾ pound) cold unsalted butter, cut into cubes

75 g (1 cup) 1-inch chunks cold brie (store in the fridge until ready to use)

75 g (½ cup) dried black currants

375 mL (1½ cups) buttermilk

Egg Wash

1 egg

1 tablespoon water

Coarse sugar, for garnish

1. **Make the scones:** In a large bowl, whisk together the flour, sugar, baking powder, baking soda, garlic powder, onion powder, and salt to combine. Drop in the butter and rub into the flour mixture by rolling each cube of butter between your thumb and index finger until mostly incorporated, about 7 minutes. It will have a fine, fluffy texture but should hold together when squeezed. (Alternatively, you can use a stand mixer fitted with the paddle attachment and mix on low speed for 5 to 10 minutes. Scrape the flour mixture into a large bowl.)

2. Remove the brie from the fridge. Add the brie and black currants and toss gently to evenly distribute them throughout the flour mixture. Create a well in the centre of the flour mixture. Pour the buttermilk into the well and stir quickly with a fork until a shaggy dough forms, 30 to 60 seconds. The buttermilk should be fully incorporated, and there may still be some dry, crumbly bits in the bottom of the bowl.

3. Dust a work surface generously with flour. Stack the shaggy dough, a handful at a time, onto the work surface to form a layered mound. On the final handful, press the dough into any dry mix in the bottom of the bowl to push as much as possible into the dough. Press down on the dough with your hands to shape it into a rough 10-inch circle, about 1¼ inches thick. (The circle doesn't have to be perfect.) Cut the dough in half, and then place one half top side down on the other half. Press down on the

recipe continues

dough again to form it into another 9-inch circle, about 1¼ inches thick. (The stacking and cutting process will create layers within the scones.)

4. Cut the round of dough into 8 equal pie wedges. Transfer the scones to a container in a single layer and chill in the freezer for 6 hours. If you plan to bake the scones later, allow them to freeze, and store them in a resealable plastic bag or airtight container in the freezer for up to 1 month. Bake from frozen.

5. **Prepare the egg wash and bake the scones:** Preheat the oven to 325°F (160°C). Line a baking sheet with parchment paper.

6. Remove the scones from the freezer and arrange on the lined baking sheet 2 to 3 inches apart. In a small bowl, whisk together the egg and water. Using a pastry brush, brush the tops of the scones evenly with the egg wash. Sprinkle with the coarse sugar for a sweet, crunchy top. Bake for 45 minutes, or until golden brown, rotating the pan after 35 minutes. Remove from the oven and transfer the scones to a wire rack until cool enough to handle. Enjoy warm or at room temperature. Store the scones in a vented plastic container at room temperature for up to 2 days.

Triple Chocolate Scones

YIELD 16 scones

Somewhere between a scone and chocolate cake, chocolate scones are pure decadence—dark and rich, barely sweet with a delicate and fudgy crumb, studded with semisweet chocolate chips and a drizzle of chocolate icing for good measure. These untraditional scones have a reputation of converting even scone purists.

Scones

574 g (3¾ cups + 1 tablespoon)
   all-purpose flour

50 g (½ cup) Dutch-processed cocoa powder

38 g (3 tablespoons) granulated sugar

4½ teaspoons baking powder

1½ teaspoons baking soda

½ teaspoon Diamond Crystal kosher salt

340 g (¾ pound) cold unsalted butter,
   cut into cubes

60 to 90 g (½ to ¾ cup) semisweet
   chocolate chips

375 mL (1½ cups) buttermilk

Egg Wash

1 egg

1 tablespoon water

Chocolate Drizzle

60 g (½ cup) semisweet or dark
   chocolate chips

2 tablespoons unsalted butter

1. **Make the scones:** In a large bowl, whisk together the flour, cocoa powder, sugar, baking powder, baking soda, and salt to combine. Drop in the butter and rub into the flour mixture by rolling each cube of butter between your thumb and index finger until mostly incorporated, about 7 minutes. It will have a fine, fluffy texture but should hold together when squeezed. (Alternatively, you can use a stand mixer fitted with the paddle attachment and mix on low speed for 5 to 10 minutes. Scrape the flour mixture into a large bowl.) Add the chocolate chips and toss to distribute evenly.

2. Create a well in the centre of the flour mixture. Pour the buttermilk into the well and stir quickly with a fork until a shaggy dough forms, 30 to 60 seconds. The buttermilk should be fully incorporated, and there may still be some dry, crumbly bits in the bottom of the bowl.

3. Dust a work surface generously with flour. Stack the shaggy dough, a handful at a time, onto the work surface to form a layered mound. On the final handful, press the dough into any dry mix in the bottom of the bowl to push as much as possible into the dough. Press down on the dough with your hands to shape it into a rough 10-inch circle, about 1¼ inches thick. (The circle doesn't have to be perfect.) Cut the dough in half, and then place one half top side down on the other half. Press down on the dough again to form it into an 11 to 12-inch circle, about ¾ inch thick. (The stacking and cutting process will create layers within the scones.)

recipe continues

4. Use a 2½-inch round cookie cutter to punch out rounds, cutting them as close together as possible to maximize the yield. Gather the scraps and press them together (don't knead or reroll) and punch out more rounds. Transfer the scones to a container in a single layer and chill in the freezer for 4 hours. If you plan to bake the scones later, allow them to freeze, and store them in a resealable plastic bag or airtight container in the freezer for up to 1 month. Bake from frozen.

5. **Prepare the egg wash and bake the scones:** Preheat the oven to 325°F (160°C). Line a baking sheet with parchment paper.

6. Remove the scones from the freezer and arrange on the lined baking sheet, 2 to 3 inches apart. In a small bowl, whisk together the egg and water. Using a pastry brush, brush the tops of the scones evenly with the egg wash. Bake for 35 minutes, or until firm to the touch, rotating the pan after 25 minutes. Remove from the oven and transfer the scones to a wire rack set over a baking sheet to cool completely.

7. **Meanwhile, prepare the chocolate drizzle:** In a small heat-resistant bowl, melt the chocolate chips and butter in the microwave on high in 10-second intervals, stirring well after each interval, until the chocolate is shiny but with a few unmelted chips remaining in the mixture, about 30 seconds total. Remove from the microwave and stir until completely melted.

8. **Finish the scones:** Using a spoon, drizzle the melted chocolate on top of the scones. Let sit to harden for 5 to 10 minutes. Store the scones in a vented plastic container at room temperature for up to 2 days.

Gingerbread Scones

YIELD 16 scones

Sugar and spice and everything nice! These scones are truly festive and a must for wintery holiday mornings. A healthy dose of fancy molasses and freshly grated ginger root make these scones a rich dark brown with just a bit of bite. Powder the tops with icing sugar mixed with edible lustre dust for a glittery, snowy scone landscape.

Scones

574 g (3¾ cups + 1 tablespoon)
    all-purpose flour
38 g (3 tablespoons) granulated sugar
25 g (3 tablespoons) brown sugar
4½ teaspoons baking powder
1½ teaspoons baking soda
1 tablespoon ground ginger
1 tablespoon ground cinnamon
1½ teaspoons ground nutmeg
½ teaspoon Diamond Crystal kosher salt
340 g (¾ pound) cold unsalted butter,
    cut into cubes

300 mL (1¼ cups) buttermilk
60 mL (¼ cup) fancy molasses
1 heaping tablespoon peeled and grated
    fresh ginger

Egg Wash

1 egg
1 tablespoon water

For garnish

1 tablespoon icing sugar
1 teaspoon edible ivory lustre dust (optional)

1. **Make the scones:** In a large bowl, whisk together the flour, granulated sugar, brown sugar, baking powder, baking soda, ground ginger, cinnamon, nutmeg, and salt to combine. Drop in the butter and rub into the flour mixture by rolling each cube of butter between your thumb and index finger until mostly incorporated, about 7 minutes. It will have a fine, fluffy texture but should hold together when squeezed. (Alternatively, you can use a stand mixer fitted with the paddle attachment and mix on low speed for 5 to 10 minutes. Scrape the flour mixture into a large bowl.)

2. In a large measuring cup, combine the buttermilk, molasses, and grated fresh ginger.

Stir well with a fork to fully dissolve the molasses until no lumps remain.

3. Create a well in the centre of the flour mixture. Pour the buttermilk mixture into the well and stir quickly with a fork until a shaggy dough forms, 30 to 60 seconds. The buttermilk mixture should be fully incorporated, and there may still be some dry, crumbly bits in the bottom of the bowl.

4. Dust a work surface generously with flour. Stack the shaggy dough, a handful at a time, onto the work surface to form a layered mound. On the final handful, press the dough into any dry mix in the bottom of the bowl to push as much as possible into

recipe continues

the dough. Press down on the dough with your hands to shape it into a rough 10-inch circle, about 1¼ inches thick. (The circle doesn't have to be perfect.) Cut the dough in half, and then place one half top side down on the other half. Press down on the dough again to form it into an 11 to 12-inch circle, about ¾ inch thick. (The stacking and cutting process will create layers within the scones.)

5. Use a 2½-inch round cookie cutter to punch out rounds, cutting them as close together as possible to maximize the yield. Gather the scraps and press them together (don't knead or reroll) and punch out more rounds. Transfer the scones to a container in a single layer and chill in the freezer for 4 hours. If you plan to bake the scones later, allow them to freeze, and store them in a resealable plastic bag or airtight container in the freezer for up to 1 month. Bake from frozen.

6. **Prepare the egg wash and bake the scones:** Preheat the oven to 325°F (160°C). Line a baking sheet with parchment paper.

7. Remove the scones from the freezer and arrange on the lined baking sheet 2 to 3 inches apart. In a small bowl, whisk together the egg and water. Using a pastry brush, brush the tops of the scones evenly with the egg wash. Bake for 35 minutes, or until golden brown, rotating the pan after 25 minutes. Remove from the oven and transfer the scones to a wire rack to cool completely.

8. **Meanwhile, prepare the icing sugar topping and finish the scones:** In a small bowl, stir together the icing sugar and lustre dust, if using. (You can dust the scones with just icing sugar.)

9. Using a fine-mesh strainer or sifter, dust the scones with the icing sugar. Store the scones in a vented plastic container at room temperature for up to 2 days.

NOTES

_____

_____

_____

_____

_____

_____

_____

_____

Clotted Cream

YIELD about 250 mL (1 cup)

Clotted cream—the holy grail of afternoon tea delights—is a classic British preparation made by slowly baking unpasteurized cream over low heat until it solidifies, or "clots" into a rich spread. The most famous clotted cream is made in Devon and Cornwall, where the seaside grass eaten by the cows gives a certain terroir to the dairy. Mild in flavour, it tastes only of pure milk, similar to stiffly beaten whipping cream, with a texture somewhere between cream cheese and sour cream. A beautiful canvas for fruity flavours, it is traditionally spread upon scones and eaten with jam.

As unpasteurized milk is not available on our side of the pond, pasteurized cream will have to do! If you have access to local or small-scale dairy that is minimally processed (for example, low-temperature pasteurized or non-homogenized) this is a wonderful substitute, but if not, grocery store cream will work just fine. You may find the yield is slightly reduced, but it should still clot and taste delicious atop your scone.

Serve with scones and jam, bake into Clotted Cream and Potato Quiche (page 283), swirl into soups, or eat straight from the spoon!

500 mL (2 cups) heavy (35%) cream, low-temperature pasteurized if available

1. Preheat the oven to 170°F (77°C).

2. Pour the cream into an 8-inch square shallow ceramic or glass casserole or baking dish. The cream requires lots of surface area, so be sure it does not come more than 1 to 1½ inches up the side of the baking dish. Cover tightly with foil. Carefully transfer to the oven and bake for 12 hours. Some ovens are programmed to turn off after a certain amount of time as a safety feature, so if this is your first time making clotted cream, be sure to keep an eye on the oven, checking it occasionally.

3. After 12 hours, carefully remove the baking dish from the oven gently and steadily. Remove the foil. At this stage, you should see a skin or crust has formed on the top of the cream. Let sit at room temperature until it is completely cool, around 1 hour, depending on the temperature of the environment.

4. Once cooled, cover the baking dish with a lid or plastic wrap and place in the fridge overnight for another 12 hours.

5. After 12 hours, remove the baking dish from the fridge. Using a large soup or serving spoon, gently skim the thickened top layer of clotted cream from the milky, liquid layer below into a separate small bowl or container (reserve the liquid for thinning if needed or for another use; see Peaches and Cream Scones, page 207). Don't worry about the skin, or if some of the liquid gets into the cream—once stirred, it will all come together.

6. Gently stir the clotted cream to create a uniform texture. If the cream is too thick for your liking, you can mix in some of the reserved milk to thin. Store the clotted cream in an airtight container in the fridge for up to 5 days.

Whipped Crème Fraîche

YIELD 875 mL (3½ cups)

Crème fraîche, or fresh cream, is soured dairy that is delightful served alongside fresh berries or baked treats, and even swirled into savoury soups and sauces. Rich and silky, it is thickened and acidified by the natural fermentation of bacterial cultures. Soured creams are present in many cultures across the globe—think the soured cremas of Mexican and Central American cuisine, smetana in Poland and Eastern Europe, or yogurt in Turkish, Greek, and Persian delicacies.

In our version, we like to whip the cream and buttermilk to a firm peak before setting the mixture to culture. The result is a fluffy, light-as-air topping that is perfectly flavourful and versatile.

500 mL (2 cups) heavy (35%) cream
60 mL (¼ cup) cultured buttermilk

1. Combine the cream and buttermilk in a large ceramic, glass, or plastic bowl (not metal). Whisk with a hand mixer for 5 to 10 minutes, starting on low speed and gradually increasing to high as the mixture thickens and until you have created stiff peaks.

2. Scrape down the sides of the bowl. Cover with a clean piece of paper towel and secure with an elastic band around the rim of the bowl. We recommend paper towel as opposed to a lid or kitchen towel, as this ensures the towel is perfectly clean and that the mixture can easily breathe during the culturing process.

3. Let sit in a warm area of your kitchen for 6 to 12 hours or until tangy and soured. The longer you allow the mixture to culture, and the warmer the environment, the more sour it will become. Once you have reached your desired flavour, place in the fridge for at least 2 hours to allow it to firm up prior to serving. Transfer the chilled crème fraîche into an airtight container and store in the fridge for up to 10 days. You may notice that your crème fraiche continues to culture and sour in the fridge over time. This is normal and perfectly safe to consume until it tastes noticeably off.

NOTES

Classic Lemon Curd

YIELD 500 mL (2 cups)

A classic British treat, fruit curds are surprisingly easy to prepare and come together quickly with few ingredients. This egg-based spread can seem intimidating but is a much less delicate preparation than you might think. The simple combination of eggs, sugar, lemon juice (or fruit purée, see Peach Curd, page 261) and butter, plus a dash of elbow grease and baking magic, yields a rich, creamy, fruity spread that is equally as delicious spread on scones, crumpets, or waffles, baked into tartlets and pies, piped into cream puffs, or swirled into yogurt.

There are many ways to make lemon curd, but we prefer the double-boiler method, which disperses the heat for a foolproof process—the only trick is to keep the mixture moving, whisking continuously to prevent the eggs from scrambling or coagulating. Many recipes use only egg yolks, but we opt for half whole egg and half yolk for a fluffy, custard-like texture. Whisk until your mixture has turned light in colour and the texture is thickened—you will know it when you see it! Then, mount with butter, or monter au beurre, by whisking soft butter into the warm curd one teaspoon-size chunk at a time. This technique will give your spread viscosity and richness and lends a lovely sparkle to the finished curd.

2 eggs
2 egg yolks
200 g (1 cup) granulated sugar
Zest of 1 lemon
125 mL (½ cup) lemon juice
113 g (½ cup) unsalted butter, room temperature

1. Set up a double boiler by adding about 2 inches of water to a medium saucepan with high sides. Place a large metal bowl over top, ensuring the bottom of the bowl does not touch the water. Bring the water to a simmer over medium heat.

2. Meanwhile, place the eggs, egg yolks, sugar, lemon zest, and lemon juice in the bowl over the water and whisk constantly, until smooth and lump free. As the water heats and starts to boil, it will gently start to cook the curd. Manage the heat so that the water underneath is at a simmer (not a rolling boil). Continue whisking constantly until the mixture is fluffy and light in colour, with a slightly thickened texture, 10 to 12 minutes.

3. Dip a spoon into the curd, and then draw a line on the back of the spoon with your finger. The line should stay clear and not fill in. Remove the bowl from the heat, and whisk in the butter, a teaspoon at a time, until it is melted and incorporated. Whisk continuously to ensure the mixture emulsifies and the butter does not split and become greasy.

4. Transfer the curd into a small, clean container. Scrape out the bowl, leaving behind any crust or hardened bits around the edges. Place a piece of plastic wrap directly on top of the curd to ensure a skin does not form, and transfer to the fridge for 2 to 3 hours to chill and firm up. Store in an airtight container in the fridge for up to 1 month.

Sweet Pastries

Scone Granola with Ancient Grains

YIELD 530 g (5½ cups), serves 5 to 7

Make your morning a whole lot sweeter with our scone granola (known as scone-ola in our house!), combining the wholesome goodness of rolled oats and heirloom grains with the decadence of buttermilk scone bits, wildflower honey, and creamy yogurt chips. Pair with your favourite jam and vanilla yogurt, enjoy in a bowl with milk, or use as a crunchy ice cream topping for a hearty treat.

Granola

182 g (2 cups) rolled oats

16 g (¾ cup) puffed quinoa

2 tablespoons hemp hearts

1 tablespoon millet

¼ teaspoon Diamond Crystal kosher salt

2 tablespoons brown sugar

2 tablespoons coconut oil

100 g (⅓ cup) liquid honey

¼ teaspoon pure vanilla extract

Mix-Ins

3 to 4 Signature Buttermilk Scones
    (page 196; you need 100 g/1½ cups
    toasted scone croutons)

100 g (½ cup) yogurt chips

100 g (1 cup) slivered almonds (optional)

20 g (1 cup) freeze-dried strawberries or
    raspberries (optional)

1. **Make the granola:** Preheat the oven to 250°F (120°C). Line a baking sheet with parchment paper.

2. In a large bowl, stir together the rolled oats, puffed quinoa, hemp hearts, millet, and salt. Set aside.

3. In a small saucepan, combine the brown sugar and coconut oil over low heat, stirring constantly to prevent scorching, until just melted into a syrup, 3 to 5 minutes. Remove from the heat and whisk in the honey and vanilla.

4. Pour the warm sugar mixture over the dry ingredients. Mix well with your hands, ensuring the grains are thoroughly coated in syrup. Tip the mixture onto the lined baking sheet and spread it out into an even layer, pressing with a flat hand to compress it together. Bake for 35 minutes, or until golden brown. Remove from the oven and let cool completely on the baking sheet at room temperature for 1 hour. Increase the oven temperature to 275°F (140°C).

5. **Make the scone croutons:** Line a baking sheet with parchment paper. Dice the buttermilk scones into ¼ to ½-inch cubes. Place the scone cubes on the lined baking sheet in a single layer. Be sure not to overload the sheet. (Use 2 sheets if needed.) Toast until the croutons are dehydrated and firm, 25 to 30 minutes. Cool completely on the baking sheet.

6. **Finish the granola:** Break apart the cooled granola with your hands and transfer to a large bowl. Toss with 100 g (1½ cups) of the scone croutons, yogurt chips, almonds (if using), and freeze-dried berries, if using. Store immediately in an airtight container at room temperature for up to 3 months. (An airtight container will keep the granola crunchy longer; exposure to air will soften it.)

Victoria Sponge with Lemon Marmalade and Coconut Chantilly

YIELD three 3-inch cakes

Named after Queen Victoria, the Victoria sponge is a classic teatime treat. Traditionally, it is made by weighing four eggs in their shells and matching this weight exactly in flour, sugar, and butter, and then sandwiching layers of the resulting sponge with strawberry jam, buttercream, or Chantilly, and topping with a dusting of icing sugar. In our version, we chose to substitute the berry preserve for our Lemon Cream Marmalade (page 147)—a light and fresh alternative that pairs seamlessly with the dense, crumbly vanilla sponge. A dollop of coconut cream whisked with icing sugar transforms this classic British treat into a little tropical creation without straying too far from its roots. Garnish with curls of lemon zest and voila!

Before you make the sponge, it is important to weigh the shell-on eggs; they should weigh about 200 g total. Scale the same weight each for the sugar, butter, and flour.

Sponge

200 g (1⅓ cups) all-purpose flour

2 teaspoons baking powder

½ teaspoon Diamond Crystal kosher salt

200 g (¾ cup + 2 tablespoons) unsalted butter, room temperature

200 g (1 cup) granulated sugar

4 large eggs, room temperature (about 200 g; weighed with shell on)

2 tablespoons whole milk, room temperature

Coconut Chantilly

1 (400 mL/14-ounce) can full-fat coconut milk, stored in the fridge overnight

110 g (1 cup) icing sugar, plus more for garnish

Filling

250 mL (1 cup) Lemon Cream Marmalade (page 147), divided

2 tablespoons boiling water

For garnish

Zest of 1 lemon

1. **Make the sponge:** Preheat the oven to 325°F (160°C). Lightly spray an 11 x 7-inch baking pan with cooking oil spray and line the bottom with parchment paper.

2. In a large bowl, whisk together the flour, baking powder, and salt.

3. Cream the butter and sugar together in the bowl of a stand mixer fitted with the paddle attachment on medium-high speed for about 5 minutes or until light and fluffy. Add the eggs, one at a time, mixing after each addition, then add the milk and mix until well combined. The mixture may look separated but will come together once the dry ingredients are added.

4. Reduce the speed to medium-low and gently mix the dry ingredients into the butter mixture until no dry patches remain. Be careful not to overmix, as this may result in a tougher cake.

5. Scrape the batter into the prepared pan, ensuring the top is even by gently flattening with a rubber spatula. Bake until golden brown and a skewer inserted in the centre

recipe continues

of the cake comes out clean, about 20 minutes. Remove from the oven and allow the cake to cool completely in the pan.

6. Meanwhile, make the coconut Chantilly: Remove the can of coconut milk from the fridge. Skim 100 g (½ cup) of the hard coconut cream from the top into the bowl of a stand mixer fitted with the whisk attachment (or into a medium bowl if using a hand mixer). Discard or reserve the coconut water for another use.

7. Add the icing sugar and begin to whip the coconut cream mixture at low speed so that the sugar does not puff into the air. Once the sugar is incorporated, slowly increase the speed to high and continue whipping until light and fluffy, 5 to 8 minutes. Cover the bowl with plastic wrap and refrigerate until ready to use.

8. Punch out the sponge rounds: Once the cake is cool, place a cutting board on top of the baking pan, and flip upside-down so that the cake falls out onto the cutting board. If the cake sticks to the pan, use an offset spatula or butter knife to gently dislodge the sides and try again. Flip the cake back to right side up. Use a serrated bread knife to even out the top of the cake and expose the inside crumb. Using a 3-inch round cookie cutter, punch out 6 round pieces of cake.

9. Fill and assemble the cakes: In a small bowl, mix together 1 tablespoon of the Lemon Cream Marmalade with the boiling water to make a syrup. Generously brush the sponge rounds with the syrup. Place a dollop of marmalade on 3 of the sponge rounds, and then top with a spoonful of the coconut Chantilly. Place the remaining sponge rounds cut side down on top of the marmalade and Chantilly to form sandwiches. Generously dust the tops of the cakes with icing sugar. Top with a curly zest of lemon. Serve immediately.

TIP: This sponge cake freezes well. After the cake is completely cool, remove from the pan, wrap tightly with plastic wrap and store in the freezer for up to 2 months or until ice crystals start to form. Defrost at room temperature until it can be cut easily, about an hour. Assemble and serve.

NOTES

Clotted Cream and Oat Petticoat Tail Shortbread

YIELD 16 cookies

Shortbread is a classic example of perfection in simplicity. Originating from Scotland, shortbread is traditionally made with only flour, butter, and sugar in a 3:2:1 proportion. In our rustic, breakfast-y version, we substituted a portion of the butter for a generous helping of Clotted Cream (page 239) for a delicate, milky flavour. Additionally, cutting in a small portion of oat flour and cornstarch gives these biscuits a melt-in-your-mouth, flaky texture. A quick chill in the freezer before baking allows them to hold their shape—especially important for these adorable "petticoat tail" shaped shortbread, named after the frilly petticoats that women wore under their skirts during the twelfth century. Enjoy with a cup of strongly brewed builder's tea for breakfast, because cookies for breakfast is always a good idea!

This recipe is particularly proportion dependent, so we highly recommend using weight measurements (grams) as opposed to volume (cups/teaspoons). This will ensure the dough comes out as intended.

57 g (4 tablespoons) unsalted butter, room temperature

170 g (¾ cup) cold Clotted Cream (page 239)

100 g (½ cup) granulated sugar, plus 1 or 2 teaspoons for sprinkling

240 g (1½ cups + 5 teaspoons) all-purpose flour

45 g (½ cup) oat flour

2 tablespoons cornstarch

1. Preheat the oven to 325°F (160°C). Line a baking sheet with parchment paper.

2. In the bowl of a stand mixer fitted with the paddle attachment (or by hand in a medium bowl with a hand mixer), combine the butter, clotted cream, and sugar. Beat until well combined and creamy, but not fluffy, 4 to 5 minutes. Scrape the sides of the bowl.

3. In a small bowl, whisk together the all-purpose flour, oat flour, and cornstarch, until well combined and free of clumps.

4. With the mixer running on low speed, gradually add the dry ingredients to the butter mixture until just combined into a coarse, crumbly dough with no dry patches remaining. (If mixing with a hand mixer, add the dry ingredients in 2 or 3 additions, allowing the flour to incorporate before adding the next addition.) Be careful not to overmix, which will lead to tough shortbread.

5. Turn the dough out onto a lightly floured work surface. Cut the dough into two equal portions. Working with one portion of dough at a time, shape the dough into a flat 7-inch disc, about ½ inch thick. Repeat to shape the second portion, and transfer both discs onto the lined baking sheet. Dock the dough by pricking it all over with a fork (play around with different

recipe continues

patterns). This will allow steam to escape while baking, ensuring fewer bubbles and a lovely, flat top to your biscuits. You can use the back of a butter knife, chopstick, or fork to make little ruffle details around the edge of the cakes, traditional of the petticoat tail shape. Bake the shortbread until the dough feels firm to the touch and has little to no give, 40 to 45 minutes. Shortbread should be pale with very little browning, so if you notice any golden brown, reduce the oven temperature to 300°F (150°C). Remove from the oven.

6. While the shortbread is still piping hot, sprinkle sugar generously over the short-bread and gently press it into the surface with the palm of your hand. The heat from the shortbread will slightly melt the sugar granules, causing them to stick to the sur-face. While the shortbread is hot, use a sharp kitchen knife to cut each shortbread cake into 8 wedges. Cutting the shortbread while hot will ensure crisp edges with min-imal crumbling. Let the shortbread cool completely.

7. Once cooled, gently lift and tip each shortbread wedge to remove any excess sugar. Store the shortbread in an airtight container at room temperature for up to 3 weeks (the shortbread get better as they age).

TIP: This shortbread is a lovely canvas for many different flavour additions. Try adding the zest of a lemon and 1 teaspoon of finely ground lavender buds into your clotted cream mixture for lemon lavender cookies, or dip halfway in tempered chocolate for a chocolate covered treat.

VARIATION: If you are using a traditional 8 to 9-inch stoneware or ceramic shortbread pan, press the entire batch of dough into the pan, dock the dough, and bake for 50 to 60 minutes at 300°F (150°C). This will yield a shortbread that is double the thickness, so you can expect more browning to enable the shortbread to bake throughout. To check for doneness, look for minimal give when pressed in the centre and an even golden colour throughout.

NOTES

_____

_____

_____

_____

_____

Sour Cherry and Rhubarb Jubilee Bars

YIELD nine 2½-inch square bars

Truly delightful with a cherry on top, these bars are inspired by the famous dessert cherries jubilee—a classic dish made with fresh cherries and cherry liqueur, which is then flambéed and served spooned over vanilla ice cream. In our updated version, we use a heaping spoonful of our Sour Cherry and Rhubarb Jam (page 69), drizzled with liqueur and set ablaze for a brief moment until the alcohol dissipates. This caramelizes the sugars in the filling, deepening and intensifying the cherry flavour and lending a rich, slightly boozy, and mature nuance.

Paired with a scone crumb crust, these bars are lovely enough for teatime and nostalgic enough for a casual picnic in the park. Enjoy them traditionally with a scoop of vanilla ice cream.

Scone Crust

6 to 7 Signature Buttermilk Scones (page 196; you need 250 g/2 cups scone crumbs)

1 tablespoon granulated sugar

65 g (3 tablespoons) golden syrup

Filling

200 g stemmed and pitted sour cherries*

200 g topped, tailed, and diced rhubarb

45 mL (3 tablespoons) Sour Cherry and Rhubarb Jam (page 69)

60 mL (¼ cup) kirsch (cherry liqueur), divided

1 tablespoon cornstarch

Streusel Topping

150 g (1 cup) all-purpose flour

75 g (⅓ cup) granulated sugar

½ teaspoon ground cinnamon

113 g (¼ pound) cold unsalted butter, cut into cubes

1. Preheat the oven to 275°F (140°C). Line a baking sheet and an 8-inch square baking pan each with parchment paper.

2. **Prepared the scone crust:** Dice the buttermilk scones into ¼ to ½-inch cubes. Arrange the cubed scone on the lined baking sheet in a single layer. Be sure not to overload the tray (you can use a couple of baking sheets to give your scone bits lots of room for air circulation). Toast until the croutons are firm, dehydrated, and no longer have any give, 25 to 30 minutes. Cool completely on the baking sheet. Transfer to a food processor and pulse to a fine crumb.

3. Measure 250 g (2 cups) of the scone crumbs into a large bowl. Add the sugar and mix with a fork until evenly distributed. Pour in the golden syrup and mix with a rubber spatula or by hand until well combined and no clumps of syrup remain. The texture will be similar to wet sand. When you squeeze a handful of crumbs, it should hold together. Add an extra drizzle of golden syrup if needed. Scrape the scone crumb mixture into the prepared pan and press it firmly and evenly into the bottom of the pan with your hand or a rubber spatula to make a flat crust. Par-bake the crust for 15 minutes until ever-so-slightly darkened and firm to the touch. Remove from the oven and set aside. Increase the oven temperature to 350°F (180°C).

recipe continues

4. Meanwhile, make the filling: In a medium saucepan, combine the sour cherries, rhubarb, Sour Cherry and Rhubarb Jam, and 2 tablespoons of the kirsch. Heat over medium-low heat until warm and the juices start to run from the fruit, 3 to 5 minutes. If using a gas stove, turn off the flame. If using an electric stove, reduce the heat to low.

5. Pour the remaining 2 tablespoons of kirsch into a large metal spoon or ladle, and, holding the spoon over the pan, ignite with a match. Immediately pour the flaming kirsch into the warm fruit mixture and blaze until the flames dissipate. If using a gas stove, turn it back on to medium-low heat. If using an electric stove, increase the heat to medium-low.

6. Add the cornstarch and continue cooking, stirring continuously, until the liquid at the bottom of the pan has thickened slightly and a spoon dragged along the bottom creates a line for a moment before filling in, about 5 minutes. Remove from the heat and set aside to cool.

7. Make the streusel topping: In the bowl of a stand mixer fitted with the paddle attachment (or in a medium bowl if mixing by hand) combine the flour, sugar, and cinnamon, and gently mix on low speed until all the ingredients are evenly distributed. (If mixing by hand, use a fork.)

8. With the mixer running on low speed, gradually drop in the cold butter, a cube at a time. Once all the butter is incorporated, increase the speed to medium-low. The mixture will look dry and sandy. After 11 or 12 minutes, you will start to see the crumbs coming together. Stop the mixer and scrape down the sides of the bowl. Increase the speed to medium-high and mix for another

4 to 6 minutes, until marble-size pieces begin to form. Do not overmix; you do not want to form a dough. (If you are working by hand, rub the butter into the flour mixture until the desired texture is achieved, similar to when making scones or pastry.) Set aside in the fridge.

9. Assemble the bars: Pour the cooled fruit mixture over the par-baked crust in an even layer. Generously sprinkle the streusel over top. Bake until the streusel starts to turn golden brown, 25 to 30 minutes. Allow the bar to cool before slicing and serving. Store in an airtight container in the fridge for up to 5 days.

TIP: This crust is a perfect way to use up day-old scones. If you happen to have a few scones left over, pop them in your freezer. When you have a handful saved up, defrost at room temperature until they are soft enough to dice.

VARIATION: If you can't find golden syrup, you can substitute 1:1 with liquid honey.

*You will need about 260 g of whole cherries. See **A NOTE ON MEASURING FRUIT** (page 19).

Orange Blossom Angel Food Cake with Fresh Peaches

YIELD one 10-inch tube cake, serves 8 to 12

Like pure sunshine wrapped in a fluffy cloud, this cake is a true joy to make and serve. Stunning in flavour and texture, it is light as air on account of the firmly whipped egg whites and omission of butter (not something we do often!). For this recipe, every effort is made to achieve the highest rise possible. Fold the ingredients together ever so delicately so as not to collapse any aeration in the batter. Also, allow your cake to cool upside down. This will help ensure it won't fall when it is still hot from the oven.

Delicately scented with orange blossom water and frosted with a simple milk glaze, this treat is one we like to enjoy with floral white teas to perfectly balance its lightness of flavour and texture. Lovely for breakfast or as a teatime alternative to scones with Whipped Crème Fraîche (page 241) and jam.

Orange Blossom Angel Food Cake

300 g (1½ cups) granulated sugar, divided

150 g (1 cup) all-purpose flour

2 tablespoons cornstarch

12 egg whites

2 tablespoons orange blossom water

1½ teaspoons cream of tartar

½ teaspoon Diamond Crystal kosher salt

Orange Blossom Glaze

110 g (1 cup) icing sugar

45 mL (3 tablespoons) heavy (35%) cream

1 tablespoon orange blossom water

For garnish

2 to 3 peaches, pitted and cut into
   1-inch-thick wedges (2 cups/500 mL)

Fresh florals (optional)

1. Preheat the oven to 325°F (160°C).

2. **Make the orange blossom angel food cake:** Whisk together 100 g (½ cup) of the sugar, flour, and cornstarch in a medium bowl until well combined and free of lumps.

3. In the bowl of a stand mixer fitted with the whisk attachment, combine the egg whites, orange blossom water, cream of tartar, and salt, and whisk on medium speed until foamy, about 5 minutes. With the mixer running, gradually pour in the remaining 200 g (1 cup) sugar in a steady stream, and then increase the speed to high and continue to whisk until soft, floppy peaks form, 4 to 5 minutes. Remove the bowl from the mixer. Gently fold in half of the dry ingredients using a rubber spatula until no dry patches remain, and then add the remaining dry ingredients and fold until all the ingredients are fully incorporated. Run the spatula across the bottom of the bowl to ensure no dry patches remain.

4. Scrape the batter into an ungreased 10-inch tube pan. Run a butter knife through the batter in a circle to ensure there are no air bubbles. Place the pan on a baking sheet so that the pan is not resting directly on the oven rack. Bake until the top of the cake is no longer sticky to the touch, 40 to 45 minutes. Remove from the oven and immediately invert the pan so the cake doesn't

recipe continues

collapse and stays light and airy. Allow the cake to cool completely in the pan. If your pan has feet, simply rest upside-down on the feet. If not, place upside down on a wire rack to cool completely.

5. Meanwhile, prepare the orange blossom glaze: Place the icing sugar in a small bowl. Add the cream and orange blossom water and mix until no lumps remain and the glaze streams in thick ribbons from a spoon.

6. Finish the cake: Once the cake is completely cool, gently run an offset spatula or butter knife around the sides of the pan to loosen the cake. Place a plate or cutting board on top of the pan and invert it. Gently lift the pan, and the cake will fall out onto the plate. Spoon the orange blossom glaze over the cake, spreading it over the top and pushing it gently over the sides for a pretty dripping effect. Top with a crown of fresh sliced peaches and florals (if using) and serve immediately. (You can store the cake, without the glaze and garnishes, tightly wrapped in plastic wrap in the fridge for up to 1 week. Glaze and garnish just before serving.)

TIPS: Angel food cake freezes beautifully! After removing from the pan, wrap the cake tightly with plastic wrap and store in the freezer for up to 2 months or until ice crystals start to form. Defrost at room temperature for about an hour or until the cake feels soft and spongy. Glaze, garnish, and serve.

Save your egg yolks to make Classic Lemon Curd (page 242) or Peach Curd (page 261). Half of the cake can be used to make a Sunshine Peach Trifle (page 261).

VARIATION: This cake is also delicious without the glaze, sliced and toasted until the edges are a deep golden brown. Serve warm with jam and Whipped Crème Fraîche (page 241).

NOTES

_____

_____

_____

_____

Sunshine Peach Trifle

YIELD one 3 L (12-cup) trifle, serves 8 to 10

This lovingly layered dessert is made with cubes of angel food cake, blanketed with fluffy whipped mascarpone, peach curd, and fresh fruit. Though the traditional British trifle is typically made with custard and whipped cream, we opted to incorporate a fresh fruit curd and whipped mascarpone frosting, typically found in the Italian layered dessert tiramisu. The cheese lends a lovely complexity of flavour, and the layers of bright and cheerful curd made with fresh peaches cuts right through the overall sweetness of this spoonable dessert. Using mascarpone instead of whipped cream also means this dish freezes beautifully, so you can always have a trifle ready, just in case!

Peach Curd

300 g (1¾ cups) peeled, pitted, and diced
    ripe peaches*

125 mL (½ cup) water

4 egg yolks

135 g (⅔ cup) granulated sugar

2 tablespoons lemon juice

113 g (¼ pound) unsalted butter,
    room temperature

Mascarpone Cream

750 mL (3 cups) heavy (35%) cream

135 g (⅔ cup) granulated sugar

2 teaspoons pure vanilla extract

475 g (2 cups) mascarpone cheese,
    room temperature

Peach Syrup

2 tablespoons Sunshine Peach Jam (page 77)

1 tablespoon boiling water

For assembly

350 g (2 cups) peeled, pitted, and 1-inch-thick
    wedged ripe peaches*

½ Orange Blossom Angel Food Cake
    (page 257), cut in 1-inch cubes

1. Make the peach curd: Combine the diced peaches and water in a small saucepan and simmer, uncovered, over medium-low heat until the peaches are soft and almost no liquid remains, 5 to 10 minutes. Pour the softened peaches into a food processor or blender and purée until smooth.

2. Set up a double boiler by adding about 2 inches of water to a medium saucepan with high sides. Place a large metal bowl over top, ensuring the bottom of the bowl does not touch the water. Bring the water to a simmer over medium heat. Meanwhile, place the peach purée, egg yolks, sugar, and lemon juice in the bowl over the water and whisk constantly, until the mixture is fluffy and light in colour, with a slightly thick-ened texture, 10 to 12 minutes. Dip a spoon into the curd, and then draw a line on the back of the spoon with your finger. The line should stay clear and not fill in. As you whisk, you will also begin to see the lines from the whisk hold their shape as the curd thickens. Remove the bowl from the heat, and whisk in the butter, a teaspoon at a time, until it is melted and incorporated.

recipe continues

Whisk continuously to ensure the mixture emulsifies and the butter does not split and become greasy.

3. Transfer the curd into a small, clean container. Place a piece of plastic wrap directly on top of the curd to ensure a skin does not form. Transfer to the fridge until ready to use.

4. **Make the mascarpone cream:** In the bowl of a stand mixer fitted with the whisk attachment, (or in a large bowl with a hand mixer) combine the heavy cream, sugar, and vanilla and beat on high speed until medium-stiff peaks form, 5 to 8 minutes. Add the mascarpone and beat on medium speed until just incorporated, 1 to 3 minutes. Cover with a lid or plastic wrap, and set aside in the fridge.

5. **Prepare the peach syrup:** In a small bowl, combine the Sunshine Peach Jam and the boiling water. Stir to dissolve until it is the consistency of a thin syrup.

6. **Assemble the trifle:** Layer one-third of the mascarpone cream in the bottom of a medium glass bowl, tray, or trifle dish. Top with a layer of angel food cake cubes, drizzle with the peach syrup, and then add a layer of fresh peach slices and dollops of peach curd. Repeat layers of cream, cake, syrup, peaches, and curd again until you reach the top of the dish, 2 to 3 layers of each. We like to finish the top with mascarpone cream, cubes of cake, and peach slices.

TIP: This trifle freezes beautifully! Wrap tightly in plastic wrap and store in the freezer for up to 2 months or until ice crystals start to form. Defrost at room temperature until soft throughout.

*You will need about 900 g of whole peaches (total combined weight needed for the diced and wedged peaches). See A NOTE ON MEASURING FRUIT (page 19). For preparation instructions, see the chart UNIQUE FRUIT PREPARATION (page 19). (Blanching the peaches will make them more resistant to oxidizing/browning so they look bright and beautiful in the trifle.)

NOTES

_____

_____

_____

_____

_____

_____

_____

_____

Soft Pretzels with Strawberry and Chocolate Dip

YIELD 6 pretzels

Inspired by Belgian cookie trays, a pretzel shaped pastry is so playful and fun to make! We opted for a softly baked pretzel for this recipe, dusted in cinnamon sugar. Typically, a simmering bath in baking soda and water just before baking gives pretzels their quintessential golden colour and chewy crust. However, for this recipe, a quick dip in a tap-warm baking soda solution keeps the crust of the pretzels delicate, fluffy, and dessert-y, without losing their pretzel character.

The pretzel shape begs to be pulled apart and dipped, so serve these pastries with a strawberries and cream dip made with white chocolate and our Strawberry, Raspberry, and Cream Jam (page 35).

Soft Pretzels

338 g (2¼ cups) all-purpose flour, divided, plus more for dusting

2 tablespoons brown sugar

56 g (¼ cup) melted unsalted butter, divided

250 mL (1 cup) warm (115°F/46°C) whole milk

½ teaspoon Diamond Crystal kosher salt

2¼ teaspoons (8 g packet) instant yeast

2 tablespoons baking soda

375 mL (1½ cups) warm water

50 g (¼ cup) granulated sugar

2 teaspoons ground cinnamon

Strawberry Chocolate Dip

150 g (⅓ pound) white chocolate, chopped

75 mL (⅓ cup) heavy (35%) cream

2 tablespoons Strawberry, Raspberry, and Cream Jam (page 35)

1. **Make the soft pretzels:** In the bowl of a stand mixer fitted with a paddle attachment, add 75 g (½ cup) of the flour, brown sugar, 2 tablespoons of the melted butter, warm milk, salt, and yeast. Mix on medium-low speed to incorporate the ingredients evenly, and then slowly add the remaining 263 g (1¾ cups) flour in 2 additions, mixing after each addition until incorporated, until a smooth dough forms, 10 to 12 minutes.

2. Transfer the dough into a large bowl greased with butter or cooking oil spray. Cover with plastic wrap and let rise in a warm area until doubled in size, about 1 hour.

3. Preheat the oven to 350°F (180°C). Line a baking sheet with parchment paper.

4. Once the dough has doubled in size, turn it out on a floured work surface. Slightly knead the dough until smooth, uniform, and elastic to ensure an even rise. Then, cut the dough into 6 equal portions. Roll each piece into a thin rope about the width of a pencil (they will puff up substantially when baked) and twist into a pretzel shape.

5. In a wide, shallow bowl, dissolve the baking soda in the warm water (as hot as you can comfortably touch). Dip the pretzels, one at a time, into the solution for about 5 seconds, and then lay them on the lined baking sheet, leaving about 2 inches

recipe continues

between each pretzel. Bake until golden brown, 5 to 8 minutes. Remove from the oven and let sit on the baking sheet to cool.

6. Place the remaining 2 tablespoons melted butter in a small bowl. On a large plate or wide bowl, stir together the granulated sugar and cinnamon.

7. Once the pretzels are cool enough to handle and no longer delicate, brush them with the melted butter and fully dredge in the cinnamon sugar mixture. Place the coated pretzels on a serving tray or platter in a single layer.

8. **Make the strawberry chocolate dip:** Place the white chocolate in a medium bowl. Heat the cream in a small saucepan gently over low heat until it is steaming and warm but not boiling. Pour the warm cream over the chocolate and stir with a rubber spatula until the chocolate is melted and the ganache is smooth and silky. Add the Strawberry, Raspberry, and Cream Jam, and stir until smooth.

9. Serve the pretzels immediately with the dip, as these are most magical served as fresh as possible. You can keep the dip warm in a fondue pot or double boiler if the pretzels will be sitting out on a table.

NOTES

Spiced Persimmon Pull-Apart Bread

YIELD one 8-inch round loaf

Afternoon tea treats are notoriously finger foods, meant to be delicately nibbled with teacup in hand. A contemporary spin on this tradition, pull-apart breads are a beautiful offering for teatime, their slowly consumable nature making for a fun and engaging experience.

For a rustic elegance, we love this modified brioche dough formed in a bouclette or looped rosette style. In this way, each petal can be delicately pulled from the loaf, ensuring clean fingers, while pockets of spiced jam, dusting of cardamom sugar, and sprinkle of rose petals add a lovely, barely there bouquet.

150 mL (⅔ cup) warm (115°F/46°C) whole milk
38 g (3 tablespoons) granulated sugar
2¼ teaspoons (8 g packet) active dry yeast
350 g (2⅓ cups) all-purpose flour
½ teaspoon Diamond Crystal kosher salt
2 egg yolks
80 g (⅓ cup + 1 teaspoon) soft unsalted butter, plus more for brushing and serving

1½ teaspoons pure vanilla extract
80 g (¼ cup) Persimmon, Cardamom, and Rose Jam (page 119), plus more as needed

For garnish
55 g (½ cup) icing sugar
1 teaspoon ground cardamom
Sprinkle of dried culinary rose petals (optional)

1. Generously grease an 8-inch round cake pan with cooking oil spray or butter.

2. Combine the warm milk, sugar, and yeast in a small bowl, and stir until dissolved. Let sit for 10 to 15 minutes for the yeast to activate. It will begin to froth.

3. Place the flour and salt in a stand mixer fitted with the dough hook attachment, and mix on low speed just to combine evenly. Add the egg yolks, activated yeast mixture, butter, and vanilla, and knead on medium-low speed until the dough comes together into a smooth, stretchy ball around the hook and pulls away from the sides of the bowl, 10 to 15 minutes.

4. Grease a medium bowl with cooking oil spray or butter. Transfer the dough

onto an unfloured work surface and knead by hand briefly just to ensure uniformity. The dough should not be sticky or require any flour. Shape the dough into a tight ball and place in the bowl. Cover with plastic wrap or a kitchen towel and let rise in a warm area until doubled in size, about 2 hours.

5. Once the dough has doubled in size, turn it out onto a very lightly floured work surface. Punch down the dough, kneading briefly to ensure uniformity, about 30 seconds. Shape the dough into a flat disc, wrap tightly with plastic wrap, and chill in the freezer for 20 to 30 minutes, until the dough feels firm and cool to the

recipe continues

touch (do not freeze fully). Chilling the dough will make it easier to work with—it will be less sticky and have less spring back as it is rolled out.

6. Remove the dough from the freezer and unwrap. On a lightly floured work surface, use a rolling pin to roll out the chilled dough until about ¼ inch thick. Using a 3-inch round cookie cutter, punch out as many circles as possible. Collect the scraps, reroll, and punch out more circles until all the dough has been used.

7. Working with 3 circles of dough at a time, arrange the circles in a vertical row, slightly overlapping them by a third. Spoon about ½ teaspoon of the Persimmon, Cardamom, and Rose Jam down the centre of the dough. Starting at the end closest to you, roll up the dough into a small log. Cut the log crosswise into 2 rosettes and place cut side down into the prepared pan. Repeat with another 3 dough circles and ½ teaspoon of jam, until you have formed all the dough and evenly spaced them in the pan (a random pattern is fine). Cover with plastic wrap and place in a warm area and let rise until doubled in size, about 1 hour.

8. Preheat the oven to 350°F (180°C).

9. Once proofed, the rosettes will look puffy and fill the pan. A light press with your finger will leave a small divot in the dough without bouncing back. If you like your pull-apart bread extra jammy, you can add a few dollops of jam between the petals of the rosettes.

10. Melt 1 or 2 tablespoons of butter in a small saucepan or microwave in a heat-resistant bowl. Brush the top of the bread thoroughly and generously with the melted butter. Bake until golden brown, 20 to 25 minutes. The bread will slightly contract and begin to pull away from the sides of the pan toward the end of baking. Allow the bread to cool completely in the pan. Once cooled, you will be able to easily lift or tip the bread out of the pan.

11. Stir together the icing sugar and cardamom in a small bowl. Using a fine-mesh sieve or sifter, dust the top of the bread with the icing sugar mixture just before serving. Sprinkle with dried rose petals, if using. Delightful served fresh from the oven with soft butter on the side.

NOTES

_____

_____

_____

_____

_____

_____

_____

Tea Sandwiches and Savoury Delights

Classic Cucumber Tea Sandwiches with Creamy Spinach Spread

YIELD 10 tea sandwiches

Fresh cucumber finger sandwiches are one of the most traditional of afternoon tea delights. The most classic tea sandwich is a simple assembly of white bread lightly coated with butter and layered with slices of cucumber. For our elevated version, we substituted the white bread with brioche, a yeast bread enriched with butter. Freshly chopped spinach and a plethora of herbs whipped into cream cheese can be made quickly and ahead of time.

Spinach Spread

227 g (8 ounces) cream cheese, room
    temperature
30 g (1 cup) roughly chopped baby spinach
2 tablespoons finely chopped fresh flat-leaf
    parsley leaves
2 tablespoons finely chopped fresh dill

Tea Sandwiches

10 slices brioche bread (1 loaf)
1 large English cucumber
2 tablespoons unsalted butter, softened,
    more to taste

1. **Make the spinach spread:** Place the cream cheese in a medium bowl and use a rubber spatula to break down and soften the texture. Add the spinach, parsley, and dill and gently fold into the cream cheese until uniformly combined. Transfer the spread into a metal strainer set over a medium bowl (the spinach may weep liquid), cover with plastic wrap and transfer to the fridge until ready to use.

2. **Assemble the tea sandwiches:** Stack 2 to 4 slices of bread on top of each other. Using a sharp serrated bread knife with a gentle sawing motion, cut off the crusts. Let the knife do the work and resist the urge to push down on the knife which will lead to pinched edges. Then, cut the stack of bread in half vertically. Continue cutting the pieces of bread, keeping the original stacks to ensure the tops and bottoms of your sandwiches match up perfectly.

3. Cut both ends off the cucumber. Slice the cucumber into 3 to 4 equal lengths, about 3 inches long. Then, using a mandoline (⅓ to ¼-inch setting) or a sharp kitchen knife, thinly slice the cucumber pieces lengthwise into rectangles. You'll need at least 10 cucumber slices, one for each sandwich. (Use the best, largest centre slices.) Place the cucumber slices between 3 or 4 layers of paper towel to absorb excess moisture.

4. Arrange the slices of bread on a large work surface. Keep the tops and bottoms of the bread paired up exactly as you cut them. Spread a thin layer of butter on the top halves. Spread a thick layer of herb spread on the bottom halves, top with a slice of cucumber, and then close the sandwiches. Tie with a little piece of twine or strip of parchment paper.

Mini Fleur de Sel Bagels with Preserved Lemon Spread, Pickled Onions, and Smoked Salmon

YIELD *16 bagel sandwiches*

Our extended family gatherings are never complete without bagels and lox, so inspired by our New Jersey roots, we have elevated a mini bagel and lox to tea-sandwich status with a sprinkle of fleur de sel, fresh herbs, and homemade pickled onions. Bagels are surprisingly easy to make, especially in mini size when they are particularly forgiving. We prefer ours boiled in the classic New York style for a glossy, crunchy crust and dense, chewy middle.

A schmear of cream cheese is a must—whipped with homemade preserved lemons and scallion—while quick-pickled pink onions add a pop of flavour and vibrant colour to this classic sandwich.

Preserved Lemon
(Yield: 125 mL/½ cup; you will have extra)

1 lemon

1 heaping tablespoon Diamond Crystal kosher salt

Quick Pickled Onions

1 medium red onion, thinly sliced

125 mL (½ cup) white vinegar

60 mL (¼ cup) rice vinegar

1 teaspoon liquid honey (optional)

1 teaspoon Diamond Crystal kosher salt

Preserved Lemon Spread

227 g (8 ounces) cream cheese

15 g (¼ cup) finely chopped fresh dill

18 g (3 tablespoons) finely chopped spring onion

1 tablespoon preserved lemon, finely chopped, or to taste (recipe above)

Zest of ½ lemon

Mini Bagels

2¼ teaspoons (8 g packet) active dry yeast

400 mL (1⅔ cups) warm water, divided

2 tablespoons granulated sugar

2 teaspoons Diamond Crystal kosher salt

600 g (4 cups) all-purpose flour, divided, plus more for dusting

Fleur de sel, for garnish

Poaching Liquid

2 L (8 cups) water

60 mL (¼ cup) malt syrup or liquid honey

1 tablespoon baking soda

2 teaspoons Diamond Crystal kosher salt

15 to 20 slices smoked salmon, for serving

1. **Prepare the preserved lemon:** Wash the lemon well, scrubbing the fruit with mild soap and hot water. Using a sharp kitchen knife, slice off the stem and blossom ends of the lemon so that the flesh is revealed. Set the fruit upright on your cutting board on one of the flat ends, and, working vertically, carefully slice off the zest and pith in sections, rotating the lemon as you work. You will now have a completely bare lemon. Cut the lemon in half.

recipe continues

2. Chop the sections of lemon peel into small pieces (the tiniest of cuts). Place the brunoise lemon peel in a small non-reactive bowl or container, such as a glass jar, and add the salt. Place a strainer over top of the container. Squeeze the lemon halves to release all of their juices. Discard the lemon membranes. Use a spoon to combine the ingredients. Cover with a tight-fitting lid. Let sit at room temperature for at least 12 hours or up to 24 before using. Store in the refrigerator for up to 2 months. (Preserved lemon is delicious in a variety of culinary applications, such as salad dressings and marinades.)

3. Prepare the quick pickled onions: Pack the sliced red onions into a 250 mL (8-ounce) mason jar. Combine the white vinegar, rice vinegar, honey (if using), and salt in a small saucepan and heat over high heat until steaming but not boiling. Pour the hot liquid over the onions to fill the jar, leaving ¼ inch of headspace. Seal with a lid, and let cool to room temperature for 1 to 2 hours depending on the temperature of the room. Store sealed in the fridge until ready to use or up to 4 months.

4. The next day, make the preserved lemon spread: Place the cream cheese in a medium bowl, and use a rubber spatula to start breaking down and soften the texture. Add the dill, spring onion, 1 tablespoon of the preserved lemon, and lemon zest, and mix thoroughly with a rubber spatula until well combined. Cover and set aside in the fridge.

5. Make the bagel dough: In a small bowl, stir together the yeast with 250 mL (1 cup) of the warm water and sugar. Let sit and bloom for about 5 minutes to activate the yeast, or until the mixture appears foamy.

6. In a stand mixer fitted with a dough hook, combine the yeast mixture, the remaining 150 mL (⅔ cup) warm water, salt, and 150 g (1 cup) of the flour. Begin to mix on low speed, and slowly add 375 g (2½ cups) flour in 3 additions (a total of 525 g/3½ cups), beating after each addition just until incorporated, until the dough has come together, 10 to 12 minutes. The dough will be tacky and sticky. If it feels too dry, add 1 or 2 tablespoons more water and mix until incorporated and the dough is smooth.

7. Grease a medium bowl with cooking oil spray or olive oil. Set aside.

8. Lightly flour a work surface. Turn out the dough and knead by hand, gradually working in as much of the remaining 75 g (½ cup) flour as possible as you knead, until completely smooth, 15 to 20 minutes. If you are working in a dry kitchen, you may only be able to incorporate a portion of this flour. In a more humid kitchen, for example during the summer months, you may find that the dough can take up to 150 g (1 cup) more flour—the more flour you can incorporate, the better! By the end of the kneading process, the dough should be strong enough to be stretched tissue thin and transparent without tearing. Place the dough in the greased bowl. Cover with a damp kitchen towel and let rise in a warm area for about 1 hour or until doubled in size.

9. Position the racks in the upper and lower thirds of the oven and preheat to 425°F (220°C). Line 2 baking sheets with parchment paper.

10. Once the dough has doubled in size, punch down the dough, and then re-cover and let rise for 10 minutes.

11. **Meanwhile, prepare the poaching liquid:** In a large, wide saucepan, combine the water, malt syrup, baking soda, and salt. Bring to a boil over high heat. Once it boils, reduce the heat to a simmer.

12. Once the dough has completed its second rise, turn it out onto an unfloured work surface. Using a bench knife, cut the dough into 16 equal pieces (about 60 g each). Pre-shape the pieces into balls. Working one ball at a time, tuck the edges of the dough underneath to make a dome shape, and then place the ball seam-side down on the work surface. Cupping your hand on top of the ball, roll the ball to twist the edges further underneath the ball to form a perfectly round shape. Then, push your finger through the middle of the ball to form a bagel. Widen the hole to be about 1 inch in diameter (wider than you might think). Remember that these are New York–style bagels. They will puff during the last proofing stage, and the hole will end up much smaller after baking. Repeat with all the pieces.

13. Place the bagels on the lined baking sheets. Cover with plastic wrap and let rest for 10 to 15 minutes. Gently press the dough with your finger; if the little divot left by your finger remains and does not pop back, the dough is fully proofed and ready to boil.

14. **Poach the bagels:** Ensure your poaching liquid is at a simmer, not a rolling boil (you do not want the bagels to be tossed around as they cook). Gently transfer as many bagels as will comfortably fit in the pot.

The bagels should be able to bob and move freely in the liquid. Boil for 1½ minutes, turning halfway through using a slotted or wooden spoon. Use a slotted spoon to remove the bagels from the poaching liquid and transfer to a wire rack set over a baking sheet or kitchen towel to drain. Immediately sprinkle the damp bagels with fleur del sel. Repeat to poach the remaining bagels.

15. **Bake the bagels:** Once all the bagels are boiled and drained, place them on the lined baking sheets, 2 to 3 inches apart. Bake for 14 to 18 minutes, until golden brown, rotating the pans halfway through. Let the bagels sit on the baking sheet just until cool enough to handle—they are most magical warm and fresh from the oven.

16. Serve as a bagel and lox board to allow your guests to assemble their own bagel sandwiches. Store the leftover bagels in a vented plastic container at room temperature for up to 2 days.

Spelt Digestive Biscuits with Strawberry Goat Cheese and Rose Honey

YIELD 28 biscuits; ½ cup Strawberry Goat Cheese

In this darling take on cheese and crackers, soft unripened goat cheese is whipped with fresh strawberries, piled high atop a homemade digestive wheat round, and drizzled with rose honey. Goat cheese can be easily infused with a variety of fruits, herbs, and flavourings, and we like to switch this one up seasonally.

As for the cracker, there is historically little variation to this recipe, so we have stuck with the classic proportions. For a heartier flavour, however, we cut in a small portion of spelt flour, which adds a nutty, toasted, and slightly sweet nuance that pairs perfectly with the strawberry spread.

Digestive Biscuits

195 g (1½ cups) whole wheat flour

60 g (½ cup) spelt flour

55 g (½ cup) icing sugar

50 g (¼ cup tightly packed) brown sugar

1 teaspoon baking powder

½ teaspoon Diamond Crystal kosher salt

113 g (¼ pound) cold unsalted butter, cut into cubes

60 mL (¼ cup) cold whole milk

Strawberry Goat Cheese

85 g (½ cup) hulled and diced fresh strawberries

140 g (½ cup) soft unripened goat cheese, room temperature

1 teaspoon liquid honey

½ teaspoon rose water

Rose Honey

2 tablespoons liquid honey

1 teaspoon rose water

Dried culinary rose petals, for garnish

1. **Make the biscuits:** Position the racks in the upper and lower thirds of the oven and preheat to 325°F (160°C). Line 2 baking sheets with parchment paper.

2. In a large bowl, whisk together the whole wheat flour, spelt flour, icing sugar, brown sugar, baking powder, and salt.

3. Drop in the butter and rub into the flour with your hands until it forms a fine, crumbly texture. (Alternatively, you can use a stand mixer fitted with the paddle attachment and mix on medium-low speed for 5 to 8 minutes.)

4. Pour in the milk, and work into a dough with a fork (or in the stand mixer fitted with the paddle attachment on medium-low speed), until just incorporated and a dough has started to form.

5. Turn out the dough onto a lightly floured work surface. Knead the dough until smooth. Use a rolling pin to roll out the dough to about ¼-inch thickness. Using a 2½-inch round cookie cutter, punch out 28 rounds. Arrange the cookies on the lined baking sheets, evenly spaced. Gather the

recipe continues

scraps and reroll until all the dough has been cut. Dock the dough by pricking each biscuit with a fork or toothpick in pretty patterns. This will allow steam to escape for a perfectly flat biscuit.

6. Bake for 20 minutes or until golden brown, rotating the pans halfway through. Remove from the oven and let the biscuits cool completely on the baking sheet or a wire rack before serving, 10 to 15 minutes. Store the biscuits in an airtight container at room temperature for up to 3 weeks.

7. **Meanwhile, make the strawberry goat cheese:** Place the diced strawberries in a mini food processor and purée. (If working by hand, mash the strawberries into a rough purée in a medium bowl using a potato masher or the back of a fork.)

8. Transfer the purée into a fine-mesh sieve set over a small bowl, and gently push the purée around with a spoon to release as much liquid as possible. You will notice the purée will begin to look drier and will stick less and less to the strainer as water drips out. Discard any liquid. As strawberries vary in ripeness and texture, the amount of liquid released may vary. Riper and juicier strawberries will yield the smoothest and most flavourful purée and will also release the most liquid.

9. Place the goat cheese in a medium bowl. Use the back of a fork to break down and soften the texture. Add the strawberry purée, honey, and rose water. Mix thoroughly using the back of a fork until completely smooth and uniform. The cheese can be stored in an airtight container in the fridge for up to 3 days.

10. **Make the rose honey:** In a small bowl, use a spoon to stir the honey and rose water to a uniform, syrupy consistency.

11. Transfer the strawberry goat cheese to a small, clean serving bowl. Drizzle with the rose honey and sprinkle with rose petals. Serve with the digestive biscuits on the side, or spread cheese on each cracker to serve as canapes or open-face tea sandwiches.

NOTES

Classic Pastry

YIELD enough for two 9-inch crusts or four 6-inch galettes

This is our go-to classic pastry recipe. Superbly balanced, flaky, and tender, this pastry can be used in a plethora of applications including fruit pies, savoury pies, galettes, hand pies, tartlets, quiche—basically any recipe where a crust is needed. A sprinkle of fresh thyme, grate of lemon zest, or dash of spices can instantly transform this blank canvas to pair perfectly with any sweet or savoury filling.

150 mL (⅔ cup) ice-cold water
320 g (2 cups + 2 tablespoons) all-purpose flour
2 tablespoons granulated sugar
½ teaspoon Diamond Crystal kosher salt
227 g (½ pound) cold unsalted butter, cut into cubes

1. Pour the ice-cold water into a measuring cup and place in the freezer while you are preparing the rest of the ingredients. You want the water as cold as possible when it is added to the dough.

2. Combine the flour, sugar, and salt in the bowl of a stand mixer fitted with the paddle attachment. Mix on low speed just to combine. Drop in the butter, one cube at a time, and mix on medium-low speed until the mixture appears sandy, about 5 minutes. Don't worry if larger chunks of butter are still visible; this is what will make your crust flaky and tender.

3. Pour in the ice-cold water and continue to mix until the mixture just comes together to form a shaggy dough, 1 to 2 minutes. (It is better to leave crumbly bits at the bottom than to overwork the dough, which may make it tough.)

4. Turn out the dough onto a floured work surface. Pack together and shape the dough into a ball. If the dough feels crumbly and has trouble sticking together, give it a knead or two. Cut the dough ball into 4 equal portions for small applications such as galettes or 2 equal portions for large applications such as full-size quiches and pies. Shape each portion into a flat disc, and tightly wrap in plastic wrap and chill in the fridge for 2 hours before using, or store in the freezer for up to 2 months (or until ice crystals form). If frozen, defrost in the fridge overnight before using.

Clotted Cream and Potato Quiche

YIELD one 9-inch quiche, serves 6 to 8

For this recipe, clotted cream is whipped into the egg custard for the silkiest, smoothest, creamiest quiche imaginable. Inspired by scalloped potatoes, thinly sliced Yukon Gold layered within the custard give a lovely, stratified texture while maintaining its buttery softness and milky white appearance. Serve with baby greens dressed simply in olive oil and lemon juice for a perfect contrast to this rich and decadent lunch.

½ batch Classic Pastry (page 281)

Filling
1 large Yukon Gold potato, peeled
3 eggs
60 mL (¼ cup) heavy (35%) cream
60 mL (¼ cup) whole milk

125 mL (½ cup) Clotted Cream (page 239)
½ teaspoon ground nutmeg
½ teaspoon Diamond Crystal kosher salt
Cracked black pepper, to taste
114 g (1 cup) grated white cheddar cheese
65 g (1 cup) grated Parmesan cheese

1. Make the Classic Pastry and place in the fridge to chill for about 2 hours as directed.

2. Preheat the oven to 375°F (190°C).

3. Remove the chilled dough from the fridge and transfer to a generously floured work surface. Use a floured rolling pin to roll out the chilled pastry dough into a 14-inch circle, about ¼ inch thick. Roll the dough around the rolling pin. Unroll the dough over a 9-inch pie dish with a depth of at least 2 inches. Press the dough into the bottom and sides of the pan. Trim any excess dough if necessary, crimp or flute the edges for a frilly border, and transfer to the fridge to chill for at least 30 minutes.

4. **Meanwhile, start making the filling—prepare the potato:** Set up a medium bowl of ice-cold water. Slice the potato crosswise into thin rounds, the thinner the better. (Using a mandoline makes quick work of this preparation.) As you are cutting, place the potato slices in the bowl of cold water to prevent them from oxidizing and turning grey.

5. **Blind bake the pastry shell:** Remove the chilled pie shell from the fridge. Line the shell with parchment paper and fill with pie weights, dried beans, or rice to ensure the crust holds its shape while baking. Blind bake for 10 to 15 minutes, until you notice the edges just starting to turn golden brown. Remove from the oven and dump out the weights. The bottom will still be blonde. Dock the dough by pricking all over the base of the crust with a fork. Return to the oven and bake for another 8 to 10 minutes, until the bottom begins to turn golden brown. Remove from the oven and set aside. Reduce the oven temperature to 325°F (160°C).

6. **Finish making the filling—prepare the egg mixture:** In a medium bowl, whisk together the eggs, heavy cream, milk,

recipe continues

clotted cream, nutmeg, salt, and pepper until combined, about 1 minute.

7. Assemble and bake: Place the blind-baked pie shell on a baking sheet. Scatter a thin layer of cheddar cheese evenly across the bottom of the pie shell. Fan a layer of thinly sliced potatoes in a circular pattern over the cheese, starting from the outside and working your way into the centre. Repeat layers of cheddar cheese and potato to fill the shell to about ½ inch from the top, finishing with the final layer of cheddar. (You should be able to get 3 or 4 layers of potato and cheddar, depending on the thickness of your potato slices.)

8. Pour the egg mixture into the crust to cover the filling, and top with a generous layer of Parmesan. Carefully transfer the baking sheet into the oven, and bake until the top is puffy and golden brown and a skewer easily pierces through the layers of potato, about 1 hour. Let cool for 15 minutes before serving or enjoy at room temperature.

NOTE: This quiche makes great leftovers. Cover tightly with plastic wrap and store in the refrigerator for up to 4 days or in the freezer for up to 1 month or until ice crystals form.

Caramelized Shallot, Fig, and Blue Cheese Galette

YIELD two 6-inch galettes

Galettes are incredibly versatile, as their simple pie dough can be seasoned with any number of herbs or spices and filled with as many combinations of fruits, veggies, or pastry creams as you can imagine. This savoury version brings together a classic palate of flavours—sweet maple caramelized shallots, figs, and blue cheese—in a flaky and crumbly crust.

Delicate yet bold, these little tarts can be assembled ahead of time and kept in the fridge or freezer—simply pop in the oven just before serving for a freshly baked addition to your teatime or as a light supper.

½ batch Classic Pastry (page 281)

Caramelized Shallots

45 mL (3 tablespoons) olive oil

1 tablespoon unsalted butter

5 shallots, thinly sliced crosswise

Pinch each of Diamond Crystal kosher salt
 and cracked black pepper

2 tablespoons sherry cooking wine

2 tablespoons pure maple syrup

Filling

80 g (¼ cup) Sundried Fig, Apple, and
 Brandy Jam (page 127)

60 g (¼ cup) caramelized shallots
 (recipe at left)

30 g (¼ cup) crumbled blue cheese,
 plus more for garnish

227 g (1¼ cups) quartered fresh black
 Mission figs (about 6 figs)

Fresh thyme leaves

For assembly

1 egg

1 tablespoon water

Extra-virgin olive oil

Flaky sea salt, for garnish

1. Make the Classic Pastry and place in the fridge to chill for 2 hours as directed.

2. **Meanwhile, make the caramelized shallots:** Heat the olive oil and butter in a medium skillet over medium-low heat. Add the shallots and a pinch each of salt and pepper and cook for about 15 minutes, stirring occasionally, until the shallots are soft, transparent, and starting to turn golden brown.

3. Pour in the sherry cooking wine and maple syrup and deglaze the pan, using a rubber spatula to scrape up any browned bits from the bottom of the pan. Reduce the heat to low, and cook for another

20 to 30 minutes, stirring frequently, until the mixture is thick and jammy, and the shallots appear browned and caramelized. Set aside.

4. Preheat the oven to 350°F (180°C). Line a baking sheet with parchment paper.

5. Remove the chilled dough from the fridge and transfer to a floured work surface. If not already divided, cut the dough into 2 equal portions. Working with one portion of dough at a time, roll out the dough into an 8-inch circle, about ¼ inch thick. Dust the dough with flour if needed

recipe continues

to prevent it from sticking to the work surface or rolling pin. The edges can be inexact—this will only add to the galette's rustic aesthetic. Place the circles on the baking sheet.

6. Fill the galettes: Spoon a generous layer of Sundried Fig, Apple, and Brandy Jam (about 2 tablespoons) into the centre of each round of dough, leaving a 1-inch border of exposed dough. Top each with about 2 tablespoons of caramelized shallots and 2 tablespoons of crumbled blue cheese. Fan the fig slices on top of the filling, starting with an outer circle and working your way in. Fold the 1-inch border of the dough over the edge of the filling, making occasional pleats to hold it in place. Cup your hands around each finished galette to encourage a round shape. Place the baking sheet in the freezer, and chill for about 10 minutes to give added stability.

7. Meanwhile, in a small bowl, beat the egg with the water.

8. Remove the baking sheet from the freezer and brush the dough with the egg wash. Drizzle a bit of olive oil over the figs, and sprinkle flaky sea salt evenly over the dough and fruit. Bake for about 20 minutes, or until golden brown, rotating the pan halfway through. Immediately transfer the galettes to individual plates or a cutting board. Crumble some additional blue cheese on top and sprinkle with thyme. Serve warm or at room temperature.

NOTE: These galettes can be stored in a sealed container in the fridge for up to 3 days or in the freezer for up to 2 months or until ice crystals start to form. If frozen, defrost at room temperature for about 20 minutes, and then toast in a 300°F (150°C) oven for 5 to 10 minutes or until warm throughout.

NOTES

Roasted Grape, Rosemary, and Brie Strata

YIELD six 5-inch casseroles

Somewhere between a savoury bread pudding, casserole, and Thanksgiving stuffing, stratas are an elegant and hearty offering for an afternoon tea or light meal. Cheese board inspired, this recipe is made traditionally with cubed sourdough bread saturated in a custard of eggs, milk, and seasonings, studded with whole grapes, and creamy brie cheese. We love to drizzle these with a little bit of wildflower honey for sheen and a hint of sweetness.

1 tablespoon unsalted butter
26 g (½ cup) thinly sliced sweet onion
4 eggs
175 mL (¾ cup) whole milk
60 mL (¼ cup) heavy (35%) cream
2 tablespoons grainy mustard
1 teaspoon salt
½ teaspoon ground nutmeg

240 g (4 cups) cubed sourdough bread
340 g (1⅓ cups) cold cubed brie
50 g (½ cup) pecans, toasted and chopped
1 teaspoon finely chopped fresh rosemary leaves
200 g (1½ cups) fresh black grapes
Liquid honey, for garnish

1. Melt the butter in a medium saucepan over medium-low heat. Add the onions and cook, stirring frequently, until softened and golden brown, 15 to 30 minutes.

2. Meanwhile, whisk together the eggs, milk, cream, mustard, salt, and nutmeg in a medium bowl until smooth. Set aside.

3. In a large bowl, place the cubed bread, brie, caramelized onions, pecans, and rosemary, and toss to combine. Add the grapes and toss gently to avoid staining the rest of the ingredients.

4. Divide the bread mixture evenly between six 5-inch mini casserole dishes, filling to the top. Pour the egg mixture over top and press the bread mixture down with a fork to ensure all the dry ingredients are fully saturated in custard. Cover with lids or plastic wrap, and chill in the fridge for at least 1 hour and up to 24 to allow the bread to absorb as much custard as possible. Top up the ramekins with more custard if necessary. (You can skip chilling, but the strata will have a drier, more chunky texture.)

5. Preheat the oven to 350°F (180°C).

6. Place the casserole dishes on a baking sheet. Carefully transfer the sheet to the oven and bake, uncovered, for 45 minutes or until golden brown and just set. Drizzle with honey just before serving.

NOTE: These can also be made in a muffin pan for a wonderful grab-and-go breakfast or lunch.

Soda Bread Grilled Cheese Sandwich with Apples and Gruyère

YIELD one 8-inch loaf, enough for about 6 sandwiches

You can never go wrong with a grilled cheese sandwich, and this sweet and savoury version is no exception. For the canvas, we have opted for an Americanized spin on Irish soda bread—a quick and easy bread to whip together that uses buttermilk and baking soda as the leavening agent as opposed to yeast. So, no blooming, rising, or kneading necessary! The addition of egg, butter, sour cream, and black currants gives the bread a rich, dense crumb—a perfect pairing for ooey-gooey Gruyère, crisp sliced apple, and a dollop of our Spiced Tomato and Tawny Port Jam (page 183). Fresh yet comforting, these sandwiches are sure to go down easy!

Soda Bread

250 mL (1 cup) cold buttermilk

250 mL (1 cup) sour cream

1 egg

600 g (4 cups) all-purpose flour, plus more for dusting

50 g (¼ cup) granulated sugar

1 teaspoon baking soda

1 teaspoon Diamond Crystal kosher salt

57 g (4 tablespoons) cold unsalted butter, cut into cubes

150 g (1 cup) dried black currants

For each sandwich

2 tablespoons unsalted butter, soft for buttering the bread and frying

2 thick slices soda bread, cut from the centre of the loaf (recipe at left)

2 to 4 slices of Gruyère cheese

4 thin slices of red apple

1 tablespoon Spiced Tomato and Tawny Port Jam (page 183)

Flaky sea salt, for garnish

1. **Make the soda bread:** Preheat the oven to 400° F (200°C).

2. In a large bowl, whisk together the buttermilk, sour cream, and egg until fully combined. Set aside.

3. In a separate large bowl, whisk together the flour, sugar, baking soda, and salt until evenly combined. Drop in the cubes of cold butter, and rub into the flour with your hands until it resembles pea-size crumbs, 5 to 10 minutes.

4. Add the black currants and toss to evenly distribute within the flour mixture.

Then, create a well in the centre and pour the egg mixture in. Fold together with a rubber spatula or wooden spoon until the dough is too stiff to stir.

5. Turn out the dough onto a generously floured work surface. Knead the dough until smooth and no dry patches remain, 3 to 5 minutes. If the dough feels sticky or wet, knead in more flour, up to an additional 38 g (¼ cup).

6. Transfer the dough into a cast-iron skillet, Dutch oven, or 9 to 10-inch round cake pan

recipe continues

and form a rustic dome shape. Bake for 45 to 55 minutes, until golden brown. Allow to cool slightly before slicing. The bread can be stored tightly wrapped in plastic wrap at room temperature for up to 3 days.

7. Assemble the sandwich: Spread a thin layer of butter on each slice of bread.

8. Melt the remaining butter in a large skillet over low heat. Once the butter is sizzling, place the slices of bread buttered side down in the skillet. Working quickly, arrange 2 or 4 slices of cheese across both pieces of bread. Top one piece of bread with apple slices and top the other piece with small dollops of Spiced Tomato and Tawny Port Jam, to taste. Cover with a lid, and cook for 3 to 5 minutes, or until the cheese is melted. Check the bottom often to ensure it is not burning. Flip the jammy slice of bread over on top of the apple slices to form a sandwich and cook, uncovered, until golden brown on the bottom. Carefully flip the sandwich and cook until golden brown on the other side.

9. Transfer the sandwich to a plate or cutting board, and let cool slightly, about 5 minutes, just until you can cut the sandwich without the toppings oozing out of the sides. Sprinkle with flaky sea salt.

Cottage Hand Pies with Creamy Root Vegetables and Thyme

YIELD twelve 4 or 5-inch hand pies

A vegetarian twist on the traditional British meat pie, these darling hand pies, or pasties, combine hearty root vegetables, herbs, and spices for a creamy, savoury delight. With some simple pastry work, these pockets of goodness are perfect to serve for a little lunch on the go, or a light supper. These hand pies can be nibbled delicately with little mess, and—even better—they are easy to prepare and freeze ahead of time to be freshly baked, warm and steamy when the time comes to serve.

Crust

1½ batches Classic Pastry (page 281)

Filling

1 Yukon Gold potato, peeled and finely diced

1 carrot, peeled and finely diced

1 parsnip, peeled and finely diced

1 stalk celery, finely diced

2 tablespoons olive oil

1 tablespoon Diamond Crystal kosher salt, more to taste

1 teaspoon finely chopped fresh rosemary leaves, divided

1 teaspoon finely chopped fresh thyme leaves, divided

57 g (4 tablespoons) unsalted butter

3 shallots, finely diced

2 tablespoons all-purpose flour

500 mL (2 cups) vegetable stock

500 mL (2 cups) whole milk

125 mL (½ cup) heavy (35%) cream

72 g (½ cup) fresh or frozen peas

Freshly cracked black pepper, more to taste

Flaky sea salt, for garnish

1 egg, whisked, for brushing

1. Make the Classic Pastry and place in the fridge to chill for about 2 hours as directed.

2. Preheat the oven to 375°F (190°C). Line 3 baking sheets with parchment paper.

3. **Make the filling:** Combine the potato, carrot, parsnip, and celery in a large bowl. Toss the vegetables with the olive oil, salt, ¾ teaspoon of the rosemary, and ¾ teaspoon of the thyme. Spread the vegetable mixture evenly on a lined baking sheet and roast until the vegetables are tender, about 15 minutes. Remove from the oven.

Reposition the racks in the upper and lower thirds of the oven, and increase the temperature to 425°F (220°C).

4. Meanwhile, melt the butter in a large, deep saucepan or stock pot over low heat. Add the shallots and cook, stirring frequently, until softened and transparent but not brown. Dust the shallot with the flour and continue cooking, stirring frequently, until the flour is toasted and pasty, about 5 minutes. Pour in the stock, milk, and

recipe continues

cream and return to a simmer, whisking continuously, until smooth and thickened, 20 to 30 minutes.

5. Scrape the pan of roasted vegetables directly into the stew and mix to combine. Stir in the peas. Season with more salt and pepper to taste. Remove from the heat.

6. **Assemble the hand pies:** Beat the egg in a small bowl and set aside.

7. Remove the chilled dough from the fridge and transfer to a generously floured work surface. Use a rolling pin to roll out the pastry dough to ¼ to ½-inch thickness. Using a 4½-inch round cookie cutter, punch out as many rounds as possible. Gather the scraps and reroll until all of the dough is cut, about 12 rounds. Scoop a heaping spoonful or two of stew in the centre of 6 rounds, leaving ½ inch exposed border. Using a pastry brush or the tip of a finger, brush the egg onto the edges of the rounds. Place the remaining rounds over the filling. Using a fork, press down on the edges to seal the tops to the bottoms.

8. Place the hand pies on the other 2 lined baking sheets (6 pies per sheet, evenly spaced). Brush the tops of the pies with the egg for a nice, golden sheen. Sprinkle with flaky sea salt, cracked black pepper, the remaining ¼ teaspoon rosemary, and the remaining ¼ teaspoon thyme. Cut a small X in the centre of each pie for ventilation. Bake for 35 to 45 minutes or until golden brown, rotating the pans halfway through. Serve warm.

NOTE: These hand pies freeze beautifully. Place the pies on a baking sheet in a single layer and wrap tightly with plastic wrap. Transfer to the freezer. Once frozen, you can layer them in an airtight container and store in the freezer for up to 6 weeks or until ice crystals form. Bake from frozen in a 425°F (220°C) oven until golden brown, 35 to 45 minutes.

NOTES

Savoury Cheese Sables with Cranberries and Walnuts

YIELD *about 16 sables*

The perfect contrast of sweet and salty, these savoury short biscuits are so easy to prepare yet so elegant. With almost equal portions of cheese, butter, and flour, they are perfectly crumbly and melt in your mouth. Sables are the French cousin of the classic Scottish shortbread, differing mainly in the shaping technique—while shortbread is typically rolled flat and cut, sables are formed into a log, chilled, and sliced. In our cheesy version, we added colourful bits of cranberry and crunchy walnuts, with a sprinkle of the eternally sophisticated herbs de Provence—an homage to its French heritage.

As this recipe is particularly proportion dependent, we highly recommend using weight measurements (grams) as opposed to volume (teaspoons/cups). This will ensure the dough comes out as intended.

90 g (½ cup + 1½ tablespoons) all-purpose flour
2 teaspoons cornstarch
50 g (⅓ heaping cup) walnuts, toasted and roughly chopped
50 g (⅓ heaping cup) dried cranberries
½ teaspoon ground pink peppercorn

¼ teaspoon Diamond Crystal kosher salt
113 g (¼ pound) unsalted butter, room temperature
100 g (1 cup) grated Parmesan cheese
2 teaspoons herbs de Provence

1. In a medium bowl, combine the flour, cornstarch, walnuts, cranberries, pink peppercorn, and salt. Mix together with a fork to evenly combine.

2. In the bowl of a stand mixer fitted with the paddle attachment, cream the butter, Parmesan, and herbs de Provence on high speed until light and fluffy, about 5 minutes. Reduce the speed to medium, and add the dry ingredients in 2 additions, mixing after each addition until just combined and no dry patches remain.

3. Place a sheet of plastic wrap on a work surface. Turn out the dough onto the plastic wrap and shape into a log. Wrap the plastic wrap around the log, twisting the ends like a candy wrapper until the log is tightly formed. Then, press down on the log with even pressure to square off each side into a rectangular shape, 6 to 10 inches long (6 inches for larger cookies; 10 inches for smaller cookies). Place the wrapped log in the freezer to chill for at least 2 hours before using or up to 1 month. If using from frozen, soften at room temperature for 1 hour or overnight in the fridge.

4. Preheat the oven to 350°F (180°C). Line a baking sheet with parchment paper.

5. Remove the chilled dough from the freezer and cut crosswise into ¼ to ½-inch-thick slices. If the dough is too firm and frozen, allow it to sit at room temperature until the dough is still cold but sliceable. Place the cut dough evenly spaced 1 inch apart on the lined baking sheet. Bake for 15 to 20 minutes, or until slightly golden brown with little give when lightly pressed with a finger. Store in an airtight container at room temperature for up to 3 weeks.

Drinks

Jammy Lemonade

YIELD 2 L (2 quarts) for eight 250 mL (8-ounce) drinks

As delightful as a warm summer's day, a dollop of your homemade jam adds a fruity sweetness and lovely colour to your lemonade. Any jam will do, but we tend to favour red berry fruits, which add a beautiful, summery depth of flavour. For the base lemonade, we like to keep the sweetness level low to account for the addition of jam and allow the fruit flavours to shine.

1 L (4 cups) water
200 g (1 cup) granulated sugar
125 mL (½ cup) jam of your choice
500 mL (2 cups) freshly squeezed lemon juice (about 9 lemons)
Ice cubes, for serving

1. Combine the water and sugar in a large saucepan over medium heat and simmer just until the sugar dissolves, stirring frequently. Transfer to a pitcher. Add the jam and stir well to combine.

2. Pour in the lemon juice and stir well to combine. Serve in glasses poured over ice cubes.

NOTES

Lilac Sweet Tea

YIELD 1 L (1 quart) for four 250 mL (8-ounce) drinks

Lilacs are one of the first springtime blooms to appear, and they mark the beginning of iced tea season. Thus, a lilac sweet tea is only fitting to celebrate this special time of year. Cold brewing your iced tea is perhaps the easiest and least fussy method for preparing iced tea, as well as yielding a delicate yet flavourful infusion that is free of any bitterness. We like to make our sweet tea with a bold long leaf breakfast tea, such as an Assam or Ceylon blend. Loose leaf is preferred for cold steeping, as the tea leaves are given the space to unfurl and swim freely.

15 g (¼ cup) strong loose-leaf black tea
1 L (4 cups) cold water
125 mL (½ cup) Pink Apple and Lilac Blossom Jelly (page 101)

1. In a large non-reactive container or pitcher with a lid, combine the loose-leaf tea and cold water. Stir, cover with the lid, and infuse in the fridge for at least 8 hours or overnight.

2. When you are ready to make the sweet lilac tea, place a fine-mesh sieve over a pitcher and strain the tea. Discard the tea leaves. Add the Pink Apple and Lilac Blossom Jelly to the pitcher and stir well to dissolve.

VARIATION: For this recipe, we added the jelly to the cold tea, which results in pieces of jelly floating within the tea for a little bit of fun and unexpected texture (similar to boba or aloe vera juice). If you prefer a textureless tea, remove 125 mL (½ cup) of water from the steeping liquid. When you are ready to sweeten the tea, add 125 mL (½ cup) of boiling water to the Pink Apple and Lilac Blossom Jelly to melt the jelly and allow to cool to room temperature, about 30 minutes. Add the jelly to the cold infusion and place in the fridge to chill.

NOTES

Strawberry Daiquiri Poptail

YIELD 6 ice lollies and 1 cocktail

We just couldn't resist pairing Strawberry, Raspberry, and Cream Jam ice lollies with a classic daiquiri for a little spin on the traditional strawberry daiquiri. These pink ice lollies are so fun to dip and lick, creating a lovely pink ombre effect in the glass, especially if sipping on a warm summer day.

Jam makes a perfect and easy base for ice lollies, so feel free to use the ice lollies part of the recipe sans booze for your little ones—let them choose their favourite jam to make their own summertime creation!

Ice Lollies

400 mL (1⅔ cups) water

125 mL (½ cup) Strawberry, Raspberry, and Cream Jam (page 35)

45 mL (3 tablespoons) freshly squeezed lemon juice

Simple Syrup

100 g (½ cup) granulated sugar

125 mL (½ cup) water

Daiquiri

2 ounces light rum

1 ounce freshly squeezed lime juice

½ ounce simple syrup, to taste (recipe at left)

6 to 8 ice cubes, for shaking

1. Make the ice lollies: In a measuring pitcher, combine the water, Strawberry, Raspberry, and Cream Jam, and lemon juice, and stir well to combine and break down the jam into the water. Pour the mixture into ice-pop moulds, leaving ½ inch of space at the top to allow for expansion after freezing, and place them in the freezer until completely frozen, at least 8 hours or overnight.

2. Make the simple syrup: Combine the sugar and water in a small saucepan and simmer over medium heat until the sugar is dissolved, stirring occasionally. Remove from the heat, transfer to a 250 mL (1-cup) mason jar with a lid, and let cool. Seal tightly, and store in the fridge for up to 1 month.

3. Make the daiquiri: Combine the rum, lime juice, and simple syrup in a cocktail shaker. Add the ice cubes and shake until well chilled. Strain into a rocks glass. Garnish with an ice lolly.

Lavender London Cream

YIELD one 375 mL (12-ounce) drink

The London Fog—strongly brewed Earl Grey tea topped with steamed milk—is a tea shop essential. In our extra special version, we have transformed this everyday drink into pure teatime indulgence. White chocolate, toasted in the oven until it turns a lovely caramelized golden brown and then added to the steamed milk, is a decadent pairing with Earl Grey tea. Topped with a hefty dollop of whipped cream that melts right into the drink, this half-hot-chocolate-half-tea-latte is sure to make any day just a little extra luxurious.

Toasted White Chocolate (Yield: about 80 g)

85 g (½ cup) roughly chopped white chocolate

Drink

2 teaspoons loose-leaf Earl Grey tea
    (or 2 tea bags)

1 teaspoon dried culinary lavender blossoms,
    plus more for garnish

175 mL (¾ cup) boiling water

125 mL (½ cup) heavy (35%) cream, divided

125 mL (½ cup) whole milk

40 g (¼ cup) toasted white chocolate shards,
    plus more for garnish (recipe at left)

1 to 2 teaspoons granulated sugar, or to taste

1. **Make the toasted white chocolate:** Preheat the oven to 250°F (120°C). Line a baking sheet with parchment paper.

2. Place the chocolate in a small ceramic or glass casserole dish and bake for 40 to 50 minutes, stirring well every 10 minutes, until the chocolate is fully melted and smooth and has turned golden brown. (Don't worry if the chocolate turns grainy or matte at first, it will become smooth as it cooks.) Remove from the oven and use a rubber spatula to spread the caramelized chocolate in a thin layer on the parchment paper. Transfer to the fridge to harden, 10 to 15 minutes.

3. Once hardened, peel the chocolate away from the parchment paper and crumble into fine shards. Place in an airtight container and store in the fridge—you will have extra.

4. **Make the drink:** Place the Earl Grey tea and lavender blossoms in a metal tea infuser or disposable tea sachet in a large 375 mL

(12-ounce) mug. Pour in the boiling water and steep for 4 minutes.

5. **While the tea is steeping, whip the cream:** Pour 60 mL (¼ cup) of the heavy cream into a small bowl. Whip by hand using a whisk or with a hand mixer until it is fluffy and holds its shape.

6. Remove the tea infuser or sachet from the tea. If using a paper tea sachet, squeeze the bag firmly on the side of the cup to get every drop.

7. **Finish the drink:** Combine the milk, remaining 60 mL (¼ cup) heavy cream, and 40 g of toasted white chocolate shards in a small saucepan over low heat and whisk constantly until the chocolate is melted and the milk is steaming, but not boiling. Remove from the heat. Stir in 1 or 2 teaspoons of sugar, to taste.

8. Pour the hot chocolate into the tea concentrate. Top with 2 or 3 hefty dollops of whipped cream. Garnish with lavender blossoms and crumbles of toasted white chocolate.

Chamomile, Milk, and Honey

YIELD one 375 mL (12-ounce) drink

In one of our favourite before-bed treats, a spoonful of bee pollen and a sprinkle of cinnamon transforms simple chamomile tea into a warm and cozy delight. Bee pollen is essentially the field-gathered flower pollen that honeybees bring back to the hive which, mixed with the magic of Mother Nature, is packed into the comb and serves as nutrition for the bees. Herbalists tout bee pollen for its potential anti-inflammatory and healthful qualities; however, it also serves to add body and wildflower flavour for a rich and creamy latte.

3 g (3 tablespoons) dried chamomile blossoms (or 3 tea bags)
2 teaspoons bee pollen, plus more for garnish
1 teaspoon dried culinary lavender blossoms
1 cinnamon stick
175 mL (¾ cup) boiling water
125 mL (½ cup) whole milk
2 teaspoons liquid honey, or to taste
Sprinkle of ground cinnamon, for garnish

1. Place the chamomile, bee pollen, lavender blossoms, and cinnamon stick in a glass jar or carafe. Pour in the boiling water and steep for 5 minutes.

2. In a small saucepan, heat the milk over low heat until steaming but not boiling. Froth with an electric milk frother if you have one, but it is not necessary.

3. Once the tea is steeped, mix gently with a spoon to further dissolve the bee pollen. Strain the tea through a fine-mesh sieve into a mug, pushing with the back of a spoon to squeeze out every last drop. Drizzle in the honey and stir to dissolve. Top with the warm steamed milk and garnish with a sprinkle of cinnamon.

NOTES

Banana Brunch Punch

YIELD 1.5 L (1.5 quarts) for six 250 mL (8-ounce) drinks

We had no choice but to include a cocktail based on our Banana, Bourbon, and Vanilla Bean Jam (page 177), and considering it is the quintessential breakfast jam, a brunch punch just seemed right! Banana classically lends itself to rum drinks, but this fruity bourbon concoction is the perfect lazy midday brunch. With a hint of retro inspiration, this golden pitcher is sure to brighten up your morning, even if it is the hair of the dog that bit you.

4 to 6 ice cubes, for shaking

125 mL (½ cup) Banana, Bourbon, and Vanilla Bean Jam (page 177)

4 ounces bourbon

175 mL (¾ cup) fresh orange juice

175 mL (¾ cup) fresh pineapple juice, cold

4 fresh pineapple rings

1 orange, cut into cubes

500 mL (2 cups) sparkling white wine, cold

250 mL (1 cup) sparkling water, cold, or to taste

For Garnish

Pineapple leaves

Orange slices

1. In a cocktail shaker, combine the ice, Banana, Bourbon, and Vanilla Bean Jam, bourbon, and orange juice, and shake well.

2. Strain the mixture into a large pitcher or punch bowl. Add the pineapple juice, pineapple rings, and orange, and stir well to combine. Top with the sparkling wine and sparkling water, stir, and garnish each with a pineapple leaf and orange slice.

NOTES

Magic Ginger and Lemongrass Tonic

YIELD two 250 mL (8-ounce) drinks

We almost always have a big jar of this magical tonic in our fridge at home. With its blend of healthful and anti-inflammatory ingredients and bold flavours, it is as delicious as it is beautiful. Make this tonic by the batch and warm it by the cup, or sip over ice—either way, it is sure to offer some TLC for body and mind alike.

1 (4-inch) piece fresh ginger, scrubbed and roughly chopped

4 (2-inch) pieces fresh turmeric, scrubbed and roughly chopped

1 whole skin-on lemon, roughly chopped

4 stalks lemongrass, lightly bruised and roughly chopped

3 sprigs fresh rosemary, roughly chopped

3 cinnamon sticks

45 mL (3 tablespoons) dried culinary rose buds

For serving

Ice cubes (if serving cold)

Pure maple syrup, to taste

Lemon slices

Rosemary sprigs

1. Combine the ginger, turmeric, lemon, lemongrass, rosemary, cinnamon sticks, and rose buds in a 1 L (4-cup) mason jar or glass vessel with a lid. Fill to the top with boiling water and let sit at room temperature until cool, about 2 hours. Once cooled, seal tightly and store in the fridge for up to 1 week. This tonic will continue to infuse with time and only gets better with age. Continue to top up the water as needed when it runs low.

2. Enjoy reheated or poured over ice cubes. Sweeten with maple syrup to taste. Garnish each glass with slices of lemon and a sprig of rosemary.

NOTES

Baked Apple Toddy

YIELD one 250 mL (8-ounce) cocktail

In our version of this classic cocktail, we substituted the sugar for a heaping bar spoon of Baked Apple and Brown Sugar Jam (page 115) for a warm and toasty drink that is sure to put a fire in your belly on those chilly winter nights.

2 tablespoons Baked Apple and Brown Sugar Jam (page 115)
1 ounce rye whisky
½ ounce lemon juice
60 mL (¼ cup) boiling water

For garnish
Apple slice
1 star anise
1 cinnamon stick

1. Combine the Baked Apple and Brown Sugar Jam, whisky, and lemon juice in a cocktail beaker. Muddle with a wooden muddler or bar spoon for about 1 minute to break down the pieces of apple in the preserve and infuse flavours into the alcohol.

2. Pour in the boiling water, stir gently, and steep for 1 to 2 minutes. Strain the toddy through a fine-mesh sieve into a glass cocktail mug. Garnish with the apple slice, star anise, and a cinnamon stick.

NOTES

Acknowledgments

Thank you, thank you, thank you to everyone—our families, our friends, our staff, and our customers—who was kind, patient, and understanding while we wrote this book.

Thank you to Miriam and Max, for your ever-present love and support, and without whom Kitten and the Bear would have never even existed. Thank you for always believing in us.

Thank you to Margaret, for every plum pitted and every window washed, and for manifesting our success.

Thank you to Paul, for all of your guidance, wisdom, and for always being there, tool belt and moving truck at the ready.

Thank you to Melody, for elevating this book with your gorgeous artwork, and for always being so generous with your talents. Thank you for being our chief teacup hunter, aesthetic sounding board, and kindred spirit.

Thank you to Teddy, for your loyalty, questionable humour, and for always being there to lighten the mood. Thank you for being the master of the scone and allowing us the joy of being your honorary family. A hero arises!

Thank you to Andrea, our unbelievable editor, for seeing in us what we did not see in ourselves. Thank you for your boundless patience and teaching us so much along this journey.

Index